"*Italian American* is a book you must have on your shelves.
It is filled with so much passion and so many stories,
featuring food I not only grew up with but crave and
cook daily. Angie and Scott are great chefs and fabulous
people, and every bit of warmth and hospitality that you
feel when you walk into their restaurant, Don Angie,
pours out of every page of this magical book."
　　　—Michael Symon, James Beard Award–winning
　　　　chef, *New York Times* bestselling author, and
　　　　restaurateur

"A book I have been waiting for since I tasted the best
lasagna in the world! I love the West Village in New York
City. It is brimming with restaurants, eateries, and cafés,
but few as polished and delicious as Don Angie. That the
restaurant's owners are now sharing some of their amazing
recipes for all home cooks is remarkable. Thank you,
Scott and Angie!"
　　　—Martha Stewart

"Scott and Angie have honored their Italian-American
roots, Southern Italian flavors, family traditions, and
experimented with new ingredients in such a beautiful
way. Their ancestors redefined and created a new type
of cuisine when they came to America, which is exactly
what Scott and Angie are doing today."
　　　—Jean-Georges Vongerichten, chef and
　　　　restaurateur

Italian

American

Italian American

Red Sauce Classics and New Essentials

Angie Rito & Scott Tacinelli

with Jamie Feldmar

PHOTOGRAPHS BY CHRISTOPHER TESTANI

CLARKSON POTTER/PUBLISHERS
New York, NY

for our little meatball,
Roman James

contents

scott's mom as a young girl
eating with her grandfather

ADDario family gathering

5/12/46   1940

Angie's grandma with her sisters
and cousins as young children

Angie's grandparents on their
wedding day

scott's parents during
a wedding toast

introduction

This book is about family.
Italian-American cooking *always* is,

when you get down to it. We're both the grandchildren and great-grand-children of immigrants from Southern Italy, and while our families worked, celebrated, squabbled, and reminisced, the one constant was food. A lot of food. Italian-American cooking is about family, and the spirit of generosity, manifesting in an abundance of good things to eat at all times.

We grew up eating the kind of food that East Coasters refer to as "red sauce"—a vast genre aptly named for the rich, red tomato sauce that usually appears as the centerpiece of every meal. But whether you call it "red sauce" or simply "Italian-American," both terms refer to a distinct style of cooking that's separate from traditional Italian cuisine.

Italian-American food has become a genre in its own right, marked by popular dishes like spaghetti and meatballs, multitiered chicken and egg-plant parms, and hearty baked pastas laden with molten cheese. It's a cuisine that took on a life of its own as Italian immigrants adapted to living in a new country and made do with what was available, resulting in a whole new style of cooking that can't be found in the motherland.

Today, many American chefs attempt to "modernize" or refine Italian cui-sine, which often means focusing on Northern Italian fare, marked by rich risottos, silky fresh pastas, and wine-braised meats. But Italian-American food is something else entirely. It's a cuisine developed from the foods of the Italian south, where most Italian immigrants to the US, including those in our family, came from. This is the land of extruded dried pastas, tomato sauce, and olive oil in copious amounts. This is where unassuming trattorias run by time-tested nonnas turn out some of the most soulful, delicious, and comforting meals we've ever had, and where the recipes our families have handed down through generations come from.

Italian-American food hasn't always gotten the respect it deserves in highfalutin culinary circles, but it's become something of an obsession for us, to redefine what the term means and to bring it to as many people as pos-sible. At our restaurant Don Angie in New York City, we strive to both honor and breathe new life into the cuisine, resulting in dishes that proudly strad-dle the line between Italian and American, in all of their multicultural glory.

New York is where so many of our ancestors first set foot in this country, building the foundation for the city's now-legendary Little Italy (although most Italians have long since moved away). There are classic red-sauce joints aplenty in this town, with names like Ferdinando's and Bamonte's and Don Peppe's, and we love them all. We regularly seek out the oldest of the old-school spots, ideally ones with bad lighting, chintzy décor, and a heavy dose of nostalgia. Places like these just feel like home to us, and we can't get enough of them.

Scott's grandparents SAM & Jenny on their wedding day

Scott's grandparents Ernest & Lorraine in Central Park

But as much as it's true that New York is a city steeped in tradition, it's also a city pulsating with the vibrant mix of a thousand different cultures and cuisines all at once. And though red sauce is the food of our people, we've been lucky to expand our worldview through countless hours spent cooking and eating our way across the greatest melting pot in the world.

For years, we lived in a tiny apartment above a Chinese restaurant on the Lower East Side, where we first tasted the chrysanthemum greens we'd later use in our version of a Caesar salad. We've taken countless trips to Kalustyan's, a legendary international spice shop in an Indian neighborhood known as "Curry Hill," familiarizing ourselves with new-to-us ingredients like Urfa biber, Tasmanian pepperberries, and Persian black lime. Working our way across the city's kitchens, we befriended coworkers from all over the globe who introduced us to their own food traditions. Our coworker Regulo brought in his wife's delicious Dominican quipe (beef and bulgur) every week for family meal; our barista Syed invited us to his apartment in Queens for a homemade Bengali feast; a talented cook named Kanya taught Angie how to make herb-scented coconut milk for delicate Thai desserts. Through these friends and colleagues, we fell in love with flavors and ingredients from outside of our Italian-American heritage, and those elements naturally began to find their place in our own kitchen.

We have now developed our own highly personalized version of Italian-American cooking, one that's rooted in Southern Italy but enmeshed with flavors and techniques from all over the world. Our grandmothers might not use tamarind paste, guajillo chiles, or Japanese eggplants in their kitchens, but they're certainly familiar with the rhythms of adapting your recipes to fit your surroundings. Immigrants have been cooking this way for generations; we're just putting our own spin on the idea.

Italian-American dishes are the root of our cooking, but they're just the starting point. In the end, it's all about cooking with heart. Every move we make as professional chefs is done with the same spirit of generosity we grew up with. For us, it's solely about taking care of people, the way our families always have. It's about finding deep comfort in simple ingredients, and about expanding the boundaries of what you typically bring into your own kitchen. And now, by cooking your way through this book, whether you were born Italian American or not, you become a part of that tradition, too. Welcome to the family.

We both have Southern Italy
in our blood. Santo Rito, Angie's grand-

father, started apprenticing at a bakery in Sicily at the tender age of ten (although sometimes he claims he was eight). He came to the States in the 1950s, met and married Angie's grandmother Maria, who had recently emigrated from a town outside of Naples. Together, they opened an Italian bakery and deli in Cleveland that bears the family name and is still going strong today. Angie grew up working at Rito's Bakery, arranging antipasto platters, decorating cookies, and assembling sprawling pastry trays during the busy holiday seasons. Having a deli in the family was useful for feeding the constant stream of relatives that filtered in and out; you never knew when a cousin might drop by.

On Angie's mother's side, her great-grandparents Gemma and Joseph, whose parents had come from Molise, lived in Cleveland's Little Italy and sold fruits and vegetables at a stand in the local market. Angie's paternal great-grandparents, Antonio and Lidia Landino, came to Cleveland with their daughter Maria (who later married Santo) from a small town outside of Naples, where they'd been farmers. Antonio kept a sprawling backyard garden in his new home, tucked among the urban landscape on East 135th Street, presiding over it from a plastic lawn chair. In his forty years in the States, he refused to learn English. Maria also carried on the family's rich gardening

Angie's great grandparents
ANTONIO & LIDIA

tradition: When she married and had her own home, she, too, grew an impressive garden. She'd jar her fresh tomatoes every year, and the whole family would feast on peak-summer sauce during the Feast of the Seven Fishes at Christmas.

Scott's family history isn't radically different. His paternal grandfather, Ernest, was born to immigrants from a small town in the province of Benevento and grew up in the Bronx. Ernest and his wife, Lorraine, raised their family there, and Scott's father eventually moved to New Jersey to raise his. Scott's maternal grandparents, Sabino and Giovanna Addario, were born in Brooklyn to parents who had emigrated from Salerno. Sabino's mother Antonia made her long-cooked ragu over a wood-burning grill in Prospect Park on Sundays. Sabino, who went by his American nickname "Sam," sold pretzels and Italian ices from a cart and raised pigeons on his roof; Giovanna, who went by "Jennie," sent Scott home with Tupperwares full of Sunday sauce every time he visited from New Jersey. They, too, kept an impressive urban garden in their backyard in Queens, growing tomatoes, zucchini, cucumbers, peppers, parsley, and basil. In the springtime every year, Jennie made Scott and his brother each miniature Easter pies (a traditional Neapolitan savory pie, page 233, made with meat and cheese) with their initials carved into them. These labor-intensive dishes were her expression of love, as is the way for so many immigrant families.

Maybe then it shouldn't be a surprise that we met in a restaurant, in our adopted hometown of New York City. Here's how it happened:

Scott: I grew up cooking with my grandparents, and cooked a lot in college. I was the one watching Food Network late at night, trying recipes out on my friends, cooking up 2 A.M. feasts after a night at the bars. On spring break, everyone else went to Cancún, but I drove with a friend from Pennsylvania to New Orleans to eat at Emeril Lagasse's restaurant, stopping at every local BBQ joint we could find along the way. After college, I wanted to work in the music industry. I played the drums, and had an internship at Atlantic Records. I was interviewing for a job at a record label when I got offered a different job in radio sales, and I wound up working there for almost ten years. I still cooked for my friends and family but had never thought of doing it as a career. By the time I turned thirty, I realized that I wasn't emotionally fulfilled by my work, and I really wanted to spend my life doing something I was passionate about. I called my mom and said I was thinking of leaving my job and going to culinary school. She said, "I think that's the best thing you could do," and that was it for me. I quit the next day.

After graduating from culinary school, Scott landed a job as a line cook at a restaurant called Park Avenue. A few months later, Angie, fresh out of college and brand new to New York, began working there as a server.

Scott: I thought she was so cute, I couldn't take it. We'd go to Subway Bar, this divey chef hangout, after work, and we'd stay there all night just talking. We both came from Italian-American families, and she loved food as much as me. She asked me to help introduce her to the restaurant scene in New York because she was new to the city and wanted to learn. We hit all the institutions on our days off—I'll never forget going to 2nd Avenue Deli together, and Angie tried to order a pastrami and cheese. The waitress goes, "Oh, honey, we're kosher—you can't do that here."

Angie: At first we were just friends; I had just moved to New York and didn't want a boyfriend. But from the moment we first met we had some special connection that I couldn't put my finger on. Our first official date was at Blue Ribbon Brasserie—a legendary late-night chef hangout. My mind was blown by the idea that we could sit at a white-tablecloth restaurant and order a nice bottle of Burgundy at 2 A.M. That was in October of 2008, and not long after that, we booked a three-week trip to Spain. All we had were plane tickets. We stayed in hostels and ate our way around the country—it was an all-food itinerary. I realized I was in love with Scott on that trip.

Like Scott, Angie had always been passionate about food and hospitality.

Angie: My family ran a deli and bakery and I loved growing up there—the camaraderie, the hospitality, and, of course, the food. By the time I was in my late teens, I was certain that I wanted to own a restaurant one day. Still, I had this notion that I should go to college and do something more "serious" as a career first, then maybe I'd eventually have my own restaurant later in life. I studied journalism in college, but I really loved cooking—I was the one inviting friends over after a late night out, making huge pasta feasts for twenty-five people at 3 A.M. I moved to New York after graduation for an internship in film development, and needed another job to make ends meet, so I started working in restaurants, working in the front of house. But I missed cooking and really wanted to work in the kitchen. I told Scott I was considering going to culinary school, and he said, "Why don't you just try working in a restaurant kitchen, and see if you like it?" So I did, and I haven't turned back.

our wedding day
in florence, Italy

We worked separately for a while—Angie at restaurants such as Torrisi Italian Specialties and The Hurricane Club, Scott at Quality Meats. Though we both truly loved what we were doing, we were spending long, grueling hours working apart from morning until late at night—there was one year where we shared only two days off. We realized after working separately in the industry for several years that the only way for us to be in a relationship while also doing the work we're passionate about was to do it together.

We teamed up in 2013 to open Quality Italian, an Italian-American steakhouse in Midtown Manhattan, where for the first time we had the opportunity to create dishes in the kitchen together. This is when we started laying the groundwork to develop our own style of cuisine. We learned to work effectively together to oversee and operate a restaurant, from production to service, leading a large team—invaluable lessons we carry with us today.

By then, we had started a tradition of annual pilgrimages to Italy together, visiting new regions each trip to learn more about the country's broad cuisine and to understand more about where the Italian-American dishes we'd come to know and love originated. We went to the town of San Marzano in August to experience the region's annual tomato harvest, and sampled the true Sicilian granita in Catania that Angie's grandfather had told her about as a child. We explored the unique and diverse cuisines of regions we'd never been to before, such as the Austrian-inflected smoked meat platters in northeastern Italian cities like Trieste, buckwheat pasta in the northern city Trento, and traditional dishes like *sa panada* in Sardinia, a loose relative to similarly named Spanish empanadas. In 2015, we were married in one of our favorite Italian cities, Florence, and we couldn't have asked for a more perfect day. We had a multicourse lunch on the rooftop of the Grand Hotel Baglioni (where the Negroni was supposedly invented), including a pici with veal cheek ragu that inspired the Osso Buco & Prosciutto Ragu (page 117), antipasti galore, and a giant Napoleon-style cake (that cracked down the middle, but no matter).

Back in New York, a friend of ours was looking for someone to run a nineteen-seat pop-up in the back of his East Village bar, and we jumped at the opportunity. We'd be cooking behind a counter and serving people, sushi-bar style, and we loved the idea of being able to interact with our guests face-to-face in such a personal setting. The project, called "dinnertable," was a blank canvas and really allowed for us to flex our creative muscles. We began to refine our own personal

the two of us at Park Avenue Seasons, where we first met

DON Angie under construction

cuisine, rooted in family recipes, tangled up with the ingredients and techniques we'd come to love from other cultures. It was there that we developed recipes like the Stuffed Mussels with Pepperoni Rice (page 61), the Chrysanthemum Caesar (page 75), and made the very first version of our pinwheel lasagna (see page 175).

Running dinnertable was a blast—it was just the two of us, plus our then–sous chef Adam (who still works with us today), cooking up elaborate menus in a tiny kitchen with only a toaster oven and mini fridge. But as it gained traction, it seemed to become more unsustainable for us—prepping from early in the morning until dinner service, then frantically cooking, cleaning, and serving, sometimes all at once, as a line of people formed down the block. We were beginning to burn out.

Around this time, we were approached about partnering in a new restaurant downtown, and it was an opportunity to launch a concept that felt true to us and our cuisine, but with a little more infrastructure than a pop-up inside a bar. We spent months searching for the perfect space, touring ramshackle kitchens in ancient buildings (one had a five-foot ceiling, another was only accessible by crawling through a literal hole in the ground). We didn't know exactly what we were looking for until we found it—the room just felt right the second we walked in. It was a storefront in the West Village on a quaint, tree-lined block, in a beautiful corner spot with light on all sides, and a sizable (for New York) kitchen. We decided to name our new restaurant Don Angie—"Don" being a sign of respect for the boss, Angie being, well . . . you can see where this is going.

By the time Don Angie opened, we had a vision for what we wanted to cook: food rooted in the Italian-American flavors of our youth, combined with fresher ingredients, new culinary techniques, and the creative presentations and diverse influences we'd fallen for once we left home. That means there's room for lasagna (there's always room for lasagna), but instead of sloppy stacked layers of pasta and cheese, we transform it into neat cinnamon bun–like rolls to slice and bake individually. There's a Caesar salad, of course (a mainstay in most Italian-American restaurants, although not an Italian invention, if you want to get technical about it), but ours is made with delicate chrysanthemum leaves in lieu of romaine lettuce, an ingredient we learned about from our Chinese neighbors downstairs. We love to get creative

with our cooking and surprise our guests with new flavors and ideas, but we also want our food to be approachable and comforting. We try to emulate the same spirit of hospitality and generosity our families ingrained in us and share those warm feelings with our guests, cooking creatively but more essentially, with a lot of love. It's important to us to have something for everyone, in every sense of the phrase.

about this book

When we sat down to write this book, we wanted it to go beyond a Don Angie cookbook. Don't get us wrong. We're proud of the recipes at our restaurant, but the way we cook at home is different. We don't often spend hours painstakingly rolling out fresh pasta at home for dinner (okay, maybe we do *sometimes,* but only when it's a special occasion). Both of us were lucky to grow up in food-loving families surrounded by very accomplished home cooks (our parents, aunts, uncles, and grandparents), and we knew we wanted to showcase family recipes. That said, we can't help but put our own spin on things. So what you'll see within is a mix of classic and not-so-classic Italian-American dishes, some of which are based on recipes our families have been cooking for generations, and some of which are born of our own imaginations and experiences.

We start off with two chapters dedicated to antipasti (one hot and one cold), a staple of the Italian-American table and the way in which all proper red-sauce meals begin. These little predinner snacks are meant to be mixed and matched, and eaten with abandon. Make a bunch and have fun with them; antipasti are the true gateway to Italian-American cuisine.

After covering a few of our favorite salads, both old-school and new, we then move into an entire chapter dedicated to sauce, naturally. The recipes in this section—including a simple ten-minute tomato sauce and a slow-simmered Sunday gravy–style amatriciana with pork shoulder—are foundational to the cuisine; they're also a great way to get more familiar with our style of cooking. Yes, there's a Bolognese and a fra diavolo, but there's also a braised chicken ragu with mezcal and chiles and a spiced lamb and Marsala number that no nonna could be responsible for.

Of course, we have a whole section devoted to pasta—dried and fresh, and within the latter, for hand-rolled gnocchi and gnudi, as well as homemade pastas made in both the Northern and Southern Italian styles. This is separate from the freestanding lasagna and baked pasta chapter that comes next; what can we say? The world of pasta is wide and wonderful, and we're just barely scratching the surface.

An entire chapter on meatballs again mixes the traditional (a classic beef-and-veal combo modeled after our grandmothers' versions) with the less-than-traditional (shrimp parm in meatball form? Yes!). At this point, you may have filled up on antipasti and pasta, but in the true spirit of Italian cooking, the dishes keep coming with chapters featuring main courses (*secondi* in red-sauce parlance) and vegetables. To finish it off, there is a somewhat sprawling dessert section, with several cookies and so much more (cannoli! zeppole! Vietnamese coffee tiramisù!), because Angie is descended from a long line of bakers and couldn't bring herself to pare this chapter down. We're also including a few after-dinner drinks that require little more than high-proof alcohol and patience, such as homemade sambuca and citrus 'cello.

All of these recipes are home-cook friendly, meaning we call for very little in the way of special equipment or ingredients, and we strive to streamline unnecessarily fussy instructions. Most are doable on a weeknight—really. Some, like the fresh pastas and a few of the lasagnas, are time-intensive and best saved for your "project" days. Although our techniques and flavor combinations are sometimes unconventional, the end result is always worth it. Trust us on this one.

ingredients & techniques

Most of the ingredients called for in this book can be easily found at the grocery store, though some may require a special trip to an Italian deli or market. Here's a guide to a few of our most commonly called for ingredients, as well as a handful of specialty products that are worth investing in to really get the most out of the recipes. Our three main online purveyors for Italian goods are Buon'Italia, Alma Gourmet, and Gustiamo—we buy products for the restaurant from them, but they also sell retail, and are all worth checking out if you don't live near an Italian market or are having trouble finding anything that follows.

OLIVE OIL: Look for cold-pressed extra-virgin for general cooking, and keep it in a cool, dry place away from direct sunlight. We like the brand Corto, but use anything labeled cold-pressed and extra-virgin. We don't generally call for finishing oils in this book, but if you're inclined to drizzle a higher-end olive oil on top of salad or a cooked pasta just before serving, look for oil made from Taggiasca olives from Liguria (Ardoino is what we use at the restaurant; available from Buon'Italia), which has a light and fruity, fresh flavor.

FLOUR: unless otherwise noted, all flour in the book is all-purpose. We also call for the option of using quick-mixing Wondra flour in recipes that involve making smooth gravies and Mornay-style sauces in the pan, such as the Broccoli Rabe & Provolone Gratin on page 250, because it's less likely to cause lumps. If you don't have Wondra, you can still use all-purpose flour, just be sure to mix the sauce extra well. In the Pasta chapter, however, we call for a few different kinds in the base recipes for fresh pastas. They are as follows:

Durum flour: This is the finely ground powder left over from milling durum wheat. It's high in protein and gluten, and creates pasta with a stretchy texture and a slightly nutty flavor. We like King Arthur's Durum Flour or Caputo Semola di Grano Duro Rimacinata. Both are available online.

"00" flour: A very finely ground soft wheat flour, which is low in protein and makes for soft, supple pasta. We like Caputo Pasta Fresca e Gnocchi Farina di Grano Tenero Tipo "00," available online.

Semolina: This is made from milled durum wheat. It has a hard, coarse texture, similar to sand, a yellowish color, and a mild, slightly nutty flavor. Because it has a high gluten content, semolina helps pasta keep its shape and gives it a firm texture. We like Bob's Red Mill Semolina Flour and General Mills Semolina No. 1.

CANNED TOMATOES: For whole canned tomatoes, it's worth it to seek out the ones labeled "San Marzano DOP," which really are the best in the world, thanks to the unique growing conditions in San Marzano sul Sarno. They have a natural sweetness, not too much acidity, and great depth of flavor. There are multiple brands selling 28-ounce cans; look for ones specifically labeled as DOP—Denominazione di Origine Protetta ("protected designation of origin"). If you can't find that, Mutti produces a great selection of imported non-DOP alternatives, including canned crushed tomatoes (called "Polpa"), which we call for occasionally.

CHEESES: Cheese plays a huge role in Italian-American cooking. Some grocery stores have a well-stocked selection, but for the real experience, visit an Italian deli for cheeses and meats if there's one in your area. You'll be able to taste things that might not be available in the supermarket, ask questions, and get informed opinions from the experts. Many of these cheeses are also available online at the Italian grocers mentioned earlier.

Parmesan: When we use Parmesan, we use only Parmigiano-Reggiano, and ideally one aged for 24 months. Italians are nutty about their food traditions, and true Parmesan can be labeled Parmigiano-Reggiano only if it's produced in a certain area, from cows that are raised a certain way, graze on certain grass, and produce a certain type of milk. The longer it's aged, the more depth of flavor it has. Younger Parmesans tend to be saltier and less earthy, but the 24-month stuff is packed with little crunchy, umami-heavy flavor crystals. We often call for it finely grated—please do not buy the pregrated stuff, which has far less flavor. Invest in a hunk (it will last), and grate it by hand on the star-shaped holes or the finest side on a box grater.

Pecorino: Although the super-salty Pecorino Romano is more common, we generally prefer Pecorino Toscano, which has a slightly sharper, tangier flavor, similar almost to a well-aged Cheddar. Look for a version that's been aged for at least 120 days, and like Parmesan, grate it yourself on the star-shaped holes or finest side on a box grater.

Ricotta: Look for high-quality whole-milk ricotta, which might be sold in the form of a hand-dipped cone or basket in the "gourmet" part of the cheese section in a supermarket.

Stracchino: A more specialty item, this is a fresh Italian cheese with a very soft, creamy (in fact spreadable) texture and a mild, delicate flavor. It has no rind. We call for it in the recipe for Seasoned Stracchino Cheese Spread (page 39). It's available at many cheese shops and Italian markets—BelGioioso makes a good domestic product (called Crescenza-Stracchino) and imported versions are available online from brands such as Nonno Nanni—but if you can't find it, try substituting a mild Brie with the rind cut off, or Fontina, though the flavor will be a bit more pungent.

Robiolina: As called for in the Don Angie Pinwheel Lasagna (page 175) as well as the Honey Zeppole (page 283) and a few other recipes, robiolina is a fresh, soft, spreadable white cow's milk cheese sold in a tub, similar to whipped cream cheese (which you can use as a substitute if necessary). We prefer Nonno Nanni brand, available from Alma Gourmet. It's sometimes sold as robiola, which is not to be confused with robiola bosina.

Robiola Bosina: This mild cheese is made from both cow's and sheep's milk, resulting in a very rich, creamy treat. It's sold in square or slab form, similar to Brie, which you may use as a substitute. It's often available at specialty cheese shops or can be purchased online at Murray's Cheese.

Mozzarella: There are all different kinds of mozzarella, including fresh Napoli-style mozzarella di bufala, which is made from rich, creamy water buffalo milk. This is the type we call for in the Persimmon Caprese (page 87), though if you can't find di bufala, a high-quality whole-milk cow's milk mozzarella will do. The other style that we call for in this book, and somewhat on the opposite side of the spectrum in terms of mozzarella cachet, is whole-milk, low-moisture shredded mozz. (Unlike Parmesan and pecorino, it's okay to buy this one preshredded, though if you want to get fancy with it, you can buy a mozzarella block from an Italian deli and shred it yourself with a box grater.) It has excellent melting and stretching properties and is essential to many Italian-American staples.

HOW TO **Drain Ricotta**

When we instruct for ricotta to be packed and drained overnight, wrap the cheese in cheesecloth and place it in a colander or strainer set over a bowl to catch the liquid. Place a heavy pot or canned tomatoes on top of the cheese to weigh it down and put the whole setup in the refrigerator overnight before using. This removes any excess moisture that could interfere with the rest of the recipe, making it too "wet" or loose to work with properly.

Sharp provolone: While the more common mild provolone is, as its name implies, mild and mellow, sharp provolone is a whole different beast—it's pungent, salty, and firm, with an unmistakably "Italian-American" flavor that might make your mouth itch. It has a role in certain situations, like the Baked Ziti Nerano with Zucchini & Provolone (page 185), Pesto-Marinated Provolone (page 40), and Broccoli Rabe & Provolone Gratin (page 250), where its sharpness complements the other flavors, like the bitterness of the rabe, beautifully. Note that when provolone is called for coarsely grated (whether sharp or mild), it should be done on a box grater.

MEATS: Like cheese, you may be able to find some of these Italian-style meats in the grocery store, but an Italian deli (or an online source) will be a sure bet for sourcing. Fra' Mani is an excellent California-based supplier of salumi and specialty meats; they sell most of the following meats online.

Mortadella: Consider this an Italian cousin to bologna, hailing from, appropriately enough, Bologna. It's an emulsified, cooked sausage with pockets of fatback and often pistachios. It's flavored with garlic and black peppercorns, as well as mace for a hint of spice. We love it grilled (as in the spiedini on page 67), or to add fat and flavor to meatballs made with leaner meats like chicken (as in the meatballs on page 195).

Capocollo (aka *gabagool*): This type of *salumi* is named as such because it is usually made from the upper muscle of the pig that starts between the head (*capo*) and neck (*collo*). As with many Italian ingredients, a lot of variations with similar yet different sounding names have come to exist, such as capicola, capicollo, coppa, or ham-capi. What we call for in this book is the spiced, cooked, smoked version that is available in the deli case, and is more similar to ham than to a dry-cured product like prosciutto. Fra' Mani makes a really great version that's smoky, garlicky, and a little spicy all at once. If you can't find it, try using smoked ham, or even andouille sausage.

Pancetta: Italy's version of bacon, though unlike its American counterpart, it's not smoked. Instead, it's salted and cured with a variety of herbs and spices, then rolled up and sold in that form. Again, Fra' Mani is our preferred brand, though pancetta is increasingly easier to find in regular grocery stores.

'Nduja: A very spicy, spreadable salami from Calabria, sometimes sold in jars or vacuum-sealed in a soft tube. It adds heat and fat to the Chicken & 'Nduja Meatballs on page 203, and can be spread across bread or crackers as part of an antipasti platter. La Quercia and Tempesta are good brands to look for.

PEPPERS: We call for a few different types of peppers and chiles throughout the book.

Crushed red pepper flakes: We call for these mildly spicy pepper flakes most often, layering in a touch of heat to dressings and sauces. These flakes are what you'd see on the table at a pizza parlor, and are widely available in grocery stores, though try to get them from a place with high turnover (such as the incredible New York spice shop Kalustyan's, which ships nationally) to ensure freshness.

Crushed Calabrian chiles in oil: As their name implies, these are crushed, oil-packed chile peppers from Calabria, with a medium-hot, piquant flavor. We like to use the chiles in our Garlic & Chile Soffritto (page 300) and the Steak al Limone (page 235). A jar keeps forever in the fridge, and both the chiles and their flavorful oil can be added to vinaigrettes and sauces to add a kick to salads and pastas. Look for TuttoCalabria brand (available from Buon'Italia online) if you can.

Pickled cherry peppers: This quintessential Italian-American ingredient is usually sold by the jar in Italian delis or in the pickle aisle in grocery stores; our preferred brand is B&G, though Cento is also widely available. The pickled peppers come in both hot and sweet varieties (we specify which in each recipe); they add a zingy pop to sauces and more.

GARLIC: We love garlic and call for it in nearly all of our recipes, in a variety of different forms, each of which contributes a slightly different effect to the dish.

Roasted: This is what we turn to when we want a more mellow garlic flavor, but also some depth, from cloves that caramelize slowly in the oven. Make a big batch using the Roasted Garlic Puree recipe on page 300 and keep extra in the freezer.

Chopped or thinly sliced: Finely chop or thinly slice cloves and toast them in olive oil at the start of a recipe when you want a more potent, punchy garlic flavor, such as in Chicken Scarpariello with Sweet & Sour Vinegar Peppers (page 227).

Grated: We call for this often when using raw garlic, grating it on a Microplane, so the fine shards melt into the recipe and deliver a kick of sharp, spicy flavor without the unpleasant sensation of biting into a big hunk of raw garlic.

Crushed: A more rustic technique (gently crush the whole clove with the side of your knife) that infuses a subtle flavor into tomato sauce and marinades without directly inserting it.

COLATURA: A condiment with ancient roots, colatura is made by salting anchovies, storing them in barrels with a weight on top, and allowing them to ferment for months before opening a spout at the bottom of the barrel and collecting the golden liquid that pours out. Colatura was highly prized in the Roman empire: Colatura-filled pots were discovered in Pompeii, and archaeologists believe they were used as currency, with good reason. The salty, umami-heavy, slightly fishy liquid adds a craveable depth of flavor to everything it touches. Delfino is our preferred brand (available at Alma Gourmet online), and know that although bottles can be a bit expensive, a little bit goes a long way. You may substitute Vietnamese fish sauce if you can't find colatura, though it typically is more pungent and saltier in flavor, so taste and adjust amounts accordingly.

VANILLA BEAN PASTE: While nothing is as good as buying fresh vanilla bean pods and scraping the interior (which you should by all means do if you can), vanilla bean paste is a good substitute. It's thicker than extract, and has a deep vanilla flavor, with distinctive vanilla seed flecks suspended throughout; the flavor is superior to extract, which is usually mostly alcohol. Nielsen-Massey makes a good, widely available version.

Finally, a few general notes on common ingredients:

- **Citrus juice** should always be freshly squeezed.

- **Black pepper** should always be freshly ground.

- All recipes call for **kosher salt,** ideally Diamond Crystal brand, unless otherwise noted. We tested everything with this brand and have calibrated the amounts accordingly; it's worth noting that other brands of kosher salt vary in sodium content and might impart a saltier flavor. (Morton, for example, has a much higher amount than Diamond Crystal.) A few recipes call for finishing the dish with a sprinkle of flaky sea salt, such as Maldon.

- **Eggs** are large, and should be organic and free-range if possible.

- **Onions** are always yellow, unless otherwise noted.

- **Herbs** are always fresh, unless otherwise noted. If a recipe calls for dried herbs, we prefer using our own homemade version (see page 301).

- If using **store-bought chicken stock** in lieu of homemade (page 299), use an unsalted variety, as all recipes were tested with our no-salt-added homemade stock and seasoned accordingly.

- We often call for long, slender **Japanese eggplants,** which have a lower moisture content and fewer seeds, helping them keep their shape and texture intact. The big Italian ones tend to mush out while cooking, though we do call for them in a handful of specific recipes. Japanese eggplants are available at farmers' markets in season or Asian grocers year-round. We specify which type of eggplant to use in every recipe.

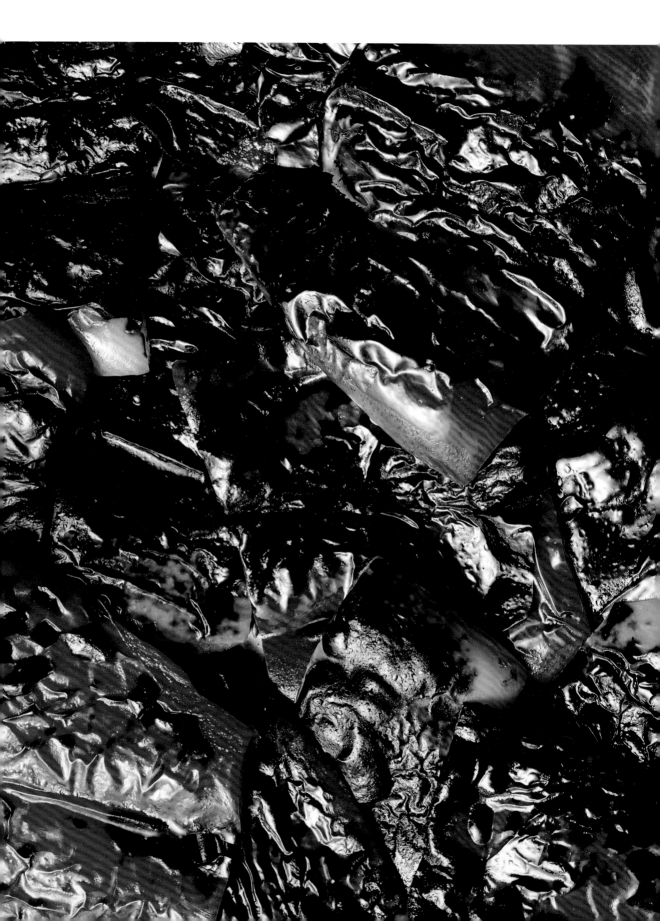

Cold Antipasti

Antipasti, while small in size, are in many respects the beating heart of a proper Italian-American meal. All these little snacky bites are intended to appear before the meal begins in earnest; and truth be told, they're usually our favorite part of the whole shebang.

Every Italian-American family has their own antipasto (the singular of antipasti) tradition. Scott's mother has used the same clear plastic platter for every family gathering over the last forty years, loading it with cheese (usually chunks of mozzarella, or provolone so sharp it makes your mouth itch), roasted red peppers, black olives, marinated artichoke hearts, and Genoa salami rolled into finger-friendly cigars. Angie's family's spread is a similar affair, often with the addition of some bootleg prosciutto that her grandpa's buddy made in his basement.

There are countless ways to mix and match antipasti on a platter. This chapter includes a variety of items, from little snacks like nuts and spreads to pair with cheeses and crisp aperitivo beverages to pickled and marinated items that go exceptionally well with Italian cured meats. We've also included some homemade cheese variations and cracker and bread recipes that pair well with all of it.

If you're strapped for time but still want to serve a whole spread, you can also doctor up some store-bought ingredients to similar effect—jarred marinated artichokes, for example, are quite good with the simple addition of fresh mint, grated garlic, and lemon juice. Or toss store-bought roasted red peppers with grated garlic, lemon juice, oregano, and red pepper flakes in some olive oil. (In fact, toss just about anything with those five things, and it'll probably be good.) And there are ways to make simple snacks look more impressive—for example, cut pieces of cheese or meat into different shapes (wedges, cubes, triangles, etc.) to add visual appeal.

The biggest challenge we find is in restraining ourselves from eating too many snacks right out of the gate—a classic platter of antipasti consists of enough food for a normal person's whole meal, but Italians like to go on to eat a bunch of pasta afterward (then a main course and vegetables, and dessert). That said, you don't have to serve a ton all at once—even one or two antipasti are a great way to start off a meal.

Pimentón-Marinated Olives

MAKES ABOUT 2 CUPS

Marinated olives have always made an appearance on our family antipasto platters, usually in the traditional garlic-and-chile Sicilian variety, or the old-school black pitted ones mixed with marinated vegetables. Our version today calls for more traditionally Spanish ingredients such as pimentón (aka smoked paprika) and sherry vinegar, inspired by the delicious tapas we had together while backpacking in Spain. It's just a little twist on a classic style.

Pop these onto any meat or cheese platter or graze on them on their own with a glass of wine or an aperitivo. You can make and eat them day-of, but the best part is that they keep well in the refrigerator and develop more flavor the longer they sit. *See photo on page 32.*

————

Drain and discard the brine from the olives. Place the olives in a zip-top bag and, using a meat tenderizer or a heavy-bottomed sauté pan, gently pound the bag or apply gentle pressure to crack the olives slightly, so that they can absorb more marinade.

In a medium heatproof bowl, mix the olives with the lemon zest, thyme, and bay leaves. In a small sauté pan, heat the olive oil and garlic over medium heat until the garlic is lightly toasted and aromatic, 2 to 3 minutes. Add the smoked paprika, oregano, and pepper flakes. Cook briefly to toast the spices (they should smell very fragrant), but don't let them burn, about 1 minute.

Immediately pour the oil mixture over the olives. Mix well. Add the sherry vinegar, red wine vinegar, salt, and sugar and stir to combine. The olives can be served right away, but the longer they sit, the more the flavors will deepen. Store in a sealed container in the fridge for up to 2 weeks. Serve at room temperature.

2 cups large Cerignola olives (or your favorite large, meaty olives — Castelvetrano will work here, too)

6 to 8 strips of lemon zest (from 1 lemon)

3 sprigs thyme

2 bay leaves

½ cup extra-virgin olive oil

4 garlic cloves, smashed with the flat side of a chef's knife

2½ teaspoons smoked paprika (preferably Spanish pimentón)

2 teaspoons dried oregano (ideally home-dried, page 301)

½ teaspoon crushed red pepper flakes

½ cup sherry vinegar

1 tablespoon red wine vinegar

¾ teaspoon kosher salt

2 teaspoons sugar

Red Onion & Poppy Jam

MAKES ABOUT 2 CUPS

We had this delicious red onion jam at a little wine and cheese bar in Florence a few days before our wedding—it was simple, but so pretty, and so delicious, with a bright flavor and vibrant color from the addition of red wine vinegar. This is our take, with the addition of poppy seeds—a classic pairing with onion, as any everything bagel–loving New Yorker will tell you. (They're also a friend to lemon, so we threw that in, too.)

The finished product is sweet, sour, and savory all at once, with a textural twist from the seeds, and a light citrusy flavor from the lemons. It's the perfect accompaniment to crackers and cheese, particularly something tangy like a Pecorino Toscano.

———

In a small pot, heat the olive oil over medium heat. Add the onions, salt, and poppy seeds and cook, stirring continually, until the onions are fragrant and translucent, about 5 minutes.

Add the lemon juice, honey, and vinegar. Increase the heat to medium-high and bring to a boil, then reduce the heat to medium-low and simmer until the liquid is thickened and reduced enough to coat the back of a spoon, about 20 minutes. Add the lemon zest and stir well to combine.

Remove the jam from the heat and transfer to a heatproof container. Place in the refrigerator to cool before serving. Leftover jam keeps, covered in an airtight container in the refrigerator, for up to 1 week.

¼ cup extra-virgin olive oil

4 cups finely diced red onions (about 2 to 3 medium onions)

1 tablespoon plus 1½ teaspoons kosher salt

¼ cup poppy seeds

½ cup fresh lemon juice (from about 2 large lemons)

1 cup honey

¼ cup Chianti vinegar or red wine vinegar

Grated zest of 1 lemon

Homemade Whipped Ricotta with Honey

MAKES ABOUT 3 CUPS

Making cheese at home might sound intimidating, but ricotta is very simple to master, and homemade versions are infinitely better than store-bought.

A few things to note: It's worth it here to invest in the best-quality milk you can find. Ideally it's from a farmers' market, or otherwise look for milk that's organic, local, and not ultrapasteurized. Ricotta recipes often call for adding only lemon juice and/or vinegar to supply the acid, but we find that the curds become very stiff that way, and leave an acidic aftertaste. We like adding a little bit of labneh or yogurt, too: It provides a little acid, which helps with the curdling process, as well as milkfat for creaminess, creating a softer, more delicate curd. To make the final product even lighter and fluffier, we even fold in freshly whipped cream. The result is a pillowy-light ricotta, perfect for snacking on with grilled or toasted bread as part of an antipasto spread. Add nuts, fresh herbs, or Cured Lemons (page 306) on top, if so desired, for an extra layer of texture and flavor. The whipped ricotta is great on its own, too, tossed into pasta or simply served with crackers.

4 cups whole milk

1½ cups heavy cream

¼ cup labneh or whole-milk plain Greek yogurt

1½ teaspoons fresh lemon juice

2½ teaspoons kosher salt

3 to 4 tablespoons honey

2 to 3 tablespoons extra-virgin olive oil

Flaky sea salt, such as Maldon

The final stage of curdling, before straining

In a blender, combine the milk, ½ cup of the cream, the labneh, lemon juice, and ½ teaspoon of the salt and blend on high until well combined, about 30 seconds.

Pour the mixture into a small, heavy-bottomed pot and bring to a gentle simmer over low heat. Cook, periodically whisking and gently scraping the sides of the pot with a silicone spatula, until small curds appear and begin to separate from the liquid, 15 to 20 minutes. The curds should be an opaque white color, while the liquid is translucent and more yellow. Once the curds form, remove from the heat and allow the ricotta mixture to rest in the warm pot for 10 minutes (see photo).

Line a sieve with a double layer of cheesecloth and place over a medium bowl. Carefully pour the ricotta mixture into the sieve to collect the curds. The liquid whey should drain quickly. Discard the whey and transfer the strained ricotta to a clean large bowl. It should have a texture similar to cottage cheese, but drier. Place the ricotta in the refrigerator until cool to the touch, about 30 minutes.

In a stand mixer with the whisk, whip the remaining 1 cup heavy cream on medium-high speed until stiff peaks form, 4 to 5 minutes. Using a rubber spatula, gently fold the whipped cream into the chilled ricotta until incorporated. Season with the remaining 2 teaspoons salt.

To serve, place the ricotta in a serving bowl. Drizzle with the honey and olive oil, and top with a small pinch of flaky sea salt. Leftover ricotta keeps, tightly sealed in the refrigerator, for up to 4 days.

Chile & Lime Candied Hazelnuts

MAKES ABOUT 2 CUPS

Hazelnuts are what we associate with Italian cuisine more than any other nut, and though they're typically used in sweets, we wanted to do something savory, borrowing a chile-lime flavor from Southeast Asia along the way. We add these to the Prosciutto & Melon Salad with Tamarind, Hazelnut & Feta (page 91); they're also great as a savory-sweet contrast to salty cheeses, or on their own as a finger-friendly snack with a crisp aperitivo beverage.

Be sure that the egg white is whipped thoroughly and evenly coats the nuts when you're mixing to ensure a uniform candy shell. And speaking of, be careful when you're removing the nuts from the oven and mixing them—you're making candy here, and hot-sugar burns are very painful.

⅔ cup sugar

2 teaspoons kosher salt

1 teaspoon sweet paprika (preferably Hungarian)

¼ teaspoon cayenne pepper

1 egg white

Grated zest of 1 lime

2 cups blanched roasted unsalted hazelnuts

2 teaspoons fresh lime juice

Preheat the oven to 325°F. Line a sheet pan with a silicone baking mat or parchment paper lightly coated with nonstick cooking spray.

In a small bowl, mix together the sugar, salt, paprika, and cayenne.

In a medium bowl, whisk the egg white with the lime zest until thick and frothy, 1 to 2 minutes. It's important to work quickly here, as the egg whites will lose their volume with time. Add the hazelnuts to the whipped egg white/lime zest mixture and fold with a rubber spatula until the nuts are evenly coated. Add the sugar-spice mixture and stir until all granules are totally incorporated into the egg mixture, and evenly coating all of the nuts. Add the lime juice and stir the nuts again to evenly coat.

Spread the nuts on the lined sheet pan and bake for 10 minutes. Coat a large spoon with nonstick cooking spray and stir the nuts with it, ensuring the sugar mixture evenly coats the nuts (not the spoon). Return the nuts to the oven for another 10 minutes. Re-oil the spoon and stir the nuts again. Return to the oven for 5 minutes more, until the nuts are shiny and the sugar coating has turned a golden brown color. Remove from the oven and let cool; do not touch the nuts with your fingers at any point until they are totally cool—the hot caramel is very hot and can burn you easily.

Once totally cool (the exterior should be completely hardened), remove from the paper or baking mat and break the nuts apart with your hands before serving. Leftover candied hazelnuts keep, tightly covered at room temperature, for up to 2 weeks.

Garlic Focaccia

MAKES ONE 18 × 13-INCH PAN (SERVES 8 TO 10)

Light, airy, and soft, this focaccia is a great entry-level bread for aspiring bakers, made with active dry yeast and pantry staples, as opposed to more complex focaccias made with natural leavening. This version has a prominent olive oil and garlic flavor, similar to garlic bread, but better, because this isn't just bread with garlic brushed on top of it—the bread is infused with garlic, then topped with more for good measure.

Eat this as is, alongside more olive oil, or perhaps with the Homemade Whipped Ricotta with Honey (page 27) or Seasoned Stracchino Cheese Spread (page 39). The focaccia comes out even lighter if you mix the dough a day in advance and chill it in the refrigerator overnight; though this step is not strictly necessary, it's good to know if you like to plan ahead. *See photo on page 33.*

2⅓ cups lukewarm (105° to 110°F) water

2¼ teaspoons (1 envelope) active dry yeast

2 teaspoons sugar

1½ cups extra-virgin olive oil

6⅓ cups bread flour

2 tablespoons plus ½ teaspoon kosher salt

¼ cup Garlic & Chile Soffritto (page 300)

½ teaspoon crushed Calabrian chiles in oil

4 garlic cloves, finely chopped

½ teaspoon dried oregano (ideally home-dried, page 301)

1 teaspoon flaky sea salt, such as Maldon

In the bowl of a stand mixer, whisk together the warm water, yeast, and sugar until the yeast is dissolved. Allow the mixture to sit until bubbling and foamy, 10 to 15 minutes.

Add ½ cup of the olive oil and whisk to combine. Attach the dough hook. Add the flour and salt and mix well on medium speed for 7 to 8 minutes to activate the gluten. The dough should be smooth and pull away cleanly from the sides of the bowl. Add the garlic and chile soffritto. Mix well on medium speed to combine, about 2 minutes.

Line a large (18 × 13-inch) sheet pan with parchment paper and coat the paper with ¼ cup of the olive oil. Place the dough on the pan. Drizzle ¼ cup of the olive oil over the dough and cover loosely with plastic wrap. Let rise in a warm place until doubled in size, about 3 hours.

Preheat the oven to 400°F.

Using your fingers, gently press the dough across the surface of the pan. Use your fingertips to create divots (being careful not to puncture the dough) across the surface of the dough. Set aside, uncovered, in a warm place for 30 to 45 minutes, until the dough has risen again and is puffy in appearance.

Place the pan in the oven and bake until the bread is lightly golden brown on top and starting to set in the pan, about 15 minutes.

Meanwhile, in a small bowl, stir together the remaining ½ cup olive oil, the Calabrian chiles, garlic, and oregano.

Remove the bread from the oven and spread the garlic-oil mixture evenly across the top, then sprinkle evenly with the flaky sea salt. Rotate the pan and return to the oven until the garlic is lightly toasted and aromatic and the focaccia is evenly golden and pulling away from the side of the pan, another 15 to 18 minutes. Cool completely in the pan.

To serve, cut into 1½-inch-wide strips (if freezing to serve later, do not cut into strips). Leftover focaccia keeps, tightly sealed in the refrigerator, for up to 3 days, or up to 3 months in the freezer. Leftovers are best served toasted.

Roasted Cauliflower & Pine Nut Spread

MAKES ABOUT 2½ CUPS (SERVES 4 TO 6)

With a tahini-esque base made out of pine nuts instead of sesame, and a flavor profile that nods toward Sicily, this funky little vegetable dip comes off like the Italian cousin to hummus. It's an intensely flavored affair: We roast the cauliflower and onion to the point of deep caramelization, which adds a lot of umami and depth of flavor. Blending it with yogurt makes it creamy, and the pine nut puree provides a final layer of richness.

Serve this snackable spread as a dip with crackers or crudités, or spread it on toasted bread or crostini. *See photo on page 33.*

Make the pine nut puree: Preheat the oven to 225°F.

Arrange the pine nuts in a single layer on a sheet pan and toast, shaking the nuts every 2 to 3 minutes and watching closely, until light golden and aromatic, 15 to 17 minutes. Remove the pine nuts but leave the oven on and increase the temperature to 450°F.

Let the pine nuts cool slightly, then set aside 2 tablespoons for garnish. Blend the remaining pine nuts in a food processor, then add the oil and blend until smooth, about 2 minutes, scraping down with a rubber spatula every 30 seconds. You should have about ½ cup of pine nut puree. Leave the puree in the bowl of the food processor and set aside.

Make the cauliflower: Line two sheet pans with parchment paper.

In a large bowl, combine the cauliflower, onion, garlic, salt, pepper, sugar, and olive oil and toss until evenly coated. Divide between the two prepared pans.

Roast until the onions and cauliflower are fully cooked and very deeply browned, rotating the pans and stirring the vegetables halfway through, about 20 minutes total.

Let the roasted vegetables cool slightly, then transfer to the food processor with the pine nut puree. Add the yogurt, feta, and lemon juice. Pulse until thick, smooth, and well combined.

Pine nut puree

½ cup pine nuts

2 tablespoons neutral oil, such as vegetable

Cauliflower

4 cups cauliflower florets (from about ½ large head, trimmed)

½ medium yellow onion, sliced into thin half-moons

2 garlic cloves, grated on a Microplane

1 tablespoon kosher salt

1 teaspoon freshly ground black pepper

½ teaspoon sugar

½ cup extra-virgin olive oil, plus more for garnish

¼ cup whole-milk plain yogurt

½ cup crumbled feta cheese (2½ ounces), plus more for garnish

1 tablespoon fresh lemon juice

Fresh basil and/or mint leaves, torn, for garnish

Transfer to a small serving bowl and garnish with additional olive oil, crumbled feta, pine nuts, and fresh basil and/or mint. Leftover cauliflower spread will keep, tightly sealed in the refrigerator, for up to 4 days.

Spiced Pignoli Brittle

MAKES ABOUT 2 CUPS

In the restaurant we use this crumbly, almost granola-esque pine nut brittle to top Eggplant Agrodolce with Spiced Pignoli Brittle (page 254), but we love snacking on it as part of an antipasto spread; it goes particularly well with many cheeses. This brittle has more of a soft, sugary texture than some of the hard, shiny brittles out there.

Pay close attention to the pine nuts at the edge of the sheet pan, taking time to remove the sheet and stir a few times, as it tends to cook from the outside in and you don't want the edges to burn. Pine nuts are sensitive—they go from toasty to burnt in seconds, so keep an eye on things in the oven. *See photo on pages 32–33.*

1 large egg white

1½ cups pine nuts

½ cup sugar

½ teaspoon kosher salt

½ teaspoon smoked paprika (preferably Spanish pimentón)

¼ teaspoon cayenne pepper

Preheat the oven to 350°F. Line a sheet pan with a silicone baking mat or parchment paper sprayed with nonstick cooking spray.

In a medium bowl, combine the egg white and 1½ teaspoons water and whisk until thick and frothy, about 1 minute. Stir in the pine nuts.

In a small bowl, combine the sugar, salt, smoked paprika, and cayenne. Using a rubber spatula, fold the spices into the egg white/pine nut mixture.

Pour the pine nut mixture in an even layer across the lined sheet pan and bake for 10 minutes. Remove the pan from the oven, stir, and spread into an even layer again. Return to the oven for an additional 5 minutes, then remove and stir and spread into an even layer again. Bake for a final 5 minutes, until golden brown, then remove, stir, and let cool to room temperature.

Serve at room temperature. Leftover brittle keeps, tightly covered at room temperature, for up to 2 weeks.

Spicy Giardiniera alla Kimchi

MAKES ABOUT 6 CUPS

This is an amalgamation of Korean kimchi, one of our favorite NYC bodega snacks, and Italian giardiniera. Traditionally, giardiniera is made by soaking chopped vegetables in a brine overnight, then topping with vinegar and spices. Here, we salt the vegetables, similar to the process of making a quick kimchi. The vegetables are seasoned as they absorb the salt and lose their natural liquid at the same time—it's a neat way of concentrating the flavor of the vegetables while enhancing their snappy texture. The finished giardiniera is crunchy, spicy, and tangy—perfect for putting on a sandwich, grain bowl, or just serving as is on an antipasto platter. If you prefer your giardiniera extra spicy, you can add a tablespoon of sriracha to the marinade as well.

You need about 1¼ pounds of cauliflower here. If you can find a head that is small, cut it into quarters through the core (as directed in the procedure that follows) and use all of it. However, most heads weigh upward of 2 or 3 pounds by themselves. If that's what you can find, then cut a 2½-pound head into quarters, leaving the core intact, before thinly slicing two of the quarters and reserving the remaining cauliflower for another use. *See photo on page 32.*

1 small (1¼-pound) cauliflower, quartered, core intact

2 large carrots, peeled

4 celery ribs, sliced crosswise on a bias into ¼-inch pieces

¼ cup kosher salt

2 large sweet pickled cherry peppers (such as B&G), seeded and chopped

1 cup white wine vinegar

6 garlic cloves, peeled

2 tablespoons colatura or fish sauce

3 tablespoons sugar

1 teaspoon crushed red pepper flakes

1 tablespoon dried oregano (ideally home-dried, page 301)

¾ cup thinly sliced scallions (4 to 6 scallions)

⅓ cup extra-virgin olive oil

Carefully slice the cauliflower into thin (¼-inch) planks on a mandoline set over a medium bowl, holding the cauliflower with the palm of your hand and keeping your fingers up. (It's okay if some small florets detach and fall into the bowl.) Use the mandoline to slice carrots into ¼-inch-thick coins into the same bowl. Add the sliced celery and salt and toss to combine. Let sit at room temperature for 45 minutes.

Meanwhile, in a blender, combine the pickled cherry peppers, vinegar, garlic, colatura, sugar, and pepper flakes and process on high until the mixture is smooth and turns bright red, about 1 minute. Set aside.

Rinse the cauliflower mixture thoroughly with cold water to remove all the salt. Drain well. Return to the bowl and add the oregano and scallions along with the red pepper mixture and olive oil. Stir well to combine.

It can be eaten immediately, but it tastes better the longer it sits. Ideally, refrigerate it for 24 hours before eating. Giardiniera keeps, tightly covered in the refrigerator, for up to 2 weeks.

Grandma Rito's Marinated Roasted Peppers

MAKES ABOUT 3 CUPS (SERVES 4)

There's always a steady supply of these roasted peppers in Angie's grandma's fridge, for any type of surprise visit. It doesn't matter whether the visitor is hungry, or what time of day it is, Angie's grandma will throw twenty snacks at you, and this is one. She used to roast bell peppers on the open flame on the stovetop, but in recent years, she's developed this broiler technique, of which she is justly proud. It allows you to char and remove the skin, but doesn't hammer the peppers into mush, so you keep all the flavor along with a nice crisp texture. She tells all her friends about it, and now we're telling you.

The longer these peppers sit, the better they are. Eat them plain, on a sandwich or salad with fresh mozzarella, as a side to grilled steak or chicken, or use them in Spicy Fra Diavolo Sauce (page 103). If you're just snacking, know that these taste best at room temperature. *See photo on page 32.*

4 large red bell peppers

¼ cup extra-virgin olive oil

1 garlic clove, grated on a Microplane

2 teaspoons kosher salt

¼ teaspoon freshly ground black pepper

1 teaspoon dried oregano (ideally home-dried, page 301)

1 tablespoon fresh lemon juice

1 sprig basil, gently bruised with the back of a knife

Preheat the broiler. Line a baking sheet with foil.

Remove the stem from each pepper by cutting around it with a sharp knife. Cut a slit down the side of each pepper and flatten it out, skin-side down. Carefully cut out and discard the ribs and seeds from the interior.

Place the cleaned peppers skin-side up on the prepared baking sheet and broil until their skin is blistered and browned and they smell very fragrant, 10 to 12 minutes. Remove from the broiler and let cool. Once cool enough to handle, remove the skin by wiping it off with a clean towel (it should slide off easily). Slice into ½-inch-wide strips.

Place the pepper strips in a large bowl and cover with the olive oil, garlic, salt, pepper, oregano, lemon juice, and basil. Stir to combine and let marinate at room temperature for a minimum of 15 minutes and up to 1 hour before serving.

Serve at room temperature, or keep in the refrigerator until ready to use. Peppers keep, tightly sealed in the refrigerator, for up to 1 week.

Angie's grandmother, Maria Rito

Shrimp Cocktail alla Puttanesca

MAKES 4 CUPS (SERVES 4 TO 6)

It's not very Italian, but who doesn't love a good shrimp cocktail? At our family's annual Feast of the Seven Fishes dinner, Angie's aunt Anna brings shrimp cocktail as part of the antipasto spread, and it's always the first thing to get finished. Wanting to revamp a classic, we thought about some of our favorite foods with a similar flavor profile: a delicious tomato-based shrimp ceviche in Acapulco, a Bloody Mary with celery seeds and black pepper, and, of course, caper and olive-studded puttanesca sauce, usually served with spaghetti. All of that, combined with a good lashing of hot sauce, form a tangy, spicy, salty marinade for raw shrimp, which "cooks" in fresh lemon juice for a souped-up version of shrimp cocktail that's all but guaranteed to be a hit with guests. Serve this with thick-cut toast or grilled bread, crostini, or crackers.

———

Cut the shrimp in half horizontally (butterfly style) into two even-sized halves. Place in a large bowl and toss with the lemon juice and salt. Let sit in the refrigerator for 45 minutes to 1 hour, until the shrimp firms up slightly and begins to look opaque.

Meanwhile, in a food processor, combine the tomatoes, sugar, capers, garlic, colatura, pepperoncini juice, black pepper, celery seed, oregano, and Tabasco. Pulse until combined, about 30 seconds.

Add the pureed tomato mixture to the shrimp, along with the celery, pepperoncini, olives, and parsley. Toss to combine thoroughly. Add the olive oil and stir to combine.

Place in a serving bowl or individual dishes and drizzle with more olive oil, if desired. Serve immediately. The shrimp will continue to firm up as they sit in the liquid, and leftovers will keep, refrigerated, for 1 day.

1 pound jumbo (21/25 count) shrimp (preferably wild-caught), peeled and deveined

½ cup fresh lemon juice (about 2 large lemons)

1½ teaspoons kosher salt

½ cup canned crushed tomatoes

1 tablespoon plus 1 teaspoon sugar

¼ cup brine-packed capers, rinsed and drained

5 garlic cloves, grated on a Microplane

1 teaspoon colatura or fish sauce

¼ cup pickling liquid from jarred pepperoncini peppers

1 teaspoon freshly ground black pepper

½ teaspoon celery seed

1 teaspoon dried oregano (ideally home-dried, page 301)

1 tablespoon Tabasco sauce

½ cup thinly sliced celery, pale yellow inner stalks and leaves only (about 4 small stalks)

2 jarred pepperoncini, thinly sliced crosswise

6 large Sicilian green olives, cracked and pitted, or 12 Manzanilla olives, pitted and halved

¼ cup chopped parsley

⅓ cup extra-virgin olive oil, plus more (optional) for drizzling

Seasoned Stracchino Cheese Spread

MAKES ABOUT 2 CUPS

We spent part of our honeymoon in Trieste, in the northeast of Italy, and fell completely in love with this unique little corner of the country. It used to be a part of the Austro-Hungarian Empire, and there are still some remnants of that style of cuisine in the region today, like this tangy, creamy spread made with stracchino cheese (see page 19). The spread is smooth and rich, imbued with a smoky-spicy flavor from the paprika and Calabrian chiles. This is a cheese spread that needs a vehicle, so serve it with crackers, crudités, and/or grilled bread to truly appreciate it, either as a stand-alone or as part of a composed cheese plate. (We even spread it on our Veal Milanese da Pepi on page 236.)

In a stand mixer with the paddle, mix the cheese on medium speed until smooth and creamy, about 1 minute. Add the onion powder, garlic powder, mustard powder, smoked paprika, chiles, lemon juice, salt, and sugar and mix on low until well combined, about 2 minutes. If necessary, pause to scrape down the sides of the bowl with a rubber spatula to ensure that all ingredients are incorporated. (You can also do this by hand with a whisk and/or rubber spatula, though it will be a forearm workout.)

Serve at room temperature. Leftover cheese spread keeps, tightly sealed in the refrigerator, for up to 4 days.

1½ cups stracchino cheese (about 12.5 ounces or 360 grams)

2 teaspoons onion powder

2 teaspoons garlic powder

1 tablespoon mustard powder

1¼ teaspoons smoked paprika (preferably Spanish pimentón)

1 teaspoon crushed Calabrian chiles in oil

2½ teaspoons fresh lemon juice

2 teaspoons kosher salt

1 teaspoon sugar

our wedding day in Florence, Italy

Pesto-Marinated Provolone

MAKES ABOUT 2 CUPS

If you're serving a meat and cheese platter and want to zhuzh up the cheese without a lot of extra effort, here's your solution: Put it in pesto. It takes all of 10 minutes to whip up and looks (and tastes!) more special than just plunking down a wedge on a plate.

You can make pesto with raw basil, but it oxidizes (turns brown) quickly that way—blanching it before blending helps preserve its color and shelf life, and, we think, enhances its flavor a bit, by concentrating the sugars in the leaves. Add a clove of garlic, grated on a Microplane, for a spicy kick, if so inclined, but note that it won't keep for quite as long in the fridge this way (about one day instead of two).

Other cheeses work here, too—try it with gouda, sharp Cheddar, or feta. *See photo on page 33.*

Fill a medium bowl with ice and water. Bring a small pot of water to a boil over high heat. Blanch the basil until vibrant green, about 5 seconds. Immediately remove the basil from the boiling water and shock it in the ice bath to prevent further cooking.

Drain the basil and pat dry with paper towels, then squeeze them again in a clean kitchen towel to wring out as much liquid as possible. It's important to get these leaves as dry as possible at this point—any excess water in the final product will cause it to turn brown.

Roughly chop the basil and add it to the blender, along with the pine nuts, parmesan, pecorino, lemon juice, and salt. Blend on high speed and slowly drizzle in the oil while blending, until it resembles a thick puree. You should have about ¾ cup of pesto.

In a large bowl, combine the provolone cheese and pesto and toss to evenly coat. The cheese can be served immediately, but will taste best after sitting in the refrigerator for 12 to 24 hours. Leftover cheese keeps, tightly covered in the refrigerator, for up to 3 days.

3 cups packed basil leaves

⅓ cup pine nuts

⅓ cup finely grated Parmigiano-Reggiano cheese

⅓ cup finely grated pecorino cheese (preferably Pecorino Toscano)

1 teaspoon fresh lemon juice

½ teaspoon kosher salt

⅔ cup extra-virgin olive oil

1 pound sharp provolone cheese, cut into ½-inch cubes

Angie's dad & his cousin Pasquale at the family deli

Savory Pizzelle Crackers with Black Pepper, Fennel & Parmesan

MAKES ABOUT 24 CRACKERS

This is a fun interpretation of a quintessential Italian-American cookie, made savory with cheese and black pepper instead of the typical chocolate, vanilla, or anise versions. Cacio e pepe was our loose flavor inspiration, and the finished product is somewhere between cracker and parmesan frico. Serve with sliced meats and cheese as part of an antipasto platter. *See photo on page 33.*

———

In a stand mixer with the paddle, combine the eggs, olive oil, granulated onion, fennel pollen, salt, pepper, sugar, parmesan, flour, and baking powder and mix on medium speed until fully incorporated, 2 to 3 minutes.

Spray a pizzelle press with nonstick cooking spray. Scoop a heaping tablespoon of batter into the press and cook until the crackers are golden brown, 1 to 2 minutes. Carefully remove with an offset spatula or butter knife and cool to room temperature on a wire rack. Repeat until all the batter is used.

Serve at room temperature. Leftover crackers keep, in an airtight container at room temperature, for up to 2 days.

Special equipment

Pizzelle press, which is available online for about $30 (you can of course use the press to make sweet pizzelle as well).

3 large eggs

½ cup extra-virgin olive oil

1 teaspoon granulated onion

1 teaspoon fennel pollen or ground fennel

1½ teaspoons kosher salt

½ teaspoon freshly ground black pepper

1 teaspoon sugar

¾ cup finely grated Parmigiano-Reggiano cheese

1 cup all-purpose flour

¼ teaspoon baking powder

Pickled Eggplant a Scapece with Sumac & Mint

MAKES ABOUT 4 CUPS

Angie's grandmother Maria grew up on a farm outside of Naples, where they'd preserve eggplant for the winter. When she moved to America, this pickled eggplant recipe came along, too, albeit without the sumac and mint, which are our modern-day additions. (That, and the fact that we prefer to use slender, firm Japanese eggplants instead of the big, mushy Italian ones.) Enjoy these as part of an antipasto platter, on a sandwich, or on their own, with nothing more than a toothpick.

Make sure to slice the eggplant paper thin and salt it well, and to cool down the pickling liquid completely before pouring it over the eggplant, all of which helps it retain its firm texture and vibrant purple color.

Make the pickling liquid: In a medium pot, heat the olive oil over medium heat. Add the garlic and cook until pale golden, 1 to 2 minutes. Add the oregano, sumac, and Calabrian chiles and stir to combine. Add the vinegar, sugar, salt, and 6 tablespoons water and bring to a boil over medium-high heat. Once boiling, immediately pour the liquid into a wide, shallow heatproof bowl, and let cool completely in the refrigerator, about 40 minutes. You should have about 2½ cups of brine.

Prepare the eggplant: Sprinkle the eggplant slices evenly with the salt and toss to coat. Set aside in a large bowl for 30 minutes.

Wrap the eggplant in a clean towel and wring to remove as much moisture as possible. Pat dry and return to the bowl.

Toss the chopped mint with the eggplant, then pour the cooled pickling liquid over the mixture. Cover and refrigerate overnight before serving.

Serve at room temperature or slightly chilled. The pickled eggplant keeps, covered in the refrigerator, for up to 2 weeks.

Pickling liquid

½ cup extra-virgin olive oil

4 garlic cloves, very thinly sliced

2 teaspoons dried oregano (ideally home-dried, page 301)

1 tablespoon plus 1 teaspoon ground sumac

2 teaspoons crushed Calabrian chiles in oil

1 cup rice vinegar

½ cup sugar

1 tablespoon kosher salt

Eggplant

1¼ pounds Japanese eggplants (about 4 large), ends trimmed, sliced ¼ inch thick lengthwise on a mandoline

2 tablespoons kosher salt

1 cup roughly chopped mint

Pepperoni & Fontina Crackers

MAKES 12 DOZEN 1-INCH CRACKERS (SERVES 6 TO 8)

These are basically fancy Cheez-Its with pepperoni. Enough said.

Okay, one more thing. These might sound a little intimidating, but they're really not that hard to pull off, and worth the extra effort—the end result is both completely delicious and unlike anything you can buy at the store. Go forth and impress your friends!

———

In a stand mixer with the paddle, combine the Fontina, butter, olive oil, pepperoni, salt, oregano, and granulated garlic. Mix on medium speed until combined, 1 to 2 minutes. The mixture will be crumbly.

Add the flour and mix until just combined, about 1 minute. Add the ice water, little by little, and mix on low until a cohesive dough forms, 30 to 45 seconds. Smooth the dough into a ball with your hands if it hasn't come fully together in the mixer. Split the dough into 2 discs and wrap with plastic wrap. Chill in the refrigerator for a minimum of 1 hour, or up to overnight.

Preheat the oven to 375°F.

Working with one piece at a time, place the dough between two pieces of parchment paper that has been sprayed with nonstick cooking spray. Roll the dough with a rolling pin until it's in a large round about ⅛ inch thick. Remove the top piece of parchment. Using a pizza wheel or paring knife, cut the dough into 1-inch squares (you can keep any imperfect squares around the edges and bake them with the rest). Using a toothpick, create a hole in the center of each square. Carefully transfer the parchment with the unbaked crackers on top to a large baking sheet. Repeat the process with the second disc of dough.

7½ ounces Fontina cheese, coarsely grated on a box grater (4 cups)

3 tablespoons unsalted butter, at room temperature

1 tablespoon extra-virgin olive oil

1½ ounces pepperoni, coarsely grated on a box grater (⅓ cup)

1 teaspoon kosher salt

1½ teaspoons dried oregano (ideally home-dried, page 301)

1 teaspoon granulated garlic

1 cup all-purpose flour

3 tablespoons ice water

½ cup finely grated Parmigiano-Reggiano cheese

Bake both pans until the crackers puff up and start to turn golden at the edges, 10 to 15 minutes, rotating the pans from front to back and switching racks halfway through. Remove the crackers from the oven. Leave the oven on and reduce the oven temperature to 200°F.

Move the crackers around on the baking sheet. Use a paring knife to carefully break up any that have stuck together. Return the crackers to the oven and bake until crispy, an additional 5 to 10 minutes. Remove from the oven and immediately sprinkle with the parmesan.

Serve at room temperature. Leftover crackers keep, in an airtight container at room temperature, for up to 2 days.

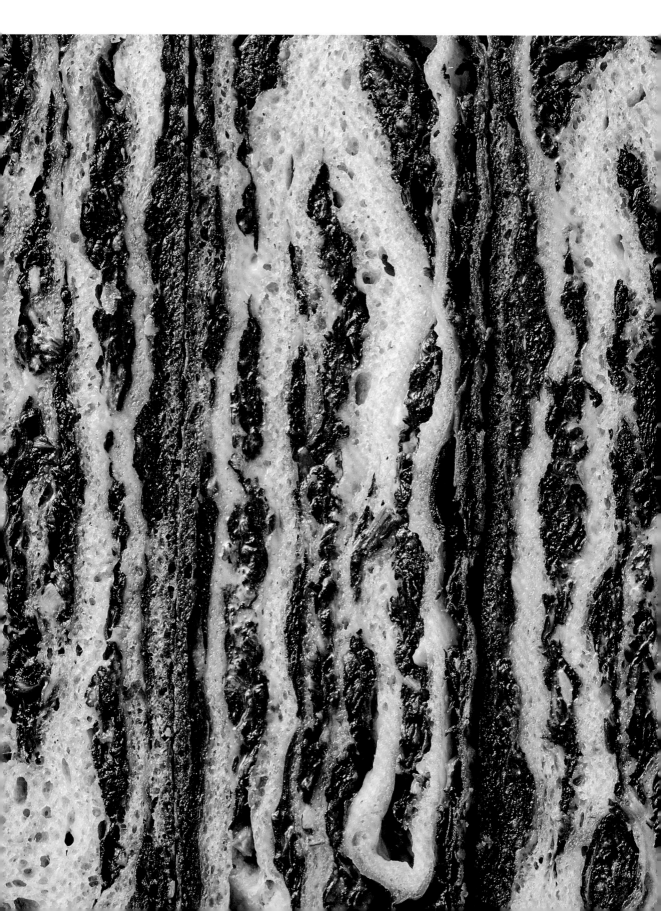

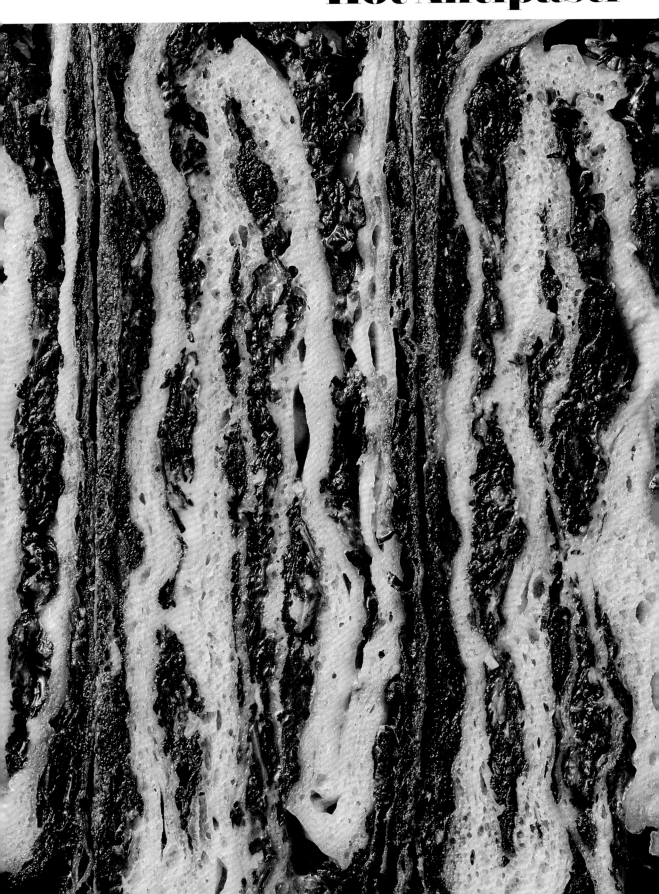

In keeping with the theme of abundance, it's not enough to just have cold antipasti before a meal—Italian Americans also load up on hot antipasti. You'll often see "hot" and "cold" antipasto sections on the menu at classic red-sauce joints, and we wanted to do them justice in their own chapter as well.

The recipes here are a mix of family recipes and our own creations. The scacciata—a sort of cheesy, veggie-stuffed focaccia—and Sicilian-style pizza rolls are our interpretations of Rito family favorites, and the stuffed artichokes are a nod to our grandmothers, both of whom made versions we loved as kids. Others are our own riffs on classics, like the Spicy Baked Clams Francesco, a kicked-up version of clams oreganata, made with our favorite hot sauce. Many of the recipes here are perfect little single servings; dishes like the mortadella spiedini on skewers and festive-looking baked mussels stuffed with pepperoni rice are great for parties.

These antipasti could work as stand-alone appetizers, or even side dishes, though we like to make a bunch and set them out as snacks before the main event (one or two as apps or hors d'oeuvres, or three or four for a full hot antipasto spread). If you're feeling really ambitious, you could mix and match hot and cold antipasto recipes from both chapters, which can be fun for holidays and entertaining. But even making just one at a time is a great way to kick off any meal.

Mushrooms al Forno with Fontina & Marsala

MAKES ABOUT 25 SMALL MUSHROOMS (SERVES 4 TO 6)

Stuffed mushrooms are one of Scott's mom's go-to moves for New Year's Eve celebrations. Hers are often filled with an umami-forward mixture of bread crumbs, cheese, and/or sausage, but we wanted a version that would use the whole mushroom (cap and stem), and really highlight their sweet, earthy flavor. So we turned to Marsala, a fortified wine from Sicily, which is a classic foil for mushrooms in Italian-American cuisine.

The result is something between a stuffed mushroom and a twice-baked potato, with a creamy, cheesy filling lightened up with tangy sour cream and fresh scallions. We use Fontina, a great melting cheese, which has a slightly funky flavor that pairs well with the earthiness of the mushrooms. Consider this finger food, ideal for entertaining or an antipasto platter, or make them as a side for a grilled steak or the Veal Milanese da Pepi (page 236).

1 pound cremini mushrooms (about 25 medium)

4 tablespoons (½ stick) unsalted butter

⅓ cup finely chopped shallot (about 1 medium shallot)

1½ teaspoons kosher salt

½ teaspoon freshly ground black pepper

½ teaspoon dried oregano (ideally home-dried, page 301)

2 tablespoons dry Marsala

½ cup sour cream

¾ cup finely grated Fontina (1½ ounces) cheese

½ cup finely grated Parmigiano-Reggiano cheese

½ cup Italian seasoned bread crumbs, store-bought or homemade (page 298)

⅔ cup thinly sliced scallions (3 to 5 scallions)

1 large egg

2 tablespoons extra-virgin olive oil

Preheat the oven to 400°F. Line a sheet pan with parchment paper.

Gently clean the mushrooms with a paper towel to remove any dirt. Carefully remove the stems, leaving the caps intact. Set the clean caps aside and roughly chop the stems into small pieces, about ¼ inch.

In a medium sauté pan, melt the butter over medium-high. Add the shallot, salt, pepper, and oregano. Cook until the shallots are translucent, about 2 minutes. Add the chopped mushroom stems. Stir well and cook until the mushrooms release their liquid and start to darken and shrink, 4 to 5 minutes. Add the Marsala. Stir well and cook until the liquid has completely evaporated, about 2 minutes. (Foamy, bubbly butter will still remain in the pan.)

Remove the cooked mushroom mixture and let cool slightly. Place in a blender along with the sour cream. Puree on high until the mixture is smooth, about 2 minutes.

Transfer the pureed mixture to a medium bowl. Add ½ cup of the Fontina, ¼ cup of the parmesan, the bread crumbs, the scallions, and the egg. Mix well

with a rubber spatula until all the ingredients are combined.

Stuff each mushroom cap with 1 to 2 tablespoons of the filling (it's okay to borderline-overstuff these caps as the filling will not run when baked). Arrange the caps on the lined sheet pan.

In a small bowl, combine the remaining ¼ cup Fontina and ¼ cup parmesan. Sprinkle the mixture evenly across the tops of the stuffed mushrooms. Drizzle the olive oil over the top of the mushrooms.

Bake until golden brown, 14 to 15 minutes. Transfer to a serving platter. Let cool slightly before serving. Leftover mushrooms keep, tightly covered in the refrigerator, for up to 3 days.

Spicy Baked Clams Francesco

MAKES 25 CLAMS

This is our riff on clams oreganata, made spicy and named after our beloved Frank's hot sauce. You see all kinds of ingredients prepared "oreganata" style in Italian-American cuisine: Our grandmothers applied it to artichokes, and fish and shrimp often get the treatment, too, but clams are tops as far as we're concerned. The key ingredients are, unsurprisingly, oregano, along with garlic, bread crumbs, and parmesan. It's one of our favorite dishes to order at a red-sauce joint to start the meal, and we always include it in our Feast of the Seven Fishes dinner, served with a buttery sauce and fresh herbs to complement the spiciness.

We like Frank's hot sauce because it has a straightforward tangy cayenne flavor, and a vinegary sharpness that pairs well with seafood. Plus, it gives the baked clams a vibrant red color. Feel free to try other hot sauces, though, and if you can't find littleneck clams, this also works with Manilas and cherrystones.

———

Prepare the clams: Place the clams in a large bowl of cold water and let sit for 20 to 30 minutes to purge any sand from them. If any shells are open, lightly tap them on the side of the bowl. If they do not close in response to the tapping, discard them, as this means they are dead. Rinse the clams with cold water and drain them in a colander. Store in the refrigerator until ready to shuck.

In a large sauté pan, heat the butter over medium heat until melted. Add the grated garlic, oregano, salt, and pepper and cook briefly, stirring often, until the garlic is fragrant and toasted, about 1 minute.

Transfer the garlic mixture to a medium bowl and add the panko, sugar, hot sauce, sriracha, chicken stock, parmesan, and olive oil. Using a spatula, gently mix to combine, carefully folding the ingredients together in a cutting motion until they resemble coarse wet sand (do not overmix or it will become too gummy).

Clams

25 littleneck clams

2½ tablespoons unsalted butter

2 large garlic cloves, grated on a Microplane

1 teaspoon dried oregano (ideally home-dried, page 301)

¼ teaspoon kosher salt

⅛ teaspoon freshly ground black pepper

1¼ cups panko bread crumbs

¼ teaspoon sugar

2 tablespoons cayenne-style hot sauce, such as Frank's RedHot

1½ teaspoons sriracha sauce

¼ cup chicken stock, unsalted store-bought or homemade (page 299)

½ cup finely grated Parmigiano-Reggiano cheese

2 tablespoons extra-virgin olive oil

3 lemons, cut into wedges, for serving

Sauce

2 tablespoons extra-virgin olive oil

2 tablespoons finely chopped garlic

1 cup dry white wine, such as Pinot Grigio

1 cup chicken stock, unsalted store-bought or homemade (page 299)

2 teaspoons kosher salt

2 teaspoons sugar

1 tablespoon plus 2 teaspoons fresh lemon juice

⅔ cup finely grated Parmigiano-Reggiano cheese

1 cup (2 sticks) cold unsalted butter, cubed

3 tablespoons chopped chives

2 tablespoons chopped dill

RECIPE CONTINUES

Preheat the oven to 400°F. Trim a piece of foil to the same size as a sheet pan and crinkle it gently with your fingers to create little ridges for the clams to balance on.

Shuck the clams (see How to Shuck Clams sidebar) and discard the top shells. Reserve the liquor (you should have about 1 cup). Arrange the clams across the sheet pan. Form a heaping tablespoon of the panko mixture into a ball, then flatten it with your fingers before placing on top of each clam.

Make the sauce: In a medium saucepan, heat the olive oil over medium-high heat. Add the garlic and cook, stirring often, until lightly toasted and fragrant, about 2 minutes. Add the wine and cook until its volume is reduced by half, about 1 minute. Add the chicken stock and reserved clam liquor (if you didn't yield a full cup, make up the difference with chicken stock), salt, sugar, and lemon juice. Bring to a boil and reduce by half, about 3 minutes.

Transfer the liquid to a blender. Open the steam vent in the lid but cover with a kitchen towel to avoid any hot splatter. Add the parmesan and butter and blend on high until incorporated. You should have about 2 cups of sauce.

Bake the clams until the breaded tops are golden around the edges, about 4 minutes.

To serve, using tongs, transfer the baked clams to a serving dish. Add the chives to the warm sauce and spoon over the clams. Top with the dill. Serve immediately with lemon wedges. Clams are best cooked and eaten day-of.

HOW TO Shuck Clams

SPECIAL EQUIPMENT
Clam knife or an old, dull paring knife (to avoid cutting yourself or damaging the blade, do not use your best knife here)

Set a fine mesh sieve over a small bowl. Hold the clam in a towel or glove to protect your hand, with the hinge nestled in your palm near your thumb, with the opening at your fingertips. Insert the knife tip between the shells, into the muscle, twisting it gently to pry the top shell open. Cut around the seal of the shell. Snap off the top shell and discard. Pour the liquor from the clam through the sieve into the small bowl. Leave the clam in the bottom shell, and place the shucked clams onto the prepared baking sheet, open side up, as you go. Reserve the liquor from all the shucked clams.

Scacciata with Swiss Chard & Spinach

MAKES 2 LOAVES (SERVES 8 TO 10)

Think of this almost like a stuffed focaccia, with thin layers of dough that are stuffed and folded over on themselves, creating a deliciously savory layered bread that slices up into a perfect handheld snack. Most regions of Sicily call it *scaccia*, but in the small town where Angie's grandfather is from, it's known as *scacciata*, and to this day it's her father's favorite thing. The greens and garlic, plus anchovies and olive oil in the filling, lend a spanikopita-like feel to the whole endeavor.

The dough is simple to make, but if you're pressed for time, you can also use 1½ pounds of store-bought pizza dough instead. We've provided step-by-step photos for the folding instructions on page 54. *See photo on pages 46-47.*

Make the dough: In the bowl of a stand mixer, whisk together the warm water, yeast, and sugar until the yeast is dissolved. Allow the mix to sit until bubbling and foamy, 10 to 15 minutes. Attach the dough hook and stir in the flour and salt on low to combine. Add the olive oil and continue mixing on medium speed until the mixture forms a smooth ball, about 2 minutes. Transfer to a clean, oiled mixing bowl, cover with plastic wrap, and set aside in a warm place until the dough doubles in size, about 2 hours.

Meanwhile, make the filling: In a large pot, heat the olive oil over medium-high heat. Add the garlic, salt, black pepper, and pepper flakes and cook until the garlic just starts to turn light golden, about 2 minutes. Stir in the anchovies and cook for another 30 seconds.

Stir in the Swiss chard and continue to cook for 5 minutes, stirring often, until the chard has wilted and released most of its liquid. Add the wine and cook until dry, stirring often, another 5 minutes.

Add the spinach and cook until completely wilted and very dry, stirring often, for another 10 minutes. Remove from the heat. Stir in the lemon juice, sugar, and parmesan until well combined. Remove the mixture from the pot and place in a medium bowl. You should have about 4 cups of the filling. Place in the refrigerator and let cool completely.

Dough

1¼ cups lukewarm (105° to 110°F) water

1 tablespoon plus 1½ teaspoons (2 envelopes) active dry yeast

½ teaspoon sugar

3¼ cups all-purpose flour

1 tablespoon kosher salt

3 tablespoons extra-virgin olive oil, plus more for the bowl

Filling

¾ cup extra-virgin olive oil

⅓ cup chopped garlic (from 1 large head or 15 cloves)

2½ teaspoons kosher salt

½ teaspoon freshly ground black pepper

½ teaspoon crushed red pepper flakes

2 anchovy fillets, finely chopped

1 pound roughly chopped Swiss chard leaves (from about 2 large bunches)

⅓ cup dry white wine, such as Pinot Grigio

16 ounces roughly chopped fresh spinach (from about 2 large bunches) or frozen spinach, thawed and drained

¼ cup fresh lemon juice (about 1 large lemon)

1 tablespoon sugar

1 cup finely grated Parmigiano-Reggiano cheese

To assemble

1 cup all-purpose flour, for the work surface

4 cups shredded whole-milk mozzarella cheese

3 tablespoons extra-virgin olive oil

RECIPE CONTINUES

Preheat the oven to 425°F. Line a baking sheet with parchment paper.

To assemble: Once the dough has doubled in size, gently punch it down and divide it into 2 equal balls. Work with one ball at a time and cover the other ball in plastic wrap until ready to use.

Place one ball of dough on a lightly floured surface and dust with more flour. Gently press the dough into a rectangular shape using your fingers, stretching as needed. Using a lightly floured rolling pin, carefully roll the dough into a thin 18 × 14-inch rectangle about ⅛ inch thick.

Set the dough with a long side facing you. Spoon 1 cup of the filling onto the middle of the rectangle and spread it out gently with a rubber spatula to fill the center of the rectangle, keeping about 3 inches of dough clear on the long edges and 1½ inch clear on the short edges. Sprinkle 1 cup of the mozzarella on top of the filling only.

Fold the top half of the long side of the rectangle into the middle, then fold the bottom half of the long side up to meet the first, overlapping by about ½ inch. You should now have a rectangle that's 18 × 7 inches.

Spread ¾ cup of the filling on top of the folded dough, spreading it evenly to fill the center of the rectangle, keeping about 1½ inches of dough clear on the short edges and 3 inches clear on the long edges. Sprinkle ¾ cup of the mozzarella over the filling only.

Fold the two short ends of the rectangle inward to meet in the middle. You should now have a rectangle that's 9 × 7 inches. Spread ¼ cup of the filling on one half of the top, keeping about 1 inch of dough clear of the edges. Sprinkle ¼ cup of the mozzarella over the filling only.

Fold the dough in half, like closing a book, so it is now 4½ × 3½ inches in size. Prick the top with a fork. Transfer to a parchment-lined baking sheet and thoroughly brush the top and sides with olive oil. Repeat the process with the second dough ball.

Bake until deeply golden brown and crisp, 35 to 40 minutes. Remove from the oven and transfer to a wire rack for at least 10 minutes. Cut into 1-inch-wide slices and serve warm or at room temperature. Leftovers keep, tightly covered in the refrigerator, for up to 4 days, or frozen for up to 2 months. Reheat scacciata in the oven at 350°F for 10 to 12 minutes.

Addario-Style Frying Peppers

MAKES 5 TO 8 PEPPERS

Every Italian-American family has a recipe for stuffed peppers, a mainstay of hot antipasto platters. This is Scott's family's, albeit with a few tweaks: The filling is bread crumbs, the way his grandmother did it, but lightened with ricotta and amped up with zingy pickled peppers. They're steamed with a little liquid (we use water and lemon, though chicken stock would be a good alternative to add additional flavor) and can be served hot or at room temperature, as is or with a little Spicy Fra Diavolo Sauce (page 103) spooned on top.

Italian frying peppers, also known as cubanelles, are light green, mild peppers with thin walls that are ideal for stuffing. They're fairly widely available, though if necessary, you can substitute bell peppers halved lengthwise (just note they will take a few minutes longer to bake).

———

NOTE: A grapefruit spoon, while not strictly necessary, is the ideal size and shape for getting the ribs and seeds out of the peppers.

½ cup Italian seasoned bread crumbs, store-bought or homemade (page 298)

½ cup whole-milk ricotta cheese

½ cup finely grated pecorino cheese (preferably Pecorino Toscano)

½ cup finely grated Parmigiano-Reggiano cheese

2 tablespoons Roasted Garlic Puree (page 300)

⅓ cup chopped seeded sweet pickled cherry peppers, such as B&G

¼ teaspoon freshly ground black pepper

1 teaspoon dried oregano (ideally home-dried, page 301)

2 teaspoons kosher salt

3 tablespoons roughly chopped parsley

1 large egg

2 anchovy fillets, finely chopped

6 to 8 Italian frying peppers (aka cubanelles)

2 tablespoons extra-virgin olive oil

2 tablespoons fresh lemon juice

Preheat the oven to 400°F.

In a medium bowl, combine the bread crumbs, ricotta, pecorino, parmesan, garlic puree, cherry peppers, black pepper, oregano, salt, 2 tablespoons of the parsley, the egg, and anchovies by hand until well incorporated.

Using a small knife, cut the top of each pepper off just below the stem. With your finger or a small spoon, remove as much of the seeds and ribs as you can without breaking the pepper.

Using your fingers, carefully press the stuffing mixture into the peppers, pushing gently to get it all the way to the end of the pepper.

In a heavy-bottomed medium sauté pan or cast-iron skillet, heat 1 tablespoon of the olive oil over medium heat. Add the peppers and cook, turning occasionally, until golden brown on all sides, 6 to 8 minutes.

Add ¼ cup water to the pan along with the lemon juice. Place in the oven and bake until the peppers are completely soft and cooked through and the filling is slightly crispy where exposed, about 15 minutes.

Top with the remaining 1 tablespoon chopped parsley and 1 tablespoon olive oil and serve immediately. Peppers keep, tightly covered in the refrigerator, for up to 3 days.

Stuffed Artichokes Oreganata

SERVES 4

This is a very nostalgic dish for us—both of our grandmothers made stuffed artichokes, and we wanted to pay homage to them with our own rendition. Angie remembers finding out as a small child, much to her horror, that her grandma's filling involved anchovies, which she's clearly gotten over. Our version today has a lot of strong, savory flavors, but they don't overpower the palate—the finished product is perfectly balanced. Serve these as an appetizer or side dish, or even as a light main with a salad—they're satisfying enough to stand alone.

Cook the artichokes: With a sharp knife, cut off artichoke stems to form a flat base. Cut across the top of the artichoke (about 1½ inches down) to expose the purple tops of the innermost petals. With kitchen shears, trim the pointed leaves of the artichokes. Using your hands, gently remove the innermost petals to expose the fuzzy choke. Use a spoon to carefully scoop out all of the fuzz, revealing the heart. Squeeze two of the lemons liberally over the cut tops and insides of the artichokes to prevent browning.

Gently place the artichokes in a medium pot, petals facing up. Squeeze the remaining 2 lemons over the artichokes and drop them in. Add the garlic, wine, salt, peppercorns, bay leaves, and mint sprigs, plus enough water that the artichokes are submerged halfway in liquid. Bring to a simmer over medium heat. Reduce the heat to maintain a steady gentle simmer, then cover and simmer until the artichokes are tender, about 45 minutes. Remove the artichokes from the pot and set aside to cool.

Make the stuffing: In a large sauté pan, melt the butter over medium heat. Add the garlic, anchovies, oregano, black pepper, dried mint, cayenne, and salt. Cook until the butter foams, the anchovies melt, and the garlic is golden, 3 to 4 minutes.

Place the panko in a large bowl and pour the butter-garlic mixture over it, mixing well. Add the chicken stock, olive oil, and parmesan and mix well to combine. The stuffing should hold together without sticking to your fingers.

Artichokes

4 medium artichokes

4 lemons, halved

3 heads garlic, halved horizontally

1 cup dry white wine, such as Pinot Grigio

3 tablespoons kosher salt

1 tablespoon black peppercorns

4 bay leaves

4 sprigs mint

Stuffing

½ cup (1 stick) unsalted butter

8 garlic cloves, grated on a Microplane

3 anchovy fillets, finely chopped

1 teaspoon dried oregano (ideally home-dried, page 301)

½ teaspoon freshly ground black pepper

1 teaspoon dried mint (ideally home-dried, page 301)

½ teaspoon cayenne pepper

1 teaspoon kosher salt

2¼ cups panko bread crumbs

1 cup chicken stock, unsalted store-bought or homemade (page 299)

¼ cup extra-virgin olive oil, plus more for drizzling

1 cup finely grated Parmigiano-Reggiano cheese, plus more for serving

Lemon wedges, to serve

Preheat the oven to 400°F.

Using your fingers, place the stuffing mixture in between every artichoke petal, starting from the outside and working your way in. Aim to use ¼ to ½ cup of stuffing per artichoke. Place the artichokes in a baking dish and drizzle the tops with the olive oil. Place in the oven and bake until golden brown, 15 to 20 minutes.

Remove from the oven and top with more grated parmesan. Serve with lemon wedges. Leftovers keep, tightly covered in the refrigerator, for 2 days.

Stuffed Mussels with Pepperoni Rice

SERVES 6 TO 8

Paella was the loose source of inspiration for this finger-friendly snack, but we made it our own by swapping out chorizo for pepperoni, a specifically Italian-American type of *salumi* (meaning, you don't really see it in Italy). Think about it—with paella, you pair chorizo with shellfish, so why not try pepperoni? Plus, the flavor is so nostalgic for us.

You see a lot of baked shellfish (think clams) in Italian-American restaurants, especially around New York, and this is a way to do something a little different. There's a great mussel flavor in every bite because you make a quick stock from the mussels while they cook, and use that same liquid to cook the rice. And the baked shells are so pretty when they come out of the oven—add this to the menu the next time you're feeling particularly festive.

Prepare the mussels: Place the mussels in a large bowl of cold water with the salt and let sit for 20 to 30 minutes to purge any sand from them.

Rinse the mussels with cold water, scrubbing them gently to remove any barnacles or mud, and drain in a colander. If any shells are open, lightly tap them on the side of the bowl. If they do not close in response to tapping, discard them, as this means they are dead. Remove any beards from the mussels by grabbing the beard between your thumb and forefinger and briskly tugging it toward the hinge of the shell.

In a large heavy-bottomed pot, heat the oil over medium heat. Add the garlic and cook until lightly toasted, 2 to 3 minutes. Add the parsley and pepper flakes and stir to combine. Add the mussels and wine. Cook, covered, until the mussels start to open, 2 to 3 minutes (discard any that do not open).

Use a slotted spoon to remove the mussels immediately from the pot and place them in a large bowl in the refrigerator to cool while making the rice. Strain the liquid that remains in the pot through a sieve and set aside (discard the aromatics). You should have about 3 cups of liquid—if you have less, add enough water to reach 3 cups.

Mussels

5 pounds mussels

1 tablespoon kosher salt

1 cup extra-virgin olive oil

6 garlic cloves, crushed

6 sprigs flat-leaf parsley

Pinch of crushed red pepper flakes

1 cup dry white wine

Rice

6 ounces pepperoni, cut into 1-inch pieces

½ cup extra-virgin olive oil

3 tablespoons tomato paste

1 anchovy fillet, finely chopped

1 tablespoon plus 1 teaspoon dried oregano (ideally home-dried, page 301)

1 medium yellow onion, finely chopped

1 garlic clove, grated on a Microplane

2 teaspoons kosher salt

1 cup dry white wine

1½ cups short-grain white rice, such as Calasparra or Arborio

¼ cup fresh lemon juice (about 1 large lemon)

Pinch of sugar

For serving

1 cup Lemon Aioli (page 306)

1 lemon, cut into wedges

RECIPE CONTINUES

Make the rice: In a food processor, finely chop the pepperoni (it should be a generous 1 cup).

In a large heavy-bottomed pot, heat the olive oil over medium-low. Add the pepperoni and cook, stirring occasionally, until the oil turns bright red, 4 to 5 minutes. Add the tomato paste, anchovy, and oregano and stir to combine. Cook for 3 minutes, stirring occasionally, then add the onion, garlic, and salt. Cook until the vegetables are soft, 4 to 5 minutes.

Add the wine and increase the heat to medium-high. Cook, stirring occasionally, until the liquid is evaporated, 3 to 4 minutes. Add the rice and 3 cups of the reserved mussel stock, and reduce the heat to medium-low. Simmer, stirring frequently, until all liquid has evaporated and the rice is soft on the outside but the inside is still a tiny bit crunchy, 20 to 25 minutes. Reduce the heat as necessary to keep from scorching.

Remove from the heat and cover. Let sit for 20 minutes to finish cooking all the way through. Add the lemon juice and sugar, stir well to combine, then cool the rice mixture in the refrigerator for 30 minutes.

Preheat the oven to 400°F.

Line two sheet pans with foil and crinkle it gently with your fingers to create little ridges for the mussels to balance on. Remove and discard the top shell of each mussel. Free the mussel from the remaining shell with a paring knife, but leave it in the shell. Stuff each shell with a heaping spoonful of the cooled rice mixture and transfer to the pans, stuffed side up.

Bake for 5 minutes, then switch the oven to broil and broil for an additional 2 to 3 minutes, until the rice topping is golden brown.

To serve: Drizzle lemon aioli over the top of each stuffed mussel. Serve immediately, with lemon wedges on the side. Mussels are best prepared and eaten day-of.

Sicilian Pizza Rolls

MAKES 8 LARGE OR 16 SMALL ROLLS (SERVES 8)

As their Italian name, *cipolline Catanesi,* implies, these little puff pastry squares are native to Catania in Sicily (where Angie's grandfather is from) and they are traditionally filled with onions (*cipolle*). Angie's grandfather makes a light, classic version with tomato sauce and onion, but we added Fontina and spicy salami to make it more like a pizza roll.

These snacky, handheld treats are very versatile. A large one might serve as lunch with salad, or you can cut them into smaller bite-size pieces before baking. Feel free to play around with different cheeses and/ or meats in the filling, too. *See photo of the completed dish on page 48.*

———

NOTE: We make our own puff pastry dough with some added olive oil for savoriness, and provide instructions for doing so below—it sounds intimidating but really isn't that hard, making full use of modern conveniences like a food processor. That said, if you don't have time or don't want to, you can also use a 1-pound package of store-bought puff pastry instead.

Make the puff pastry: In a food processor, pulse the flour, salt, and pepper to combine. Add half of the butter and pulse 3 to 4 times. Add the remaining butter and pulse another 3 to 4 times, until the butter is in pieces the size of a pea. Add the olive oil and pulse to combine. Add the ice water and pulse 3 to 5 times, until the dough has started to come together into a ball but still looks shaggy.

Working quickly, turn the dough out onto a lightly floured surface and knead with your hands until it forms a smooth ball (about 10 kneads). With a lightly floured rolling pin, roll the dough into a rectangle about 12 × 18 inches. Fold the two short ends over one another (like you're closing a book) so you have a 12 × 9-inch rectangle. Then fold it in half again the opposite direction, to create a 6 × 9-inch rectangle. Fold once more, the opposite direction, to create a 6 × 4½-inch rectangle. Wrap with plastic wrap and place in the refrigerator for at least 1 and up to 3 hours.

Puff pastry

2 cups all-purpose flour, plus more for rolling the dough

1 teaspoon kosher salt

½ teaspoon freshly ground black pepper

1 cup (2 sticks) cold unsalted butter, cubed

3 tablespoons extra-virgin olive oil

½ cup plus 1 tablespoon ice water

Filling

1 (28-ounce) can whole tomatoes (preferably San Marzano DOP)

⅓ cup extra-virgin olive oil

1 medium yellow onion, thinly sliced

1 tablespoon kosher salt

1 teaspoon freshly ground black pepper

2 teaspoons dried oregano (ideally home-dried, page 301)

1 tablespoon sugar

To assemble

1 large egg

Kosher salt

8 ounces Fontina cheese, cut into ¼-inch dice

8 ounces spicy salami, such as hot soppressata or salami Calabrese, cut into ¼-inch dice

3 tablespoons finely grated Parmigiano-Reggiano cheese

RECIPE CONTINUES

Meanwhile, prepare the filling: Place the tomatoes and their liquid in a medium bowl and break them up with your hands into small chunks no bigger than a quarter. In a medium pot, heat the olive oil over medium-high. Add the onion, salt, pepper, and oregano and cook, stirring often, until the onions have softened completely, about 5 minutes. Add the tomatoes and sugar and stir well to combine. Reduce the heat to medium and cook, stirring often to avoid sticking, until the sauce has thickened and flavors have melded, about 10 minutes. You should have about 3 cups of filling. Transfer to a medium bowl and place in the refrigerator to cool completely.

To assemble: Create an egg wash by whisking the egg with 2 tablespoons water and a pinch of salt.

Remove the dough from the refrigerator and place on a lightly floured surface. Roll the dough into a 24 × 12-inch rectangle. You can cut the dough into two and roll it into two 12-inch squares at this point if it is easier to handle. (If using store-bought dough, gently roll it out to make it into a 12-inch square.) Cut the dough into eight 6-inch squares. (If you want to make smaller, bite-size pockets, cut the dough into sixteen 3-inch squares and halve the amount of filling you put in each.)

Line two baking sheets with parchment paper. Place ¼ cup of the tomato-onion filling in the center of each dough square. Top with ¼ cup of the Fontina and ¼ cup of the salami. Brush the outside corners with the egg wash, then pinch the corners up to the middle, sealing them shut where they meet. Transfer to a lined baking sheet. Repeat to fill the rest of the dough. Any leftover filling can be reserved as a dipping sauce for the finished rolls, or saved and used for another application (mozzarella sticks!).

Brush the squares with more egg wash over the surface and sprinkle the parmesan over the top, distributing the cheese evenly across all squares. Place in the refrigerator for at least 30 minutes and up to 4 hours before baking.

Preheat the oven to 400°F.

Bake the squares until the pastry is golden brown and the cheese is bubbling, 25 to 28 minutes, rotating the pans from front to back and switching racks halfway through. Let cool slightly before serving.

Serve warm. Leftovers keep, tightly covered in the refrigerator, for up to 3 days. Reheat in a 325°F oven or toaster oven.

Mortadella Spiedini with Pickled Garlic Salsa Verde

MAKES 12 SKEWERS

Years ago, we had grilled mortadella in Bologna, Italy's mortadella headquarters and the namesake for its American cousin, bologna. It arrived drizzled with balsamic vinegar and topped with arugula to balance all of that fat, and we destroyed the whole plate in seconds. This is our homage—a fun, quick snack that you can eat with your fingers at a backyard cookout.

The *salsa verde* offers a bright, acidic counterpoint to the richness of the meat, and the mustard seeds are a nod to the classic American pairing of mustard and bologna sandwiches. This recipe is super simple, so it's important to buy the best-quality mortadella you can find and get it freshly sliced. Serve these skewers alongside the Pesto-Marinated Provolone (page 40) or really any of the antipasti from this book.

½ cup rice vinegar

2 tablespoons yellow mustard seeds

1½ teaspoons kosher salt

1 tablespoon sugar

Pinch of crushed red pepper flakes

3 garlic cloves, thinly sliced on a mandoline

6 ounces mortadella, thinly sliced

½ cup roughly chopped parsley

Grated zest of 1 lemon

2 tablespoons extra-virgin olive oil

Soak twelve 8-inch wooden skewers in water for at least 10 minutes or up to 1 hour.

In a small pot, combine the vinegar, 2 tablespoons water, the mustard seeds, salt, sugar, and pepper flakes and bring to a boil over medium-high heat. Remove from the heat and immediately place the sliced garlic into the mixture. Set aside to cool.

Cut the mortadella slices in half to create two half-moons. Carefully weave the skewers through the mortadella slices like a ribbon, working forward and backward and gently scrunching it onto the skewer, putting 3 or 4 slices on each skewer.

Prepare a grill or grill pan to medium-high heat. Add the skewers and cook, flipping once, until crispy and browned on the edges, about 2 minutes total.

Add the parsley, lemon zest, and olive oil to the garlic mixture and stir to combine. Drizzle the salsa verde mixture over the mortadella skewers and serve immediately. This dish is best made and eaten day-of.

Salami & Cheese Potato Crocchette

MAKES ABOUT 25 CROCCHETTE

Naples is the street food capital of Italy, with countless vendors manning carts full of delicious fried things; potatoes show up often. Some of our fondest memories are of strolling through Naples's boisterous streets, with music blasting from the windows and locals zipping through the crowds on scooters, stopping at tiny street stands along the way to sample all manner of deep-fried snacks. We wanted to develop something that would remind us of the city and its unparalleled street food game.

These *crocchette* are light, fluffy, and creamy, with a cheesy inside and crispy exterior. Our trick here is to work potato starch into the batter itself, so you don't have to bread and dredge each ball. This batter contains enough starch to form its own crispy shell, and it's naturally gluten-free.

Feel free to swap in different semihard cheeses (i.e., Gouda) and *salumi* (prosciutto, pepperoni). The Genoa salami that we call for is the deli cold cut, as opposed to a stick of salami.

1¼ pounds russet potatoes (about 2 to 3)

2 bay leaves

1 tablespoon black peppercorns

2 heads garlic, halved horizontally

1 teaspoon kosher salt, plus more for seasoning

3 ounces thinly sliced Genoa salami, cut into ⅛-inch dice

2 ounces sharp provolone cheese, roughly chopped into ¼-inch dice

1 large egg

¾ cup finely grated Parmigiano-Reggiano cheese

2 tablespoons potato starch

½ teaspoon granulated onion

½ teaspoon granulated garlic

½ teaspoon freshly ground black pepper

Neutral oil, such as vegetable, for deep-frying (about 6 cups)

Place the potatoes in a large pot with the bay leaves, peppercorns, and garlic. Add water to cover and season with kosher salt (about ¼ cup for every 8 cups water). Bring the water to a simmer over high heat, then reduce the heat to keep at a low simmer and cook, uncovered, until you can pierce the potatoes with a fork, 30 to 40 minutes. If you boil them too vigorously, the skin might start to come off and the potatoes will get too starchy. Drain, discard the aromatics, and set the potatoes aside until cool enough to handle.

Peel the potatoes (discard the skin) and pass them through a potato ricer or food mill over a large bowl. (If you don't have either you can press the cooked potato through a fine-mesh sieve with the back of a spoon.) You should have about 2 packed cups of riced potatoes.

Add the salami, provolone, egg, parmesan, potato starch, granulated onion, granulated garlic, the 1 teaspoon salt, and the pepper to the bowl and mix well with a large spoon until evenly incorporated. Using your hands, roll the mixture into 1½-inch spheres (about 2 tablespoons each) and arrange on a baking sheet for frying. (Uncooked, rolled crocchette can be kept in the refrigerator for up to 1 day before frying.)

Line a baking sheet with paper towels. Pour 3 to 4 inches oil into a large heavy-bottomed pot or Dutch oven and heat to 350°F over medium-high heat.

Working in batches to avoid overcrowding, fry the crocchette until golden brown and crispy, 1½ to 2 minutes, stirring occasionally. Carefully remove with a slotted spoon and set on the paper towels to drain. Season with salt while still warm.

Serve immediately. These are best fried and eaten day-of.

We both grew up eating simple green salads—often at the end of a big saucy meal—with a light, acidic vinaigrette to help cut through the heavier flavors. But today, our salads rarely involve lettuce. We're always trying to think outside the box, or rather, the bowl.

We like salads with a balance of different flavors, temperatures, textures, and colors, and we use different methods to build those layers—grilling Romano beans, for example, or blanching broccoli heads, and playing around with non-Italian ingredients such as tamarind, cilantro, and avocados.

There are some classic Italian and Italian-American salads out there that we didn't want to mess with too much, though we did want to give them our own twist. So our prosciutto and melon salad gets dressed with tamarind, mint, and candied hazelnuts; our caprese swaps tomatoes and balsamic in favor of persimmon and browned butter. And our Caesar—not technically Italian, but a staple at Italian-American restaurants across the country—uses delicate chrysanthemum leaves in lieu of romaine, an ingredient we fell for while living on New York's Lower East Side, next to Chinatown. The classics are a classic for a reason, but we do try to make them a little more exciting.

Many of these salads are substantial enough to act as a light lunch on their own; or serve them as an appetizer or side dish. Although these recipes do have bold flavors, nothing in them is terribly heavy, so you can easily pair them with some of the heartier pastas or main courses from other chapters. A few—like the persimmon caprese, or spicy crab panzanella with tomatoes—rely on using perfectly ripe seasonal produce, so try to make those when their main ingredients are at their peak. Others, like the potato salad or the wedge, are a little more evergreen, though of course we encourage you to use the best-quality ingredients you can find.

Broccoli Salad with Oregano Vinaigrette, Olives & Crispy Shallots

SERVES 4 TO 6

When Scott was growing up, his grandmother always had garlicky, vinegary marinated broccoli on hand to serve alongside meatballs and chicken parm. Hers was based on a simple mixture of vinegar and oil, but our tribute today involves a few more flavors, including mellow roasted garlic puree and crushed chiles, to make the dish feel just a bit more complex. The fried shallots at the end add crunch, a nice textural touch for a salad that's substantial but still feels fresh.

———

In a large pot, bring 4 quarts water and ¾ cup of the salt to a boil over high heat. Set up an ice bath: 3 quarts water, 3 cups ice, and the remaining ¼ cup of salt (the salt is so the broccoli doesn't lose its seasoning when you put it into the ice bath).

Add the broccoli and cook, working in batches if necessary to avoid overcrowding the pot, until a paring knife pierces the stalk easily, 1 to 2 minutes. Remove and immediately submerge in the ice bath to cool. Once cooled, drain and set aside to dry.

In a large bowl, toss the broccoli with the vinaigrette. Add the olives and red onion and gently toss to coat evenly. Spoon onto a platter or onto individual serving plates. Top with crispy shallots.

Serve immediately. Leftover salad keeps, tightly covered in the refrigerator, for up to 3 days.

1 cup kosher salt

3 pounds broccoli (about 2 large heads), cut into 2-inch spears (florets and tender stalk)

1 cup Oregano Vinaigrette (recipe follows)

¼ cup oil-cured olives, pitted and halved lengthwise

¼ small red onion, very thinly sliced

1 cup Crispy Shallots (page 305)

Oregano Vinaigrette

ABOUT 1½ CUPS

1 cup white wine vinegar

⅓ cup Roasted Garlic Puree (page 300)

¼ teaspoon crushed red pepper flakes

3 garlic cloves, grated on a Microplane

¼ cup extra-virgin olive oil

1 teaspoon dried oregano (ideally home-dried, page 301)

2 tablespoons sugar

1 teaspoon kosher salt

In a medium bowl, whisk together the vinegar, garlic puree, pepper flakes, grated garlic, olive oil, oregano, sugar, and salt until emulsified. Vinaigrette keeps, tightly covered in the refrigerator, for up to 3 days.

Chrysanthemum Caesar

SERVES 4 TO 6

This is our take on a Caesar, in distinctly New York fashion, using delicate chrysanthemum greens in lieu of lettuce. We were introduced to these greens when we lived in an apartment on the Lower East Side, near Chinatown, above a restaurant serving Yunnanese food. We wanted to find a way to incorporate them into our menu within the framework of our style of cuisine, and latched on to the idea of Caesar salad—not technically an Italian dish, but one that is for some reason served in a lot of Italian-American restaurants. We did a Caesar-style prep on the greens, with a toasted sesame bread crumb to bring it back to the original Asian influence, and a snowdrift of finely grated parmesan atop the whole surface. Use a Microplane here to grate the cheese so it's as airy and light as the salad itself.

NOTE: Chrysanthemum greens can be found at Asian grocers and, occasionally, farmers' markets. If you can't find them, use 10 to 12 ounces of mizuna (which will have a more bitter taste) or baby arugula.

Make the dressing: In a blender, combine the mayonnaise, lemon juice, ¼ cup water, both oils, the parmesan, roasted garlic puree, anchovy, grated garlic, sugar, colatura, salt, and pepper and blend on high speed until incorporated. You should have about 1 cup dressing. Set aside. (The dressing may be made up to 3 days ahead.)

Make the salad: First, to prepare an ice bath using a salad spinner, place 2 cups of ice and 8 to 10 cups water in the bottom of the spinner and place the basket on top of the ice, submerged in the water. (Set the lid aside for now.) To clean chrysanthemum greens, pick the leaves (discard any that are bruised) from the stalks and place them into the basket in the ice water. Discard the stalks. Allow the greens to sit in the ice water for at least 10 and up to 20 minutes. Pull the basket with the greens out, discard the ice and water, return the basket of greens to the spinner, and spin the greens dry. (Alternatively, if you don't have a salad spinner, use a sieve set in a large bowl to create the ice bath, then drain the ice water and dry the greens very well with paper towels.)

Dressing

⅓ cup Japanese mayonnaise, such as Kewpie

1 tablespoon plus 2 teaspoons fresh lemon juice

1 tablespoon plus ½ teaspoon neutral oil, such as vegetable

1 tablespoon extra-virgin olive oil

2 tablespoons plus 2 teaspoons finely grated Parmigiano-Reggiano cheese

2 teaspoons Roasted Garlic Puree (page 300)

Half of 1 anchovy fillet

¾ teaspoon garlic grated on a Microplane (about 2 cloves)

1 tablespoon sugar

¼ teaspoon colatura or fish sauce

¾ teaspoon kosher salt

¼ teaspoon freshly ground black pepper

Salad

1¼ pounds (about 40 stalks) chrysanthemum greens (see Note)

¼ cup toasted sesame seeds

¾ cup Crispy Garlic Bread Crumbs (page 299)

2½ tablespoons fresh lemon juice

2½ tablespoons extra-virgin olive oil

1½ teaspoons kosher salt

4 ounces Parmigiano-Reggiano cheese

In a small bowl, combine the sesame seeds and garlic bread crumbs.

In a large bowl, toss the greens with the lemon juice, olive oil, and salt. Place the dressed greens in a loose pile on a serving platter or individual plates. Drizzle the dressing deliberately and slowly over the top of the greens to dress them evenly. Top with the sesame/bread crumb mixture. Grate the parmesan with a Microplane over the top of the salad to shower the entire dish in a small mountain of cheese.

Serve immediately. The dressing and bread crumbs can be made ahead, but the assembled salad dish is best eaten straightaway.

Grilled Romano Bean Salad

SERVES 4 TO 6

Romano beans go by many names: runner beans, Italian pole beans, Italian string beans, flat beans, and more. Whatever you call them, these oversize, wide, flat beans are our favorite, being sweeter and less fibrous than other varieties. They're available on the East Coast from midsummer to early fall, perfectly timed to cookout season. If you can't find them or want to make this at a different time of year, use blanched string beans instead (see Note).

This is a summery dish, with a light acidity and freshness from the vinegar, lemon juice, and herbs, and celery and cucumber for crunch (a trick we picked up from Angie's grandma). The flavor of the marinade intensifies as it sits, so these beans will remain tasty for up to three days after you make it. Serve alongside grilled steak or pork for a warm-weather feast.

NOTE: If Romanos are out of season or unavailable, you may use the same amount of string beans, trimmed and blanched. To do this, bring a large pot with 4 quarts water and 1 cup kosher salt to a boil over high heat. Set up an ice bath: 3 quarts water, 3 cups ice, and ½ cup kosher salt (the salt is so the beans don't lose their seasoning in the ice bath). Cook the green beans for 1 minute, until cooked through but still crunchy and bright green in color, then use tongs or a spider to transfer to the ice bath and let cool completely. Remove the beans from the ice water and place on a plate lined with paper towels to dry. Proceed with the rest of the recipe as written.

1½ pounds Romano beans (see Note)

¼ cup red wine vinegar

3 tablespoons fresh lemon juice

⅓ cup extra-virgin olive oil

5 garlic cloves, grated on a Microplane

3 tablespoons sugar

2 teaspoons dried oregano (ideally home-dried, page 301)

1 tablespoon kosher salt

½ teaspoon freshly ground black pepper

6 celery ribs, pale inner stalks and leaves only, thinly sliced

1 cucumber, halved lengthwise and thinly sliced into half-moons

¼ cup roughly chopped dill leaves (about 5 sprigs)

8 to 10 mint leaves, roughly chopped

Prepare a grill or grill pan to medium-high heat. Grill the beans in batches, cooking for about 4 minutes on each side, until the beans have wilted and have defined grill marks. Set aside until cool enough to handle, then trim the ends and halve crosswise.

In a large bowl, whisk together the vinegar, lemon juice, olive oil, garlic, sugar, oregano, salt, and pepper. In the same bowl, mix together the grilled beans, celery, cucumber, and dill. Pour the vinegar mixture over the beans and toss to coat.

Let marinate in the refrigerator for at least 30 minutes and up to 1 hour before serving. Turn the beans over a few times in the bowl to ensure that they are evenly dressed with vinaigrette, and let come to room temperature before serving so that the olive oil is not solidified.

Toss with mint just before serving. Serve on a platter or in individual plates. Leftovers keep, tightly covered in the refrigerator, for up to 3 days; flavors will intensify as the beans sit and soak up more marinade.

Spicy Crab Panzanella

SERVES 4 TO 6

Panzanella is a Tuscan dish, typically made with leftover stale bread. We amp up its flavor by making croutons fried with a ton of garlic and herbs; when it's mixed with the marinated tomatoes, the combination is truly delicious. The marinated crab here is a nod to Midwestern cream cheese and crab dip, one of Angie's mom's staples for family events when she was growing up. Ours is lightened up with mascarpone and given a kick from sriracha. You can also skip the crab here to make an entirely vegetarian version. Serve this at a summer cookout, alongside grilled meat and corn on the cob.

———

NOTE: Tomatoes are the star of the show here, so if possible, use ripe heirloom tomatoes at their peak, in late summer. If that's not possible, look for vine-ripened tomatoes, large cherry tomatoes, or ripe plum or Roma tomatoes instead. (Tomatoes in general should be stored and eaten at room temperature.)

Make the garlic croutons: In a large bowl, mix together ¼ cup of the olive oil, the chopped garlic, pepper, oregano, and thyme.

In a large sauté pan or heavy-bottomed pot, heat the remaining ¼ cup olive oil and butter over medium heat until the butter is melted. Add the bread and stir to coat. Cook, stirring continually, until the bread is golden brown, about 3 minutes. Add the garlic/herb/oil mixture and stir to coat. Cook, stirring continually, until the garlic is toasted, about 2 more minutes. Remove from the heat. Season with the salt and stir to combine. They should be golden brown and crispy around the edges. Transfer the croutons to a plate lined with paper towels.

Garlic croutons

½ cup extra-virgin olive oil

2 tablespoons finely chopped garlic (about 6 cloves)

¼ teaspoon freshly ground black pepper

½ teaspoon dried oregano (ideally home-dried, page 301)

1½ teaspoons chopped fresh thyme (about 6 sprigs)

4 tablespoons (½ stick) unsalted butter

3 cups torn bread, in 1½-inch pieces (from a crust-on Italian-style loaf or focaccia)

½ teaspoon kosher salt

Marinated tomatoes

2 to 3 large heirloom tomatoes

1 tablespoon sherry vinegar

1 tablespoon fresh lemon juice

1 tablespoon Roasted Garlic Puree (page 300)

1 tablespoon sugar

2 teaspoons kosher salt

Grated zest of 1 lemon

2 tablespoons extra-virgin olive oil

3 celery ribs, thinly sliced crosswise

⅓ cup thinly sliced scallions (2 to 3 scallions)

⅓ cup finely chopped shallots (1 medium shallot)

¼ cup thinly sliced pepperoncini peppers (4 to 5 peppers)

10 basil leaves, torn

Marinated crab

⅓ cup mascarpone cheese

¼ cup mayonnaise

2 tablespoons sriracha sauce

2 teaspoons fresh lemon juice

1 teaspoon kosher salt

½ teaspoon sugar

½ pound jumbo lump crabmeat, picked clean for shells

To assemble

10 basil leaves, torn

6 celery leaves

¼ cup extra-virgin olive oil

Freshly ground black pepper

Marinate the tomatoes: Cut the tomatoes into 1½-inch pieces. You should have about 4½ cups of chopped tomatoes. In a large bowl, whisk together the sherry vinegar, lemon juice, roasted garlic puree, sugar, salt, lemon zest, and olive oil. Add the tomatoes, celery, scallions, shallots, pepperoncini, and basil and toss to coat. Let marinate for at least 10 minutes and up to 1 hour before assembling the salad.

Marinate the crab: In a medium bowl, whisk together the mascarpone, mayonnaise, sriracha, lemon juice, salt, and sugar until combined. Add the crab and fold to evenly coat with the mascarpone mixture. Refrigerate until ready to serve.

Assemble the salad: Just before serving, add the garlic croutons to the bowl of tomatoes and toss well so the tomato liquid soaks into the croutons. Spoon the tomato-crouton mixture onto a platter or into individual bowls and top with dollops of the crab mixture. Garnish with torn basil and celery leaves. Drizzle the olive oil over the top, along with freshly cracked pepper.

Serve immediately. Panzanella is best made and served day-of.

Garlicky Potato Salad with Avocado

SERVES 4 TO 6

The original version of this recipe comes from Angie's grandmother, who made a simple, tangy potato salad with a boatload of olive oil, garlic, and lemon juice; it was frequently served alongside the Steak al Limone (page 235) at family gatherings. Our take involves the addition of avocado, one of our favorite non-Italian ingredients. It adds a softness and creaminess that beats mayo any day, and we throw in a handful of celery and scallions for crunch.

NOTE: Use only the innermost ribs and leaves of the celery—those with a pale yellow color, which are tender and have a clean celery flavor—as opposed to the tougher, more fibrous outer parts.

In a medium pot, combine 8 cups cold water, ¼ cup of the salt, and the cut potatoes. Bring to a boil over medium-high heat, then reduce to a simmer and cook until the potatoes are cooked through, about 15 minutes.

Meanwhile, in a medium sauté pan, heat the olive oil over medium heat. Add the garlic and remaining 2 teaspoons salt and cook until aromatic, 1 to 2 minutes. Add the oregano and pepper flakes and cook for 30 seconds, being careful to avoid burning.

Drain the potatoes and set aside in a large bowl. Pour the olive oil and garlic mixture on top of the hot potatoes. Add the celery, scallions, lemon zest, lemon juice, red wine vinegar, and sugar. With a wooden spoon or rubber spatula, stir vigorously for 1 minute, until some little bits of the potato break off and emulsify with the oil, creating a slightly creamy texture. Most of the potatoes should remain intact.

Just before serving, halve and pit the avocado and slice the flesh into ½-inch cubes. Gently fold the avocado into the potatoes.

Transfer to a serving bowl or individual plates and serve at room temperature. Leftover potato salad keeps, tightly covered in the refrigerator, for up to 4 days.

¼ cup plus 2 teaspoons kosher salt

2 pounds baby red creamer potatoes, halved

½ cup extra-virgin olive oil

6 garlic cloves, grated on a Microplane

1 tablespoon dried oregano (ideally home-dried, page 301)

¼ teaspoon crushed red pepper flakes

1 cup diced celery, inner ribs and leaves only (about 4 to 5 inner ribs; see Note), plus ¼ cup leaves for garnish

1 cup thinly sliced scallions (6 to 8 scallions)

Grated zest of 1 lemon

2 tablespoons fresh lemon juice

2 tablespoons red wine vinegar

¾ teaspoon sugar

1 avocado

Spicy Antipasto Salad

SERVES 4 TO 6

We have a special affinity for cold antipasto platters loaded with Italian salumi, cheeses, and marinated vegetables (see the entire chapter dedicated to them earlier in this book) so it seemed fitting to create this homage to them in salad form. Think of everything you'd find on a classic cold antipasto platter and you'll have the right idea here. There's meat, cheese, olives, and peppers, but we've tweaked it a bit to add some nontraditional ingredients like delicate enoki mushrooms, scallions, and dill, which add a lighter, fresher flavor. Pureed jarred deli peppers make a spicy-sweet dressing that's great on everything from salads to sandwiches. The dressing has a very specific Italian-American flavor profile—acidic, sweet, spicy, and garlicky all at once. Angie's dad can't get enough of it.

Dress this salad just before serving for the best flavor. It makes for a colorful composed appetizer or a light meal alongside a simple piece of grilled chicken or fish.

———

NOTE: If enoki mushrooms are unavailable, substitute ¼ pound button mushrooms, stems removed, caps sliced thinly on a mandoline.

Make the dressing: In a blender, combine the cherry peppers, lemon juice, sugar, red wine vinegar, hot sauce, sriracha, garlic, oregano, and salt and blend on high until well combined. With the blender running on low, slowly drizzle in the olive and vegetable oils until incorporated. You should have about 1⅔ cups of dressing, all of which will be used in this salad.

Make the salad: In a large serving bowl, combine the cabbage, mushrooms, celery, soppressata, provolone, scallions, dill, and olives and toss together with your hands or salad tongs. Drizzle all of the dressing on top of the salad, then toss again to evenly coat all of the ingredients.

Serve immediately. This salad is best made and eaten day-of, though the dressing can be made up to 3 days in advance and held, tightly sealed in the refrigerator.

Dressing

½ cup chopped seeded sweet pickled cherry peppers, such as B&G

¼ cup plus 2 tablespoons fresh lemon juice

¼ cup sugar

¼ cup red wine vinegar

2 tablespoons hot sauce, such as Frank's RedHot

1 tablespoon sriracha sauce

1 garlic clove, grated on a Microplane

1 teaspoon dried oregano (ideally home-dried, page 301)

½ teaspoon kosher salt

¼ cup extra-virgin olive oil

¼ cup plus 1 tablespoon vegetable oil

Salad

¼ small head red cabbage, cored and thinly sliced on a mandoline (about 3 cups)

2 cups enoki mushrooms (see Note), trimmed from their base, gently separated with your fingers

6 celery ribs, thinly sliced on a bias

¼ pound sliced soppressata, cut into ¼-inch wide strips

¼ pound sliced sharp provolone cheese, cut into ¼-inch wide strips

½ cup thinly sliced scallions (3 to 4 scallions)

4 sprigs dill, coarsely chopped

½ cup halved pimiento-stuffed olives (ideally stuffed Manzanillas)

Radicchio Salad with Apple, Cilantro & Hazelnut Dressing

SERVES 4 TO 6

Growing up, our families almost always finished their meals with a bitter tricolor salad—a combination of radicchio, fennel, and other greens, dressed simply with olive oil and lemon juice. Our modern-day version is a loose interpretation: as if that bowl of bitter greens had run into a Waldorf salad somewhere in Southeast Asia. The dressing was inspired by our favorite Thai spicy peanut sauce, but we swapped peanuts in favor of the more Italian hazelnut, which pairs well with radicchio. Cilantro is a unique addition that ties into the flavor profile of the dressing, and adds another zip of color. Take the time to soak the radicchio in the ice bath, which helps crisp the leaves while drawing out some of their bitter flavor.

———

Make the dressing: Preheat the oven to 400°F. Line a sheet pan with parchment paper.

Spread the hazelnuts on the sheet pan, transfer to the oven, and toast until golden brown, glistening, and aromatic, 10 to 12 minutes.

Carefully transfer the hot hazelnuts to a food processor and add the neutral oil. Process briefly until the nuts begin to form a puree (though small chunks should still remain, about the size of gravel), about 15 seconds. Add the honey, sugar, vinegar, lemon juice, sriracha, salt, garlic, and cilantro leaves. Process again until well combined, about 30 seconds. You should have about 1 cup of dressing. Set the dressing aside until ready to use.

To assemble: Prepare an ice bath using a salad spinner: Place 2 cups of ice and 8 to 10 cups water in the bottom of the spinner along with ¼ cup of lemon juice and place the basket on top of the ice, submerged in the water. Set the lid aside for now. (Alternatively, if you don't have a salad spinner, you can use a sieve set in a bowl to create the ice bath.)

Clean the radicchio by removing any limp or discolored outer leaves. Cut the radicchio into quarters, then remove the core. Pull apart the individual leaves and place them into the ice bath, tearing any large outer leaves in half before adding.

Dressing

½ cup blanched roasted unsalted hazelnuts

3 tablespoons neutral oil, such as vegetable

2 tablespoons honey

3 tablespoons sugar

2 tablespoons rice vinegar

2 tablespoons fresh lemon juice

1½ teaspoons sriracha sauce

1½ teaspoons kosher salt

1 small garlic clove, grated on a Microplane

2 sprigs cilantro, leaves picked

To assemble

½ cup fresh lemon juice (about 2 large lemons)

1 small head radicchio (about 9 ounces)

1 apple, such as Honeycrisp or Granny Smith

1 small or ½ large fennel bulb

Grated zest of 2 lemons

2 tablespoons extra-virgin olive oil

½ teaspoon kosher salt

6 ounces robiola bosina cheese (see page 19), cut into ½-inch cubes (or the same amount of triple cream Brie, after the rind has been cut off)

¼ cup roughly chopped blanched roasted unsalted hazelnuts

5 sprigs cilantro, leaves picked

RECIPE CONTINUES

Cut the apple into quarters and trim away the core. Slice each apple wedge on the mandoline into half-moons about ⅛ inch thick, then place immediately into the ice bath with the radicchio.

Cut the fennel in half, remove the core, then carefully slice the cut side on the mandoline, into pieces about ⅛ inch thick. Add the sliced fennel to the ice bath as well, then allow the mixture to sit for 15 to 20 minutes.

Pull the basket with the radicchio, apple, and fennel from the spinner, discard the ice and water, then spin the salad dry. Spread the salad ingredients on a work surface lined with paper towels and blot the top with more paper towels. It is very important to dry the mixture as much as possible so as to not dilute the dressing.

Place the radicchio, apple, and fennel in a large bowl. Add the lemon zest, the remaining ¼ cup lemon juice, the olive oil, and salt. Using your hands or tongs, toss well to evenly coat.

Assemble the salad on a large platter or in individual plates. Scatter the cheese evenly across the top of the salad (or divide evenly among the plates). Drizzle the dressing across the top of the salad, deliberately and slowly, ensuring even coverage of the dressing across the salad. Sprinkle chopped hazelnuts on top and garnish with cilantro leaves.

Serve immediately. This salad is best made and served day-of.

Angie's dad & his great uncles playing an Italian card game

Persimmon Caprese

SERVES 4 TO 6

You see caprese salads on the Amalfi coast, near its namesake Capri, which is known for its juicy tomatoes. But we wanted to do a new take, and settled on persimmons, the sweet-yet-earthy fruits which often make an appearance on elaborate fruit platters after our annual Christmas Eve family feasts, and coincidentally sort of look like orange tomatoes. Persimmons are naturally quite sweet, but you get just the right amount of savoriness from the lemon juice, basil, and pine nuts, so the overall effect is well balanced. Feel free to make this in the summer, substituting grilled stone fruits like peaches or nectarines in lieu of persimmons.

Using high-quality mozzarella is key here, and fresh mozzarella is typically sold unseasoned, so we like to soak ours in salted cream to add richness and flavor (a tip Angie picked up while working at Torrisi Italian Specialties in Little Italy).

4 small balls (3 to 4 ounces each) unsalted fresh mozzarella or 1 large (16-ounce) ball

¼ cup heavy cream

2½ teaspoons kosher salt

4 Fuyu persimmons, unpeeled, cut into small wedges (about 12 wedges per persimmon)

2 tablespoons neutral oil, such as vegetable

¼ cup honey

3 tablespoons fresh lemon juice

4 tablespoons (½ stick) unsalted butter, cubed

4 sprigs basil, leaves picked

3 tablespoons pine nuts, toasted

½ teaspoon flaky sea salt, such as Maldon

If using the small balls of mozzarella, cut each ball into 4 pieces. If using the large 16-ounce ball, cut it into 16 pieces. In a medium bowl, whisk together the heavy cream and ½ teaspoon of the salt. Place the mozzarella into the seasoned cream and set aside to soak for at least 10 minutes or up to 30 minutes.

Heat a large cast-iron skillet over high heat. In a large heatproof bowl, toss the persimmon slices with 1 teaspoon of salt and the neutral oil. Working in batches to avoid overcrowding, place the persimmons in the pan and sear, flipping halfway through, until deep golden brown, 2 to 3 minutes total. Remove from the pan and set aside to cool.

Wipe out the bowl you seasoned the persimmons in and whisk together the honey, lemon juice, and remaining 1 teaspoon salt. Add the cooled persimmons to the bowl and toss to coat.

In a large sauté pan, heat the butter over medium-high until melted and large, foamy bubbles start to appear, 2 to 3 minutes. Swirl the pan to ensure even cooking. The butter will make loud sputtering noises, then the bubbles will dissipate and the noise will subside—this is when you should notice the white milk solids in the butter turning deep golden brown in color. Remove from the heat and pour the butter over the persimmons, tossing to coat evenly. Roughly chop half of the basil and add it to the persimmons, tossing to coat.

Scoop the mozzarella from the bowl of cream and arrange on a large platter or individual plates. Scoop the persimmons with a slotted spoon and arrange all of them on top of the cheese. Drizzle with additional brown butter sauce, if desired. Sprinkle the toasted pine nuts on top. Garnish with the remaining whole leaves of basil and the flaky salt.

Caprese is best made and served day-of.

Italian-American Wedge with Creamy Herb Dressing, Gorgonzola & Pepperoni

SERVES 4

Everyone loves a wedge, and the version we've dreamt up is inspired by the chopped salad from a local pizza joint called Antonio's in Angie's hometown. Our homage has a rich, tangy dressing loaded with herbs, and crumbly bits of pepperoni crumbs for crunch. Instead of blue cheese, we make a kind of Goddess dressing, with basil instead of tarragon, and red wine vinegar for a throwback to that vintage pizza shop flavor. Serve this very, very cold, so the iceberg retains its refreshing crunch.

———

Make the pepperoni crumbs: In a food processor, pulse the pepperoni for 1 minute until it looks ground and paste-like.

In a medium sauté pan, heat the olive oil over low heat. Add the pepperoni and oregano and cook, stirring occasionally, until most of the fat cooks out of the meat and it's starting to crisp up, about 10 minutes. Add the panko and cook until golden, about 2 minutes. Set aside on a plate lined with paper towels. You should have about 1 cup of pepperoni crumbs.

Assemble the salad: Remove the loose outer leaves of the lettuce and discard. Cut each head in half through the equator. Trim away the core on the bottom half and cut off a thin slice from the top half so that all of the halves sit flat on plates, equator-side up.

Gently tuck 8 to 10 basil leaves in between the leaves in each exposed lettuce half. Sprinkle each half evenly with equal amounts of the red wine vinegar, olive oil, and oregano, then spoon about 4 tablespoons of dressing over each serving. Add more dressing, if desired. Arrange the pepperoncini, tomatoes, red onion, and Gorgonzola over the top, and finish with black pepper. Sprinkle ¼ cup pepperoni crumbs over each half.

Serve immediately. The wedge is best made and eaten day-of.

Pepperoni crumbs

¼ pound pepperoni (from a stick), roughly chopped

2 tablespoons extra-virgin olive oil

1 teaspoon dried oregano (ideally home-dried, page 301)

¼ cup panko bread crumbs

To assemble

2 heads iceberg lettuce

1 large bunch basil (35 to 40 leaves)

2 teaspoons red wine vinegar

4 tablespoons extra-virgin olive oil

1 teaspoon dried oregano (ideally home-dried, page 301)

1 cup Creamy Herb Dressing (recipe follows)

⅓ cup sliced pepperoncini peppers (5 to 6 peppers)

16 cherry tomatoes, quartered

1 small red onion, very thinly sliced into half-moons

4 tablespoons Gorgonzola cheese (preferably Dolcelatte), crumbled

Freshly ground black pepper

Creamy Herb Dressing

MAKES ABOUT 1½ CUPS

2 anchovy fillets

1 garlic clove, grated on a Microplane

6 tablespoons labneh or plain whole-milk Greek yogurt

6 tablespoons crème fraîche

¼ cup packed roughly chopped parsley

¼ cup packed roughly chopped basil

2 tablespoons packed chopped chives

1 tablespoon white wine vinegar

4 teaspoons fresh lemon juice

1 teaspoon kosher salt

¼ teaspoon freshly ground black pepper

2½ teaspoons sugar

1 tablespoon neutral oil, such as vegetable

In a blender, combine the anchovies, garlic, labneh, crème fraîche, parsley, basil, chives, white wine vinegar, lemon juice, salt, pepper, sugar, and neutral oil and blend until smooth. The dressing may be made up to 3 days ahead.

Prosciutto & Melon Salad with Tamarind, Hazelnut & Feta

SERVES 6 TO 8

The basis for this colorful salad is prosciutto and melon, the Italian-American restaurant staple typically prepared with cantaloupe. For our version, we were loosely inspired by a Thai papaya salad, filling it with salty-sweet-funky flavors and contrasting textures. Hence, hazelnuts, candied with lime zest, which pair beautifully with the prosciutto; a striking tamarind-lime dressing made with fish sauce; and a tangy, creamy feta to smooth things out.

It's perfectly acceptable to serve this family style, but if you're having a dinner party and really want to wow, it's worth it to individually plate each portion for visual appeal. You can use plain toasted hazelnuts if you don't want to make the candied version, but try to candy them if you can—they really add both flavor and texture to this dish.

One small (2¼-pound) Galia or honeydew melon, peeled and seeded

½ cup Tamarind Dressing (recipe follows)

5 to 6 sprigs mint, leaves picked

1 cup large crumbled good-quality feta cheese (preferably French)

1 cup Chile & Lime Candied Hazelnuts (page 28) or toasted hazelnuts, roughly chopped

¼ pound prosciutto, thinly sliced

Extra-virgin olive oil, for finishing

Freshly ground black pepper

Assemble the salad: Slice the melon into 1-inch wedges, then cut each wedge into 4 to 5 pieces (you should have about 4 cups of melon).

In a large bowl, toss the melon with the tamarind dressing and half of the mint leaves.

Spoon the dressed melon onto a platter or individual plates. Sprinkle the feta on the top, followed by the hazelnuts. Top with prosciutto, loosely folding the meat to create height on the plate. Top with the remaining mint leaves. Finish with a drizzle of olive oil and freshly cracked pepper.

While you can make the hazelnuts up to a week ahead and the dressing up to 3 days ahead, this salad is best served immediately after assembling.

Tamarind Dressing

MAKES ABOUT 1 CUP

Tamarind concentrate is available in many Asian markets or online.

¼ cup plus 2 tablespoons tamarind concentrate

Grated zest of 2 limes

2 tablespoons plus 1½ teaspoons fresh lime juice

3 tablespoons sugar

1½ teaspoons kosher salt

½ teaspoon sriracha sauce

3 tablespoons extra-virgin olive oil

1½ teaspoons fish sauce

½ teaspoon garlic, grated on a Microplane

¼ teaspoon crushed red pepper flakes

In a medium bowl, whisk together the tamarind concentrate, lime zest, lime juice, sugar, salt, sriracha, olive oil, fish sauce, garlic, and pepper flakes until combined. The dressing will keep for up to 3 days in the refrigerator.

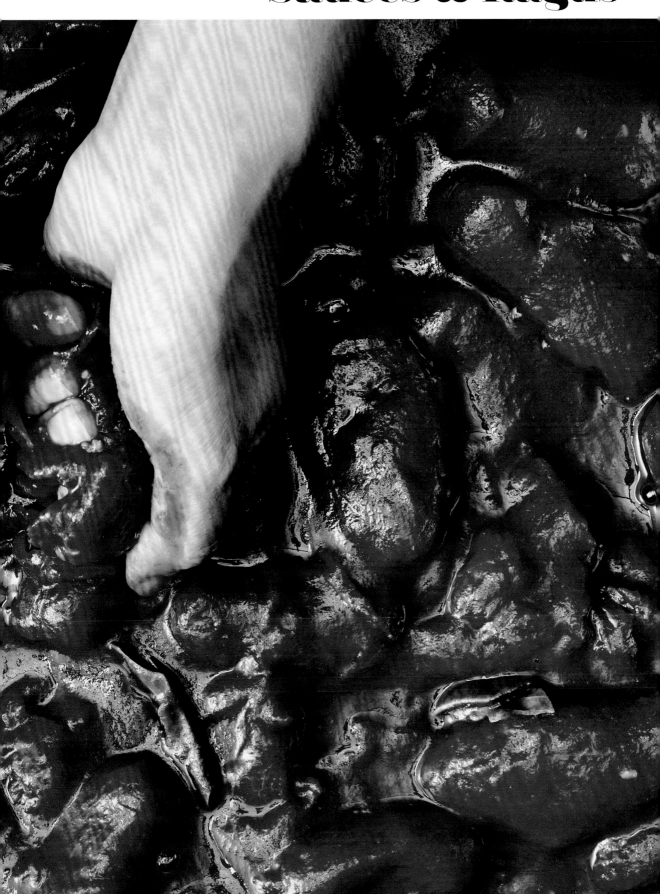

Of course this book needs a chapter on sauces, red and otherwise. In Italian-American cooking, sauce is more than a glaze or a dressing. It's the centerpiece of the table, the heart of the meal. *Red sauce* as a phrase defines an entire cuisine, and though we take plenty of liberties, the truth is that our food is still very much rooted in the red-sauce classics we grew up eating with our families.

Tomato sauce, the purest of all red sauces, is in our blood, appearing in our families in different ways. Both sides of Angie's family made tomato sauce—on her father's side, her grandmother Maria made a light, barely cooked version from her own garden-fresh tomatoes, and on her mother's side, her great-grandma Gemma prepared a richer, slow-cooked take enhanced with pork neck. Scott grew up more with what people think of as "Sunday gravy." His grandmother Giovanna ("Jennie") made a slow-cooked sauce with meat-balls, sausage, and braciole; she'd serve it over pasta or bake it into a lasagna that would feed the family for a week.

Those are the kinds of memories that we carry into these recipes. We have some more traditional offerings—a 10-minute San Marzano tomato sauce similar to Maria's recipe; a broken meatball ragu inspired by Jennie's. But we also cut loose from some of the classics—replacing the eggplants in our Egg-plant Sugo alla Norma on page 97 with slender Japanese varietals that don't mush out when cooked; adding star anise to the Italian Sausage Bolognese (page 114) to enhance its meaty flavor. We include a number of ragus (the Ital-ian term for meat-based sauces), which run the gamut from a classic, hearty recipe made with veal and prosciutto to a braised chicken and olive version, bolstered with less traditional ingredients like smoked chiles and mezcal. That's the beautiful thing about sauces—they're as much about comfort as they are about creativity. Our sauces might be rooted in nostalgia for the past, but they're very much informed by our experiences in the present.

These are some of the most versatile recipes in the book—using a simple base of meat or vegetables, you can use your imagination to come up with countless variations of flavors, textures, and ingredients. And though we pro-vide suggestions for how to pair pasta with each of these, they're not just for pasta—you can also serve sauce with meat (the Spicy Fra Diavolo Sauce on page 103 is great on top of veal or chicken), vegetables (try the Amatriciana on braised potatoes), polenta, or rice. The serving sizes here err on the side of generous, because sauces are meant to be shared. So grab a pot, gather your friends and family, and get cooking.

10-Minute San Marzano Tomato Sauce

MAKES ABOUT 7 CUPS (SERVES 4 TO 6 WITH PASTA)

Sure, a long-cooked Sunday gravy is great, but this is our go-to, ready-in-a-flash tomato sauce for weeknights, when we come home late and just want to eat something simple and comforting. It couldn't be easier to make, but it is worth seeking out canned San Marzano DOP tomatoes to get the best result.

Why? San Marzanos are considered the best tomatoes in the world, and are in fact one of the three ingredients required in making a true Neapolitan pizza. They come from a specific town near Naples, where the combination of the ashy-sandy volcanic soil from nearby Mount Vesuvius and the salty sea air create a tomato with a natural sweetness, not too much acidity, and great depth of flavor. We were lucky enough to witness San Marzanos in production during a trip to Naples a few years ago, and it was incredible—the tomatoes are only processed for thirty days a year, at the end of summer, when they are at the peak. We'll never forget the assembly line, where workers sorted out perfectly plump, bright red tomatoes and hand-tucked giant leaves of local basil into each can.

With tomatoes this good, we don't need to do much to the sauce—it's just about enhancing the natural flavors with a bit of seasoning. Put this on your favorite pasta, topping it with grated parmesan and more basil; or use it in any kind of parm preparation (from chicken on page 226 to layered eggplant on page 213)—its bright taste helps cut through heavier, fried, cheesy flavors.

2 (28-ounce) cans whole San Marzano tomatoes (make sure they are labeled DOP)

½ cup extra-virgin olive oil

8 garlic cloves, smashed with the flat side of a chef's knife

1 tablespoon plus 1 teaspoon kosher salt

¼ teaspoon crushed red pepper flakes

1 tablespoon sugar

2 sprigs basil

To serve with pasta

½ cup kosher salt

1½ pounds dried pasta, such as spaghetti, angel hair, or rigatoni

A trip to the tomato fields in San Marzano

In a food processor, pulse the tomatoes (including the liquid) until they're broken up but still chunky (you'll have about 7 cups). You can also do this with your hands, though it will produce a chunkier sauce (not a bad thing!).

In a medium pot, heat the olive oil over medium-high heat until shimmering. Add the garlic and salt and cook, stirring occasionally, until the garlic is golden and fragrant, about 2 minutes. Add the pepper flakes and stir. Stir in the tomatoes and cook until the sauce comes to a boil, 1 to 2 minutes. Immediately remove from the heat and season with the sugar, then stir in the basil sprigs.

Let the basil steep in the sauce for at least 5 minutes and up to 30 minutes, then remove the basil and garlic from the sauce before serving. The sauce is ready to be used at this point, or it can be stored in an airtight container in the refrigerator for up to 1 week, or in the freezer for up to 3 months.

To serve with pasta: In a large pot, bring 4 quarts water and the salt to a boil over high heat. Add the pasta and cook according to the package directions. Drain and add the pasta to the sauce, tossing to coat. Serve immediately.

Eggplant Sugo alla Norma

MAKES ABOUT 6 CUPS (SERVES 4 TO 6 WITH PASTA)

Scott is a huge fan of all things eggplant, and his single favorite food memory is the first time he tasted an eggplant-centric pasta called *maccheroni alla Norma* in a tiny trattoria at the top of a hill in Taormina, Sicily. It's typically made with tomatoes, eggplant, and a local cheese called *ricotta infornata*, which hails specifically from this small corner of the island. It just so happens that Angie's grandfather is from that area, and spent his youth working in a small bakery in that same hilltop town.

Local legend has it that pasta alla Norma came to be when an Italian writer tasted it and exclaimed, "This is a real Norma!" comparing it to the perfection of the Bellini opera of the same name. Fact or fiction, the name stuck, and this rich, creamy sauce has been a favorite ever since.

Eggplant is popular in Sicilian cuisine, and in turn, has become an essential Italian-American ingredient, since so many immigrants to the United States came from Southern Italy. We mix up our Norma by using Japanese eggplants, which have a lower moisture content and fewer seeds than the oversize Italian versions and pureeing them into the sauce for added eggplant flavor.

Serve this with dried short pastas like rigatoni, fusilli, gemelli, or cavatappi, whose firmer texture balances the softness and creaminess of the sauce. Top it with toasted bread crumbs and/or pine nuts for texture, and parmesan or *ricotta infornata* (for a homemade version, see page 307), the Sicilian cheese that is traditionally served with this dish, for extra oomph.

Using your hands, crush the tomatoes (including the liquid) over a medium bowl until completely broken up.

In a large heavy-bottomed pot, heat the olive oil over medium-high heat. Add the onion, garlic, and salt and cook, stirring continually, until the onions are soft and translucent but haven't taken on any color, 3 to 4 minutes. If browned bits start forming on the bottom of the pot, add a tablespoon of water and scrape off with a silicone spatula.

1 (28-ounce) can whole tomatoes (preferably San Marzano DOP)

1 cup extra-virgin olive oil

3 cups thinly sliced yellow onion (about 1 large onion)

3 garlic cloves, grated on a Microplane

1 tablespoon kosher salt

¼ teaspoon crushed red pepper flakes

½ teaspoon dried oregano (ideally home-dried, page 301)

4 cups 1-inch pieces Japanese eggplant (about 2 medium eggplants)

1 teaspoon sugar

1 cup finely grated Parmigiano-Reggiano cheese

1 small bunch fresh basil, plus more for serving

To serve with pasta

½ cup kosher salt

1 pound dried pasta, such as rigatoni, fusilli, gemelli, or cavatappi

6 tablespoons Crispy Garlic Bread Crumbs (page 299)

6 tablespoons grated Ricotta Infornata (page 307) or grated parmesan (optional)

RECIPE CONTINUES

Add the pepper flakes and oregano and cook for 1 minute. Add the eggplant and cook until its purple skin starts to turn light brown and the flesh is completely soft, 5 to 7 minutes. Add the crushed tomatoes and sugar and cook, stirring frequently, until the sauce comes to a simmer and thickens slightly, about 5 minutes.

Scoop out 2 cups of the sauce (including the eggplant) and transfer to a blender with the grated parmesan and ¼ cup water. Carefully blend until smooth (open the steam vent in the lid and cover the opening with a towel to avoid hot splatter), starting on low and increasing to high speed, 1 to 2 minutes. Return the blended sauce to the pot, stir, and cook until the sauce thickens, about 5 minutes. Remove from the heat, tear the basil leaves by hand, and add to the pot (reserve some for serving). Stir until incorporated.

The sauce is ready to be used at this point, or it can be stored in an airtight container in the refrigerator for up to 1 week, or in the freezer for up to 3 months. Reheat over medium-low, stirring in ½ to 1 cup water to reach desired consistency, as this sauce has a tendency to thicken up as it cools.

To serve with pasta: In a large pot, bring 4 quarts water and the salt to a boil over high heat. Add the pasta and cook according to the package directions. Drain and add the pasta to the sauce, tossing to coat. Top with the remaining basil and the bread crumbs. If desired, top with ricotta infornata or more parmesan. Serve immediately.

the extended Landino family in Italy

Cacciatore-Style Ragu with Mushrooms & Pancetta

MAKES ABOUT 6 CUPS (SERVES 4 TO 6 WITH PASTA)

Cacciatore means "hunter" in Italian, and this ragu delivers on the rich, earthy flavors that its name implies. Cacciatore recipes almost always apply to chicken, and most call for tomatoes and peppers, but this is our translation, with flavors that remind us of the forest, like wild mushrooms and robust herbs. It's a thick, chili-esque ragu, packed with crumbly braised ground meat and sausage-style seasonings and great over almost any type of pasta. The mushrooms and onions amp up the earthy flavor, and when you finish it with butter and cheese, it gets even creamier and more satisfying. Save this for a chilly winter night when you're in serious need of comfort.

———

NOTE: Seek out dark meat turkey or chicken (at least 10% fat) if possible here, as it's more flavorful, though if you can't find it, the fat from the pancetta will make up for it.

In a large heavy-bottomed pot, heat the olive oil and pancetta over medium-high heat. Cook for 5 minutes, stirring often, until all of the fat has rendered from the pancetta. Add the ground poultry, rosemary, thyme, pepper, fennel seeds, salt, and bay leaves and stir to combine. Cook, stirring occasionally and breaking the meat into small pieces, until the meat is browned, about 5 minutes.

Using a slotted spoon, transfer the meat to a medium bowl, leaving the fat in the pot. Set the bowl aside. Do not wash the pot.

Return the pot to medium-high heat, add the garlic, and cook until lightly toasted, about 30 seconds. Add the onion, celery, and mushrooms and stir well to combine. Cook until the onions are translucent and the vegetables release their liquid, about 10 minutes.

⅓ cup extra-virgin olive oil

8 ounces pancetta, diced

1 pound ground turkey or chicken (dark meat if possible)

1 tablespoon dried rosemary (ideally home-dried, page 301)

1 teaspoon dried thyme (ideally home-dried, page 301)

1 teaspoon freshly ground black pepper

1 teaspoon fennel seeds

1 tablespoon kosher salt

2 bay leaves

¼ cup finely chopped garlic (about 7 cloves)

2 cups diced yellow onion (about 1 medium onion)

1½ cups thinly sliced celery (about 5 ribs)

12 ounces chopped hen of the woods (maitake) or cremini mushrooms

1 cup dry white wine, such as Pinot Grigio

5 cups chicken stock, unsalted store-bought or homemade (page 299)

To serve with pasta

½ cup kosher salt

1 pound fresh egg-based pasta, such as pappardelle, tagliatelle, or linguine, store-bought or homemade (page 147)

¼ cup finely grated Parmigiano-Reggiano cheese, plus ¼ cup (optional) for serving

2 tablespoons fresh lemon juice

4 tablespoons (½ stick) unsalted butter

2 tablespoons roughly chopped parsley

⅓ cup Crispy Garlic Bread Crumbs (optional; page 299)

RECIPE CONTINUES

Add the white wine and increase the heat to high. Cook, stirring often, until all the wine has evaporated, about 5 minutes. Reduce the heat to medium and return the meat mixture and any juices to the pot, along with the chicken stock, and stir well. Bring to a simmer, then reduce the heat to medium-low and cook, stirring occasionally, until the liquid has reduced by two-thirds and large bubbles begin to form, 45 to 55 minutes. The sauce should be golden brown and thick. Discard the bay leaves.

The sauce is ready to be used at this point, or it can be stored in an airtight container in the refrigerator for up to 1 week, or in the freezer for up to 3 months.

To serve with pasta: In a large pot, bring 4 quarts water and the salt to a boil over high heat. Add the pasta and cook according to the package directions. Drain and add the cooked pasta to the pot with the ragu. Increase the heat to high and add the parmesan, lemon juice, butter, and parsley. Stir well until creamy.

Serve on a platter or in individual bowls. Top with the bread crumbs and more parmesan, if desired.

Spicy Fra Diavolo Sauce

MAKES ABOUT 5 CUPS (SERVES 4 TO 6 WITH PASTA)

Our families have an affinity for spicy things—Angie's grandfather carries around hot peppers in his pocket at all times, so he can chop them up and add them to whatever it is he's eating at the drop of a dime. (This is particularly entertaining when he is dining outside of his own home.)

"*Fra*" is an abbreviated version of *fratello*, Italian for brother, and the name of this sauce translates to, that's right, "brother devil," because it's so spicy. We use the hot pickled cherry peppers you see in the pickle aisle and puree roasted red peppers directly into the sauce to amp up the peppery flavor and the bright red color. If you prefer extra spicy, you can leave in the seeds, but proceed with caution.

Use fra diavolo any time you want a spicy version of a simple tomato sauce. It's great with sautéed shrimp or lobster over long pasta (and really any type of shellfish), in a chicken or veal parm, or on top of the Broccoli & Farro Polpette (page 196). When serving it with pasta, finish it with a pat of butter before serving for extra richness and sheen.

1 (28-ounce) can whole tomatoes (preferably San Marzano DOP)

1 cup Grandma Rito's Marinated Roasted Peppers (page 35) or store-bought

½ cup extra-virgin olive oil

2 tablespoons crushed Calabrian chiles in oil

¼ cup chopped seeded hot pickled cherry peppers, such as B&G

½ cup Roasted Garlic Puree (page 300)

2 tablespoons kosher salt

1 teaspoon sugar

To serve with pasta

½ cup kosher salt

1 pound dried pasta, such as linguine, spaghetti, or bucatini

3 to 4 tablespoons unsalted butter

Using your hands, crush the tomatoes (including the liquid) over a medium bowl until completely broken up. Set aside.

In a blender, puree the marinated roasted peppers until smooth, about 1 minute. Set aside.

In a large heavy-bottomed pot, heat the olive oil over medium-low. Add the crushed Calabrian chiles and cook for 1 to 2 minutes, stirring continually so they don't stick. Once the peppers begin to fry and make a popping sound, add the cherry peppers and cook for another 30 seconds. Add the crushed tomatoes, pureed roasted peppers, roasted garlic puree, salt, and sugar. Whisk until well combined and simmer on low, stirring occasionally, until the flavors meld, 8 to 10 minutes.

The sauce is ready to be used at this point, or it can be stored in an airtight container in the refrigerator for up to 1 week, or in the freezer for up to 3 months.

To serve with pasta: In a large pot, bring 4 quarts water and the salt to a boil over high heat. Add the pasta and cook according to the package directions. Drain and add the pasta to the sauce, tossing to coat. Stir in the butter just before serving, and serve immediately.

The chicken after it's braised

Smoky Chicken Ragu with Mezcal, Chiles & Olives

MAKES ABOUT 6 CUPS (SERVES 4 TO 6 WITH PASTA)

In restaurants, the entire staff gathers each day to eat together before service, an industry-wide tradition called "family meal." These meals usually consist of soulful, comforting dishes, and at Don Angie, braised chicken is a popular choice. A longtime member of our team, Jose, makes a mean chicken and rice when it's his turn, laced with garlic, cilantro, and chiles, and he inspired us to attempt to capture those flavors in ragu form.

This sauce comes together quickly but packs a lot of punch. It's full of smoky, comforting flavors, but still feels light enough to not knock you out for the rest of the night. We wanted to enhance the smokiness of the chiles with mezcal, but not overwhelmingly so, so we rely on lightly smoked Morita chiles here (see Note). Full of tender, hand-pulled braised chicken and meaty olives, the sauce pairs best with a more structured, chewy pasta like orecchiette. The pine nuts on top add texture, goat cheese adds tanginess, and the cilantro a dose of freshness.

———

NOTE: Moritas are 3- to 5-inch medium-hot red jalapeño peppers that have been dried and only lightly smoked, leaving them somewhat soft and fruity. If you can't find them, substitute dried or canned chipotle peppers, but use only half the amount (3 chipotles).

In a large Dutch oven or heavy-bottomed pot, heat the oil over high heat until nearly smoking.

Pat the chicken thighs dry and season all over with the salt. Add the chicken to the pot, skin-side down, carefully placing the thighs in one by one (work in batches if necessary to avoid overcrowding). Reduce the heat to medium-high and sear the chicken until the skin is deep golden brown (do not flip it), 4 to 6 minutes. Remove the chicken and set aside in a large bowl. Do not drain the oil from the pot.

Add the onion, celery, garlic, fennel, peppercorns, bay leaves, thyme, cilantro, and Moritas to the pot and cook over medium heat until the vegetables brown, 4 to 5 minutes.

¼ cup neutral oil, such as vegetable

2½ pounds bone-in, skin-on chicken thighs

1 tablespoon kosher salt

1 medium yellow onion, roughly chopped

6 large celery ribs, roughly chopped

1 head garlic, halved horizontally

½ fennel bulb, roughly chopped

1½ teaspoons black peppercorns

2 bay leaves

2 sprigs thyme

5 sprigs cilantro

6 Morita chiles, broken into halves (see Note)

½ cup tomato paste

¼ cup mezcal

6 cups chicken stock, unsalted store-bought or homemade (page 299)

1 cup meaty green olives, such as Cerignola, crushed and pitted

To serve with pasta

½ cup kosher salt

1 pound short pasta, such as orecchiette or capunti, store-bought dried or homemade (page 134)

½ cup finely grated Parmigiano-Reggiano cheese

2 tablespoons fresh lemon juice

2 tablespoons unsalted butter

½ cup crumbled goat cheese, such as Caprino Fresco

¼ cup pine nuts, toasted

¼ cup cilantro leaves

RECIPE CONTINUES

Add the tomato paste and cook for another minute, stirring often. Add the mezcal and stir. Cook until all the liquid evaporates, about 2 minutes.

Return the chicken and any juices to the pot and add the chicken stock. Increase the heat to high and bring almost to a boil, then reduce the heat to medium-low to maintain a gentle simmer. Cook, uncovered, stirring occasionally, until the chicken is very tender, 45 minutes to 1 hour. Remove from the heat. Remove the chicken and set aside until cool enough to handle. Strain the cooking liquid through a fine-mesh sieve into a clean pot (discard the vegetables, herbs, and spices). Set aside.

Pick the chicken into small pieces, discarding the bones and skin. Add the picked chicken to the pot with the strained cooking liquid. Set over high heat and cook, stirring continually, to reduce and concentrate the liquid, until it coats the back of a spoon, 3 to 5 minutes. Add the olives and stir well to combine.

The sauce is ready to be used at this point, or it can be stored in an airtight container in the refrigerator for up to 1 week, or in the freezer for up to 3 months.

To serve with pasta: In a large pot, bring 4 quarts water and the salt to a boil over high heat. Add the pasta and cook according to the package directions. Drain and add the cooked pasta to the pot with the ragu. Add the parmesan, lemon juice, and butter and stir well until creamy.

Serve in individual bowls or on a platter and top with crumbled goat cheese, toasted pine nuts, and cilantro. Leftovers keep, tightly covered in the refrigerator, for up to 2 days.

Amatriciana with Braised Pork Shoulder

MAKES ABOUT 5 CUPS (SERVES 4 TO 6 WITH PASTA)

Amatriciana is a Roman dish that typically includes guanciale, tomato, onion, and pecorino. We give it a little substance and structure by adding braised pork shoulder, which brings more texture to the dish and mellows out the strong flavor of guanciale. Our version is closer in spirit to the long-cooked ragus made by Scott's grandma Jennie and Angie's great-grandmother Gemma than a true Amatriciana, and we're okay with that.

While Amatriciana is traditionally served with bucatini, this beefed-up (or porked-up, as the case may be) version is great with egg-based pastas like pappardelle, tagliatelle, or linguine. It's filling and very satisfying, particularly in colder months.

In a food processor, process the chilled guanciale until the fat forms a paste and the meat is finely chopped, 1 to 2 minutes. Set aside.

In a medium bowl, rub the diced pork shoulder with the salt and pepper.

In a large heavy-bottomed pot, heat the oil over medium-high heat until it just starts smoking, 3 to 5 minutes. Working in batches if necessary to avoid overcrowding, carefully add the pork shoulder to the pot and brown the meat on all sides, turning it occasionally to make sure it browns evenly, 6 to 8 minutes. Once browned, remove the meat from the pot with a slotted spoon and transfer to a medium bowl and set aside, leaving any fat behind in the pot. Do not wash the pot.

Add the guanciale to the same pot. Adjust the heat to medium-low and cook until the guanciale is completely rendered, stirring occasionally, 2 to 3 minutes. You will know when it is ready when the fat has completely melted and the small bits of meat start to turn golden brown. Add the pepper flakes and red onion and cook, stirring occasionally, until the onions are translucent, 5 to 6 minutes.

Meanwhile, using your hands, crush the tomatoes over a medium bowl until completely broken up.

¼ pound guanciale, cut into ¼-inch cubes, chilled in the freezer for 10 minutes

1¼ pounds boneless pork shoulder, trimmed of fat and sinew and cut into 1-inch cubes

1 tablespoon kosher salt

½ teaspoon freshly ground black pepper

½ cup neutral oil, such as vegetable

¼ teaspoon crushed red pepper flakes

3 cups finely diced red onion (about 2 medium onions)

1 (28-ounce) can whole tomatoes (preferably San Marzano DOP)

2 cups chicken stock, unsalted store-bought or homemade (page 299)

1 teaspoon sugar

To serve with pasta

½ cup kosher salt

1 pound dried tubular pasta, such as ziti or paccheri

4 tablespoons (½ stick) unsalted butter

1 cup finely grated pecorino cheese (preferably Pecorino Toscano), plus ¼ cup (optional) for serving

2 tablespoons fresh lemon juice

6 to 8 tablespoons Crispy Garlic Bread Crumbs (optional; page 299)

RECIPE CONTINUES

Return the seared pork shoulder to the pot, along with any juices that have collected in the bowl, the crushed tomatoes, and chicken stock. Increase the heat to medium and bring to a simmer, then reduce the heat to low to maintain the simmer. Cover and cook for 1 hour, stirring every 10 minutes.

Uncover and cook until the pork is tender and the sauce is thick enough to coat the back of a spoon, another 30 minutes or so. Stir in the sugar and taste for seasoning.

The sauce is ready to be used at this point, or it can be stored in an airtight container in the refrigerator for up to 1 week, or in the freezer for up to 3 months.

To serve with pasta: In a large pot, bring 4 quarts water and the salt to a boil over high heat. Add the pasta and cook according to the package directions. Drain and add the pasta to the sauce, tossing to coat. Stir in the butter, pecorino, and lemon juice and stir well to combine. Serve immediately in individual bowls or on a platter, topped with bread crumbs (if using), and more cheese, if desired.

VARIATION: Broken Meatball Ragu

For the ultimate Sunday gravy, add 6 to 8 cooked Classic Meatballs (page 193) broken into quarters with your hands. Stir them in at the end of the sauce recipe, just before adding the sugar and tasting for seasoning.

Scott's great-grandmother prepares Sunday Gravy in a Brooklyn park

Neapolitan-Style Short Rib & Caramelized Onion Ragu

MAKES ABOUT 6 CUPS (SERVES 4 TO 6 WITH PASTA)

We discovered this sauce, sometimes called ragu Genovese, in a tiny trattoria in the heart of Naples. The rich, onion-laden pasta arrived atop a giant mound of *maccheroni*, and though it seemed so simple, the depth of flavor that had been coaxed out of the long-cooked ragu was unlike anything we'd ever tasted. The dish is found only in Naples; the sauce never became popular in the United States, nor, as far as we can tell, anywhere else in Italy. No one knows why it's called Genovese, since nothing like it exists in Genoa, the northern Italian port city from which the name is derived, but some suspect that it may have originated there, made its way south to the port of Naples via Genovese merchants, and stayed put.

The original recipe involves braised meat, usually inexpensive roasting cuts, and a mountain of onions; it's almost always served with a tubular pasta like ziti. Ours is made with short rib because it has great flavor and lots of natural fat. We braise the meat and caramelize the onions in separate pots, then combine the two at the end, marrying all of those deep roasted flavors together in a thick, rich sauce. If you don't want to go the pasta route, this ragu would be delicious over polenta, rice, or even potatoes. *See photo on pages 112–113.*

---

1 cup plus ⅓ cup extra-virgin olive oil

8 cups very thinly sliced yellow onions (about 2 pounds)

4 cups very thinly sliced cipollini or Vidalia onions (about 1½ pounds)

3 celery ribs, very thinly sliced

3 tablespoons kosher salt

2 teaspoons freshly ground black pepper

2½ pounds trimmed boneless short rib, cut into 1-inch cubes

1 cup dry white wine, such as Pinot Grigio

8 cups chicken stock, unsalted store-bought or homemade (page 299)

2 tablespoons white wine vinegar

To serve with pasta

½ cup kosher salt

1 pound dried tubular pasta, such as ziti or paccheri

½ cup (1 stick) unsalted butter, cubed

1 cup finely grated pecorino cheese (preferably Pecorino Toscano)

3 tablespoons fresh lemon juice

⅓ cup roughly chopped parsley

In a large heavy-bottomed pot, heat 1 cup of the olive oil over medium-high heat until it is nearly smoking. Add both onions, the celery, 1½ tablespoons of the salt, and 1 teaspoon of the pepper and stir well. Increase the heat to high and continue stirring until the vegetables begin to soften and release liquid, 2 to 3 minutes. Reduce the heat to medium and continue to cook, stirring and scraping intermittently, every 8 to 10 minutes, to avoid sticking. Continue cooking and scraping the vegetables while searing the short rib in the next step.

Season the short rib evenly with the remaining 1½ tablespoons salt and 1 teaspoon pepper. In a second large heavy-bottomed pot, heat the remaining ⅓ cup olive oil over medium-high heat until it is nearly smoking. Working in batches if necessary to avoid overcrowding, add the meat in an even layer and sear until browned on all sides, about 4 minutes total.

Using a ladle, carefully remove the excess fat from the pot and discard, leaving behind about 2 tablespoons of fat. Add the wine and simmer until the volume of the liquid is reduced by half, 2 to 3 minutes. Add the chicken stock and bring to a boil over high heat, then reduce the heat to low and simmer. Cover the pot, leaving just a small crack open at the top, and simmer gently until the meat is fork-tender, 1½ to 2 hours. The liquid should be reduced to about half of its original volume and turn dark brown in color.

Meanwhile, keep watching and stirring the vegetable mixture. If the vegetables start to stick or burn, deglaze with up to ¼ cup water, adding 1 tablespoon at a time, and scraping the bottom of the pot to release any stuck or burnt bits. (You may end up repeating this deglazing process two or three times.) Cook the mixture until the vegetables are very soft, a deep golden brown, and about one-quarter of their original volume, 1½ to 2 hours.

When the vegetables are caramelized and the meat is tender, add the vegetables to the pot of meat and stir very well to combine. Stir in the vinegar. The sauce should be thick enough to coat the back of a spoon. If it's too thin, simmer over low heat until it thickens up, which can take up to 30 minutes.

The sauce is ready to be used at this point, or it can be stored in an airtight container in the refrigerator for up to 1 week, or in the freezer for up to 3 months.

To serve with pasta: In a large pot, bring 4 quarts water and the salt to a boil over high heat. Add the pasta and cook according to the package directions. Drain and add the pasta to the sauce, increase the heat to medium-high, and mix thoroughly with a spoon to coat. Add the butter and pecorino and stir well to combine. Once the butter has melted, remove from the heat. Finish with the lemon juice and parsley, stirring well to combine. Serve immediately.

Italian Sausage Bolognese

MAKES 8 TO 10 CUPS (SERVES 8 TO 10 WITH PASTA)

There seems to be a misconception about Bolognese in America, in which people think any old tomato-and-meat sauce fits the bill. But in Bologna, where the sauce originates, specific ingredients must be present to call it a Bolognese, namely pancetta, veal, pork, milk, and white wine, with minimal use of tomatoes.

Our Italian-American version uses sweet Italian sausage in place of pork, along with crushed tomatoes, star anise (which helps bring out meaty flavors in braised dishes), and a little bit of colatura, or Italian fish sauce, for more umami. We chop everything into little rice-sized pieces, as they do in Bologna, for more even cooking and to allow the flavors to meld.

The finished result is hearty, but not too heavy, and a little more sophisticated than the clunky, heavy meat sauces you see today. Its rich flavors pair well with egg-based pastas like pappardelle, tagliatelle, and garganelli, and this is also what we use in the Don Angie Pinwheel Lasagna (page 175). This recipe yields a good amount of sauce, which is great because you can always freeze half of it and save it for later.

In a food processor, working in batches if necessary, process the onions, garlic, celery, and carrots until chopped as finely as possible, similar in size to uncooked rice. Set aside. Rinse the food processor and process the pancetta until very finely chopped, the same size as the vegetables. Set aside.

In a medium bowl, mix the Italian sausage and veal together and season with the salt.

In a large heavy-bottomed pot, heat the olive oil over high heat. When it shimmers, add the meat, stirring frequently with a wooden spoon to break it up into small pieces, until evenly browned, about 15 minutes. Remove the meat with a slotted spoon and set aside. Drain any excess fat from the pot but keep the browned bits on the bottom (do not wash).

2 yellow onions, coarsely chopped

4 garlic cloves, peeled

5 celery ribs, coarsely chopped

2 carrots, coarsely chopped

4 ounces pancetta, cut into 1-inch cubes

1 pound sweet Italian sausage, casings removed

1 pound ground veal

3 tablespoons kosher salt

2 tablespoons extra-virgin olive oil

½ cup tomato paste

1 cup white wine

2 (28-ounce) cans whole tomatoes (preferably San Marzano DOP)

2 cups whole milk

2 whole star anise

2 teaspoons colatura or fish sauce, plus more to taste

1 tablespoon sugar

2 tablespoons fresh lemon juice

To serve with pasta

½ cup kosher salt

2 pounds fresh egg pasta, such as pappardelle, tagliatelle, or linguine, store-bought or 2 batches homemade (page 147)

4 tablespoons (½ stick) unsalted butter

½ cup finely grated Parmigiano-Reggiano cheese, plus ¼ cup (optional) for serving

Add the pancetta to the pot over medium heat and cook, stirring occasionally, until the fat is rendered and the pancetta is browned, 8 to 10 minutes. Add the processed vegetables and cook, stirring often, until the vegetables are very soft and have taken on a darker hue, 10 to 15 minutes.

Add the tomato paste and cook, continuing to stir, for 5 minutes, until deep orange and caramelized. Stir in the wine and cook until fully evaporated, about 5 minutes.

Meanwhile, using your hands, crush the tomatoes (including the liquid) over a medium bowl until completely broken up.

Return the ground meat to the pot. Add the milk, star anise, and tomatoes. Stir well, bring to a simmer, and cook over medium-low heat, uncovered, stirring occasionally, until the sauce thickens and is bright orange, about 2 hours. If any fat separates, whisk it back in to emulsify. Discard the star anise. Remove the pot from the heat and add the colatura, sugar, and lemon juice and stir well to incorporate and re-emulsify the sauce.

The sauce is ready to be used at this point, or it can be stored in an airtight container in the refrigerator for up to 1 week, or in the freezer for up to 3 months.

To serve with pasta: In a large pot, bring 4 quarts water and the salt to a boil over high heat. Add the pasta and cook according to the package directions. Drain and add the pasta to the sauce, tossing to coat. Add the butter and parmesan and stir well to combine. Transfer to individual plates or a serving platter. Top with more cheese, if desired. Serve immediately.

Angie's dad as a boy with family

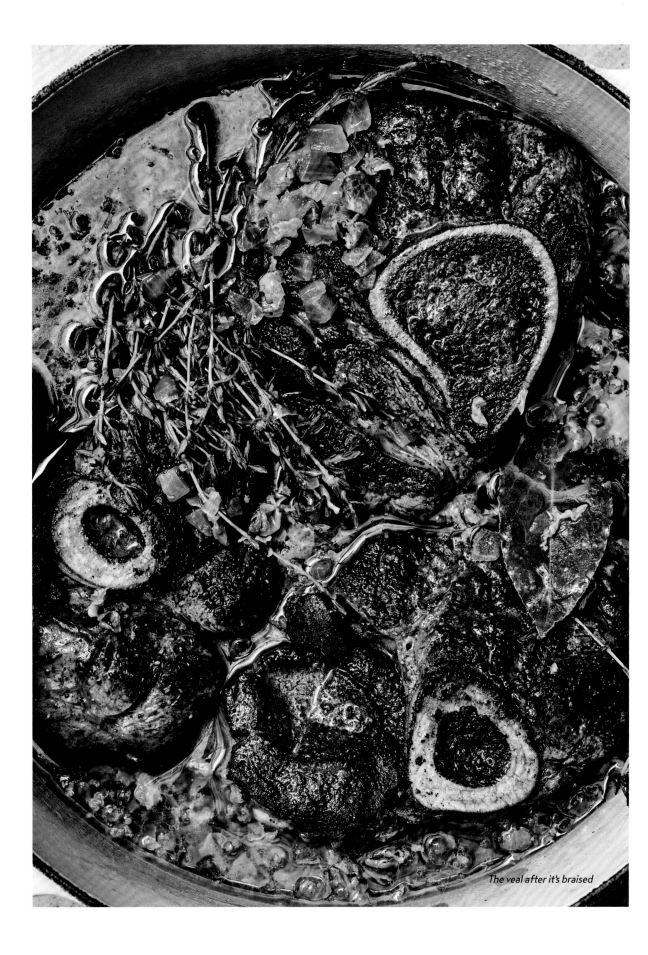

The veal after it's braised

Osso Buco & Prosciutto Ragu

MAKES ABOUT 5 CUPS (SERVES 4 TO 6 WITH PASTA)

We set out to create a rich braised veal ragu to remind us of the pasta we ate on our wedding day in Florence, and turned to Valdostana, an old-fashioned Italian-American preparation involving veal and prosciutto (it's a sort of cousin to saltimbocca, if you will). It's named for the Valle d'Aosta in northern Italy, where the dish originated, a region chock-full of hearty cold-weather dishes.

We like to use crosscut veal shank (aka *osso buco*) in this recipe because it has the bone intact and marrow exposed, which enriches the sauce with its fat and gelatin. The tender pieces of braised meat are cooked low and slow, then picked off the bone and stirred back into a sauce that's full of classic Northern Italian ingredients like prosciutto, nutmeg, peppercorn, bay leaf, and cream. Serve it over a long, flat egg noodle, such as pappardelle.

———

Cut 4 slits along the silver skin on the outside of the veal shank, being careful not to pierce the meat, cutting from top to bottom along each piece, in the same direction as the bone. (The silver skin prevents moisture from getting into the meat and slows down the cooking process, so cutting these slits creates "breathing room" that helps the meat to cook better.) Season the veal on all sides with the salt and black pepper.

In a large heavy-bottomed pot, heat 2 tablespoons of the olive oil and the prosciutto over medium heat. Cook, stirring often, until all of the fat has rendered from the meat, 3 to 4 minutes. Remove from the heat. Remove the prosciutto from the pot with a slotted spoon and set aside in a large bowl. Do not wash the pot.

Set the pot over medium-high heat. Add the remaining 2 tablespoons olive oil. Once the fat is shimmering, working in batches as necessary to avoid crowding, carefully place the veal in the pot and sear on all sides until golden brown all over, about 10 minutes total. Remove from the heat and remove the veal, placing it in the bowl along with the prosciutto, again leaving the fat in the pot.

3 pounds osso buco-style (cross-cut) veal shank, cut about 2 inches thick

1 tablespoon kosher salt

2½ teaspoons freshly ground black pepper

4 tablespoons olive oil

8 ounces thinly sliced prosciutto, cut into ½-inch squares

2 tablespoons grated garlic (using a Microplane, about 8 large cloves)

2½ cups diced yellow onions (about 2 medium onions)

¼ teaspoon grated nutmeg

3 bay leaves

8 sprigs thyme

1 cup dry white wine, such as Pinot Grigio

6 cups chicken stock, unsalted store-bought or homemade (page 299)

½ cup heavy cream

To serve with pasta

½ cup kosher salt

1 pound fresh egg-based pasta, such as pappardelle or tagliatelle, store-bought or homemade (page 147)

½ cup finely grated Parmigiano-Reggiano cheese, plus ¼ cup (optional) for serving

¼ cup fresh lemon juice (about 1 large lemon)

4 tablespoons (½ stick) unsalted butter

½ cup thinly sliced scallions, plus 2 tablespoons for garnish (4 to 5 scallions)

RECIPE CONTINUES

Set the pot over medium-high heat. Add the garlic and cook until lightly toasted and aromatic, about 1 minute. Add the onions, nutmeg, bay leaves, and thyme and stir well. Cook, stirring often, until the onions have completely softened, 10 to 15 minutes. Add the wine and increase the heat to medium-high, stirring continually and scraping the bottom of the pot until all of the liquid has evaporated, about 2 minutes.

Return the prosciutto and veal to the pot, add the chicken stock, and bring to a boil over medium-high heat. Reduce the heat to a low simmer, cover (leaving the lid just slightly ajar), and simmer until the meat is fork-tender, about 2 hours. Remove from the heat.

Carefully remove the veal from the pot and set aside until cool enough to handle. Pick the meat from the bones with your hands, shredding it as you add it back to the pot. If there's any marrow left in the bones, scoop it out into the pot as well. Discard any silver skin and the bones. The ragu should be hearty and thick, but if it's looking a little watery, allow it to simmer for up to an additional 30 minutes to reduce.

Discard the bay leaves and thyme sprigs. Add the heavy cream and stir well to combine. The sauce is ready to be used at this point, or it can be stored in an airtight container in the refrigerator for up to 1 week, or in the freezer for up to 3 months.

To serve with pasta: In a large pot, bring 4 quarts water and the salt to a boil over high heat. Add the pasta and cook according to the package directions. Drain and add the cooked pasta to the pot with the ragu. Increase the heat to high and add the parmesan, lemon juice, butter, and scallions. Stir well until creamy. Spoon onto a platter or into individual plates. Garnish with more grated parmesan (if using) and scallions. Serve immediately.

on the rooftop terrace at Hotel Baglioni with our parents on our wedding day

Spiced Lamb Ragu with Marsala & Fennel

MAKES ABOUT 6 CUPS (SERVES 4 TO 6 WITH PASTA)

When we were growing up, our families ate lamb only for Easter, but now, we'll make any excuse to eat it year-round. Lamb is a naturally flavorful meat that's bold enough to stand up to stronger spices like the ones used here, namely cumin, fennel, and allspice. We pair all that with Marsala, a fortified wine seen fairly often in Italian-American cooking, usually with veal or chicken. Marsala has a deep, full flavor that adds complexity to the other components here, and a bit of acidity as well. It's from the city of—you guessed it—Marsala, a coastal town in Sicily, an island with a long history of multicultural influences.

This is a slow-simmered, pull-apart-tender ragu that pairs best with a richer egg yolk–based pasta like the ones mentioned in the ingredients list. Or try it with rice or couscous, a borderline Sicilian/Sardinian move that wouldn't be totally out of place here.

———

Season the lamb on all sides with the salt and black pepper.

In a large heavy-bottomed pot, heat the olive oil over high heat. Add the lamb and cook, turning occasionally, until browned on all sides, about 5 minutes. Remove the lamb from the pot with a slotted spoon, place it in a medium bowl, and set aside. Do not wash the pot.

Set the pot with the lamb fat over medium-high heat. Add the garlic and cook until light golden brown, about 30 seconds. Add the onion, fennel, celery, cumin, allspice, oregano, and thyme and stir well to coat with the fat. Reduce the heat to medium and cook, stirring often, until the onions are translucent and the vegetables soften, about 15 minutes.

Add the Marsala and cook, stirring often, until all of the liquid is evaporated, about 5 minutes. Return the cooked lamb to the pot, along with the chicken stock. Stir well. Bring to a low boil, then reduce the heat and simmer, uncovered, until the sauce has turned a deep brown and reduced enough to coat the back of a spoon and the lamb is fork tender, about 30 to 45 minutes.

Ingredients

1½ pounds trimmed boneless lamb shoulder, cut into 1-inch cubes

2 tablespoons kosher salt

2½ teaspoons freshly ground black pepper

½ cup extra-virgin olive oil

¼ cup chopped garlic (about 7 cloves)

2¼ cups diced yellow onion (1 large onion)

2½ cups diced fennel (about 1 large fennel bulb), fronds reserved

1 cup diced celery (about 4 ribs)

2 teaspoons ground cumin

½ teaspoon ground allspice

2 teaspoons dried oregano (ideally home-dried, page 301)

1 teaspoon dried thyme (ideally home-dried, page 301)

¾ cup dry Marsala

6 cups chicken stock, unsalted store-bought or homemade (page 299)

To serve with pasta

½ cup kosher salt

1 pound fresh egg-based pasta, such as pappardelle, tagliatelle, or linguine, store-bought or homemade (page 147)

¼ cup finely grated Parmigiano-Reggiano cheese

2 tablespoons fresh lemon juice

2 tablespoons chopped mint, plus more to serve

4 tablespoons (½ stick) unsalted butter

Mint leaves and reserved fennel fronds, picked, for garnish (optional)

The sauce is ready to be used at this point, or it can be stored in an airtight container in the refrigerator for up to 1 week, or in the freezer for up to 3 months.

To serve with pasta: In a large pot, bring 4 quarts water and the salt to a boil over high heat. Add the pasta and cook according to the package directions. Drain and add the pasta to the ragu. Increase the heat to high and add the parmesan, lemon juice, chopped mint, and butter. Stir well until creamy. Serve on a platter or in individual plates. Top with the reserved fennel fronds and more mint, if desired.

Pasta is the cornerstone of the Italian-American canon—there is perhaps no food that's more closely associated with the cuisine than this one, and with good reason. Pasta made an appearance at every single Rito family meal, usually at the beginning, and even on "American" holidays like Thanksgiving.

It's impossible to think of Italian-American cooking without dishes like spaghetti and meatballs, penne alla vodka, or linguine with clams. These are the classics we love, and the flavors we try to keep in mind when developing pasta recipes today.

Both of us grew up eating more dried pasta than fresh—partially because it's faster, and partially because our families are from southern Italy, where dried, extruded pastas are more prevalent. But now, on special occasions and holidays, we like to break out the pasta maker and roll thin sheets of dough to fold into festive shapes or layer into lasagnas, or roll out thick ropes to cut into gnocchi or gnudi. The tactile experience of making fresh pasta can be relaxing and rewarding—and the end result is always worth the effort. Once you try it, you'll see how simple the process really is.

In this chapter, we've tried to provide recipes covering a broad range of pastas—from store-bought dried to handmade fresh. For the fresh, there are two unique styles of dough—a rich, silky version made with egg yolks and a more rustic variation without—as well as gnudi and gnocchi. The sauces cover a range of styles and flavor profiles, too, each developed to match the pasta they're paired with, though as ever, we don't believe in strict rules. You can make the sauces if you want, or not—sometimes a simple topping of butter, lemon juice, and Parmesan is enough. And we offer dried alternatives to all of the fresh pasta and sauce combinations, too, if you're not feeling up for a project.

Whatever kind of pasta you're cooking, there are a few important things to keep in mind: Make sure you have enough water in the pot for the pasta to swim around, and bring it to a rolling boil before adding the pasta, otherwise it will turn out gummy. We use 4 quarts of water for every 1 pound of pasta. And salt it well—really well, like seawater. We call for ½ cup of kosher salt per 4 quarts of water. Fresh pasta needs to cook only briefly (1 to 2 minutes), and in our experience, the cook times on the back of a dried pasta package are generally pretty accurate.

A few notes on shopping and equipment in this chapter: For dried pasta, look for bags or boxes that say "extruded with a bronze die," and noodles that look almost rough on the surface. Alma Gourmet, Buon'Italia, and Gustiamo are good online marketplaces for high-end dried pasta; we like the brands Setaro, Faella, and Martelli. For fresh pastas, we urge you to try making your own, and we have specific recommendations for the types of flours called for, which we explain further in the Northern-Style Egg Yolk Pasta (page 147) and Southern-Style Eggless Pasta (page 134) "master" recipes. If making your own fresh pasta isn't in the cards, you can still make the composed dishes using store-bought "fresh" pasta from the refrigerator section.

Pasta maker machines with a good hand-cranked roller cost about $50 to $75, and they usually come with a cutter attachment so you can turn your sheets into fettuccine or thinner, spaghetti-style noodles. Imperia is a reliable brand, or you can spring for an attachment for a stand mixer if you have one, which makes for a faster process. You don't really need any other tools for making fresh pasta, except maybe a plastic scraper for the gnocchi, and/or a ruler for measuring even shapes, though it's not strictly necessary. We tried to pick shapes here that don't require too many tools.

We take a lot of pride in our pastas at Don Angie, and make only fresh, handmade versions, which means every bowl feels special. Though this chapter runs the gamut in terms of styles, we want every recipe to feel just as special. There's a lot to learn—you can spend a lot of time here, finding the joy and value in pasta making and cookery, and the pleasure, too.

Pasta e Fagioli with Black-Eyed Peas, Collard Greens & Prosciutto

MAKES ABOUT 10 CUPS (SERVES 6 TO 8)

Angie's grandmother Dee earned the nickname "Grandma Soup" for the soul-satisfying soups she makes to start nearly every meal. This is our homage to her, in the form of the quintessential Italian-American dish sometimes referred to as "pasta fazool"—a hearty and comforting soup made with pasta and beans, along with some type of cured pork and green. Here, we took a cue from a classic American dish that also combines greens and beans—collard greens and black-eyed peas, a Southern culinary staple rooted in the culinary traditions of enslaved Africans, typically eaten on New Year's Day for good luck.

We rely on Italian ingredients like prosciutto and ditalini (little pasta tubes) to feel familiar to us, but this is a recipe rife for riffing. Feel free to swap out other types of beans and greens—lacinato kale and turnip greens are nice here, and cannellini or borlotti beans are classic. You can use any type of small pasta, too, or make your own by breaking spaghetti or linguine into little pieces.

NOTES: To cook black-eyed peas from scratch, place ¼ pound (about ½ cup) of dried peas in a medium pot and cover with 2½ cups water. Bring to a boil over medium-high heat for 2 minutes. Remove the pot from the heat and set aside, allowing the peas to soak for 1 hour. After soaking, drain the peas and rinse. Place the beans in a medium pot and cover again with 2½ cups water and ½ teaspoon of kosher salt. Bring to a boil over medium-high heat, then reduce to a simmer and cook for 30 minutes, stirring occasionally. Drain.

The sugar in the recipe is not to make the soup sweet; it's really in the service of the acid. We like to add a fair amount of citrus juice, then balance it out with a bit of sugar. This has the effect of intensifying the overall flavor of the dish, while keeping it from becoming too sour. Trust!

In a large pot, combine the olive oil and prosciutto and cook over medium heat until the prosciutto is slightly fried and its fat has rendered, about 3 minutes.

1 cup extra-virgin olive oil

¼ pound thinly sliced prosciutto, chopped into ¼-inch pieces

1 cup thinly sliced scallions (6 to 8 scallions)

7 garlic cloves, grated on a Microplane

1 teaspoon crushed Calabrian chiles in oil

2 tablespoons kosher salt

1½ teaspoons freshly ground black pepper

½ bunch collard greens (about 9 leaves), stems and ribs removed and discarded, leaves roughly chopped

Grated zest of 1 lemon

¼ cup fresh lemon juice (about 1 large lemon)

1½ cups cooked black-eyed peas (see Note) or 1½ cups canned (from a 15.5-ounce can), drained and rinsed

8 cups chicken stock, unsalted store-bought or homemade (page 299)

1½ cups dried ditalini pasta

1 teaspoon sugar

¾ cup finely grated Parmigiano-Reggiano cheese, plus ¼ cup (optional) for topping

Add the scallions, garlic, Calabrian chiles, salt, and pepper. Stir well to combine. Continue cooking over medium heat, stirring continually, until the garlic is fragrant and the scallions have wilted, about 3 minutes.

Add the collard greens, lemon zest, and lemon juice. Continue cooking over medium heat, stirring often, until the greens are wilted, 12 to 15 minutes. Add the peas and stock. Bring to a boil over medium-high heat, then reduce the heat to maintain a simmer. Simmer for 10 minutes. Add the pasta and cook until the pasta is tender, about 8 minutes.

Stir in the sugar and parmesan and serve immediately, topping with more parmesan, if desired. Leftovers keep, tightly covered in the refrigerator, for up to 4 days. Reheat gently over low heat and stir in up to 1 cup of broth or water to thin out the soup, if desired.

Cacio e Pepe Pastina

SERVES 4

Pastina is literally "tiny pasta," the most common shape being a little star, making it very popular with kids. Every Italian-American grandmother makes some version of this for her grandchildren, and ours were no different. Scott's family served pastina with escarole soup or chicken broth; Angie's in a tomato broth with carrots and eggs. Both of our mothers made us buttered pastina as kids when we were sick; it's a very easy, comforting dish that comes from a peasant food tradition and cooks up in minutes.

This is our (no pun intended) souped-up version, loaded with parmesan and a lot of freshly cracked black pepper, resulting in a flavor similar to Roman cacio e pepe. It's rich, comforting, and a little more interesting than your typical buttered pastina. Serve it as a main course with roasted vegetables or chicken on top; as a side dish; or simply on its own, à la risotto.

NOTE: Be mindful here of salting the cooking water—since pastina is so small, you can actually overseason the water. We give a specific measurement of salt to water in the procedure that follows for best results.

1 tablespoon plus
½ teaspoon kosher salt
(see Note)

6 ounces (half of a
12-ounce box) pastina

1 tablespoon extra-virgin
olive oil

¾ teaspoon freshly
ground black pepper

⅔ cup finely grated
Parmigiano-Reggiano
cheese

½ cup mascarpone
cheese

4 tablespoons (½ stick)
unsalted butter

In a large pot, bring 4 cups of water plus 1 tablespoon of the salt to a boil over high heat. Add the pastina and cook until tender, 4 to 5 minutes. Reserving ⅓ cup of the cooking water, drain the pasta and return to the pot along with the cooking water.

Add the oil, remaining ½ teaspoon salt, the black pepper, parmesan, mascarpone, and butter. Over medium-high heat, stir vigorously with a silicone spatula or wooden spoon until incorporated, 2 to 3 minutes. As the pastina comes to a boil, the starch will release from the pasta, and it should become very thick and creamy, like risotto.

Serve immediately. This dish is best made and eaten day-of, but if you do have leftovers, reheat them in a pan over low heat with a few tablespoons of water to make the pastina creamy again.

Pasta Gemma

SERVES 4 TO 6

This pasta is named for Angie's great-grandmother Gemma. Gemma's husband ran a fruit and vegetable stand in a market in Cleveland, next to his sister's egg stand. Unfortunately, Gemma's husband died suddenly at age thirty-four, leaving behind a widow and eight young children. Gemma put herself through cosmetology school to support her family as a hairdresser, but money was always tight. She often relied on her sister-in-law's eggs to flesh out a meal, and one of her specialties was essentially a thick soup made with pasta, scrambled eggs, and oil. This is our somewhat more refined homage to Gemma's dish, though it's still rooted in humble cooking traditions and back-pocket ingredients.

The technique is similar to making pasta carbonara, but instead of guanciale or bacon, we use olive oil with smoked paprika, garlic, and black pepper to emulate the flavor of smoked meat. Feel free to play with different spices as you see fit—you can swap coriander or cayenne for the smoked paprika, or omit it entirely. You could even add roasted vegetables or a handful of leafy greens like arugula to make a more substantial vegetarian meal.

––––––

NOTE: It's important here to pour the egg mixture into the pasta slowly while stirring quickly and vigorously, to ensure that the eggs don't curdle. The pasta should be lightly coated with a creamy sauce, but not soupy—think mac and cheese and you're on to the right, comforting idea.

3 large eggs

⅔ cup finely grated Parmigiano-Reggiano cheese, plus more (optional) for serving

⅔ cup finely grated pecorino cheese (preferably Pecorino Toscano), plus more (optional) for serving

½ cup kosher salt

1 pound long pasta, such as bucatini

⅓ cup extra-virgin olive oil

10 garlic cloves, finely chopped

2½ teaspoons freshly ground black pepper

1½ teaspoons smoked paprika (preferably Spanish pimentón)

1 cup thinly sliced scallions (6 to 8 scallions)

1 tablespoon fresh lemon juice

SONG OF SILVER by St. Marian's Church will help Gemma Bruno and her eight children until relief starts. (Top) Yolanda, 11; Anita, 10; Deanne, 9 (bottom); Joseph Jr., 5; Charles, 14 months; Mrs. Bruno, 33 Sue, 3; Michael, 2, and Mary, 7, at their home, 2965 Hamshire Rd., Cleveland Heights.

Song to Mean Food

A newspaper clipping for a church fundraiser held for Angie's grandma's family when her father died

RECIPE CONTINUES

In a small bowl, whisk the eggs until well beaten. Add the parmesan and pecorino and stir well to combine. Set aside.

In a medium pot, bring 4 quarts water and the salt to a boil over high heat. Add the pasta and cook according to the package directions. Reserve 1 cup of the cooking water, then drain the pasta and return it to the pot along with the reserved water.

Meanwhile, in a small pot or sauté pan, heat the oil over medium heat. Add the garlic, pepper, and smoked paprika, stirring often with a wooden spoon, until the garlic is toasted and fragrant, 2 to 3 minutes.

Add the garlic-oil mixture to the pasta in the pot and stir to combine.

Set the pasta pot over medium-low heat and slowly pour in the egg-cheese mixture with one hand while continuing to stir with the other hand, mixing vigorously to create a creamy sauce. It's important to move quickly during this step; otherwise the eggs will curdle. Once the sauce is thick and creamy, 1 to 2 minutes, remove from the heat. Add the scallions and lemon juice and stir well to combine.

Serve immediately, topped with more grated cheese, if desired.

Broccoli Soup with Broken Linguine

MAKES ABOUT 8 CUPS (SERVES 4 TO 6)

This is peasant food at its most comforting, something Angie's grandmother Maria would make for a quick lunch at home. (She'd task Angie with breaking the pasta as a child to keep her busy.) It's a one-pot affair: You're essentially infusing the oil with garlic, then adding broccoli, celery, and water to make a vegetarian stock. In goes the pasta and a touch of lemon and cheese and you're done. It's simple but soul-satisfying.

Maria learned the recipe from her mother-in-law, who was Sicilian, and we recently found a very similar recipe in an old Italian cookbook that called for a traditional Sicilian chicory, which leads us to believe that the dish was probably adapted in America with broccoli. No matter where it originated or how it exactly came to be, this is one of our favorites, and it comes together quickly for a hearty meal. Feel free to substitute cauliflower for the broccoli, if that's your mood.

Working in batches as necessary, pulse the broccoli in the food processor until it is broken up into small even pieces. You should have about 4 cups of broccoli crumbles.

In a medium pot, heat the olive oil over medium heat. Add the garlic, black pepper, and salt and cook, stirring often, until the garlic is toasted, 2 to 3 minutes. Add the celery and cook until translucent, 2 to 3 minutes.

Add the broccoli and stir to combine. Add 8 cups of water. Bring to a boil over high heat, then reduce the heat to medium-low and simmer for 30 minutes to meld the flavors.

Increase the heat to high once more to bring the soup to a boil, then add the pasta. Cook until the pasta is cooked through, about 12 minutes. Remove from the heat and stir in the lemon juice.

To serve, ladle into bowls and top with parmesan cheese. Leftover soup keeps, covered in the refrigerator, for up to 5 days.

1 pound broccoli (about 1 medium head), roughly chopped (florets and tender stalk)

½ cup extra-virgin olive oil

¼ cup thinly sliced garlic (about half of one large head)

½ teaspoon freshly ground black pepper

2 tablespoons kosher salt

½ cup finely chopped celery (about 2 ribs)

¼ pound dried linguine, broken into 1-inch pieces

2 teaspoons fresh lemon juice

½ cup finely grated Parmigiano-Reggiano cheese, for serving

Leftover Spaghetti & Meatball Frittata

SERVES 4

Depending on which life stage you're at, this is a great hangover meal, brunch centerpiece, or fun dish to make with kids. It looks almost like a cross between a frittata and a *timballo* (better known by many Italian Americans and *Big Night* fans as a timpano), and tastes rich and comforting. The idea is to bind leftover pasta and meat with egg, and while we call for classic spaghetti and meatballs in the ingredients list, you could certainly use a different noodle (angel hair, linguine, and bucatini are all good), and play around with different meatballs (the chicken and chorizo version on page 203 would be a fine choice). Because the finished product is on the more indulgent side, we like to top it with a simple, acidic herb salad to help cut some of the richness.

Make the frittata: Preheat the oven to 400°F.

In a medium bowl, whisk the eggs, milk, salt, and pepper until well combined. In a separate medium bowl, combine the cooked pasta, meatballs, and chopped tomatoes until evenly combined.

Coat the sides and bottom of an 8-inch nonstick ovenproof skillet or cast-iron pan with cooking spray. Heat the pan over medium heat and add the olive oil. Carefully place the pasta mixture in the pan and press down gently with a spoon to form an even layer. Allow the pasta mixture to sizzle for about 30 seconds, then sprinkle the parmesan and mozzarella on top and gently press down again for another 30 seconds.

Add the egg mixture to the pan, give it a small shake to ensure it evenly coats the noodles, and immediately transfer to the oven. Bake until the eggs are just set, 15 to 17 minutes. Let cool in the pan for 2 to 3 minutes, then run a butter knife around the edges to loosen. Invert onto a plate and cool to room temperature.

Just before serving, make the herb salad: In a small bowl, stir together the parsley, basil, salt, pepper, lemon juice, and olive oil.

Frittata

5 large eggs

2 tablespoons whole milk

1 teaspoon kosher salt

¼ teaspoon freshly ground black pepper

4 ounces (packed ½ cup) cooked spaghetti

1 cup crumbled cooked Classic Meatballs (page 193), without sauce (about 2 meatballs)

½ cup Oven-Dried Tomatoes (optional; page 302), or store-bought oil-packed sun-dried tomatoes, drained and roughly chopped

1 tablespoon extra-virgin olive oil

½ cup finely grated Parmigiano-Reggiano cheese

½ cup shredded whole-milk mozzarella cheese

Herb salad

10 parsley leaves

8 basil leaves, roughly torn if large

Pinch of kosher salt

Freshly ground black pepper

1 teaspoon fresh lemon juice

2 teaspoons extra-virgin olive oil

Slice the frittata into wedges with a serrated bread knife and arrange a spoonful of the herb salad on top of each slice. Leftover frittata keeps, tightly sealed in the refrigerator, for up to 3 days, and can be eaten warm or cold.

fazzoletti

fusilli

capunti

farfalle

orecchiette

Southern-Style Eggless Pasta

MAKES ABOUT 1 POUND

Eggless pasta doughs are an integral part of Italian cuisine, and common in southern Italy, where both of our families are from. There are two forms of eggless pasta dough out there: First is extruded pasta, which is typically sold dried and is probably what you've seen the most of at the grocery store. Second is this fresh eggless pasta—these are mostly shapes you can make by hand without any special equipment and have a unique, chewy texture that's a bit heartier than dried versions.

When it comes to flours, we like a mix of semolina and "00" flour here. Semolina is made from milled durum wheat. It has a hard, coarse texture, a yellowish color, and a mild, slightly nutty flavor. Because it has a high gluten content, it helps pasta keep its shape and gives it a firm texture. Bob's Red Mill makes a good version (theirs is labeled "Semolina Flour"); as does General Mills (billed as "Semolina No. 1"). We mix semolina here with a bit of "00" flour (we like Caputo brand for this, specifically their Pasta Fresca e Gnocchi Farina di Grano Tenero Tipo "00," available on Amazon), a very finely ground soft wheat flour, which helps add elasticity. The combination yields the supple-yet-sturdy texture that we're looking for.

The recipe may be humble, but there's an embarrassment of riches when it comes to all the shapes you can make with this dough (see opposite and pages 137 and 138). They don't have to be perfect—the fun is in using your hands and getting creative.

———

NOTE: Fresh pasta can be frozen for up to 1 month after it's been cut or rolled out into the desired shape. We recommend dusting the shaped pasta liberally with "00" or all-purpose flour, then arranging it on a sheet pan (in little nests if you're making long pasta) and quick-freezing to harden it for 20 to 30 minutes. This ensures that the shapes freeze individually and don't stick together. Once the pasta is frozen, you can remove it from the sheet pan and store in a zip-top bag or plastic container.

Special equipment

Pasta maker or stand mixer with the pasta attachment

2 cups semolina

2 tablespoons "00" flour, plus more for dusting

⅔ cup warm water (90° to 100°F)

To mix with a stand mixer: In a stand mixer with the paddle, mix the semolina and "00" flours together on the lowest speed. Add half of the water and mix until the dough resembles coarse sand, about 2 minutes. Add the other half of the water and continue mixing until the dough is shaggy and somewhat crumbly, 3 to 4 minutes. The dough should just come together and hold its shape when squeezed in your hand; it won't form a smooth ball. If it doesn't come together, add another 1 to 2 tablespoons of water and continue mixing until the dough feels dry to the touch and not sticky. It will probably seem drier than you think it should be, but don't worry—that's how it should feel at this point.

To mix by hand: Mound the two flours on a clean tabletop and mix together with a fork until incorporated. Make a 4- to 6-inch well in the center of the flour, add half of the water to the well, then with a fork, making 2-inch circles with your hand, slowly make your way around the well in a circular pattern, incorporating the flour into the water little by little, which should take anywhere from 30 seconds to 1 minute. Add the rest of the water to the well, and repeat the same process, until all of the water has been incorporated into the dough. Using a bench scraper, scoop any remaining flour and press it into the wet dough. Knead for 6 to 8 minutes until smooth but not sticky.

Transfer the dough to a clean surface (ideally wood or plastic, not marble, which can chill the dough) and wrap the dough tightly in plastic wrap. Let rest at room temperature for at least 30 minutes and up to 1 hour—the dough will hydrate and become smooth as it rests, and as the gluten in it relaxes, it will become much easier to work with. Pasta dough can be made up to 2 days before rolling and cutting it into specific shapes (see the Variations that follow). Bring it to room temperature before using. Once the dough has been rolled and cut, it can be kept in the refrigerator for up to 4 days before cooking.

endless variations can be made with the use of different pasta-making tools

Fusilli

MAKES 4 TO 6 SERVINGS

Fusilli is a twisted pasta that looks like a telephone cord from back in the landline days. It's an impressive shape to make by hand because it looks machine-extruded, but it's actually quite easy (and fun) to do by hand, rolling each strand all the way across a cutting board and creating a continual ridge that does a great job of catching sauce when cooked.

Special equipment
Pasta maker or stand mixer with the pasta attachment

Southern-Style Eggless Pasta (opposite)
"00" or all-purpose flour, for dusting

Make the dough as directed. If it has been refrigerated, let it come to room temperature before rolling and cutting. Cut the dough in quarters and work with one piece at a time, keeping the other pieces wrapped tightly in plastic and set aside at room temperature.

With the palm of your hand, press one piece of dough evenly on all sides into an oval shape, about ¼ inch thick, to feed into the pasta maker or stand mixer attachment.

Adjust the pasta maker or attachment to its thickest setting and feed the dough through, rolling it smoothly with the crank. Fold the rolled dough in half crosswise, matching end to end, and gently press both sides together with your hands to seal it.

Leave the pasta maker or attachment on the thickest setting and reinsert the dough, folded end first, rolling it through again smoothly with the crank. The dough should be about a foot long, as wide as your pasta maker (probably 5 to 6 inches), and about as thick as two nickels.

Attach the cutter to the pasta maker according to the machine's instructions. Set the cutter to the tagliatelle measurement. Dust the dough with "00" or all-purpose flour and cut ½ inch off the bottom corners on a diagonal to get the sheet to fit evenly in the cutter.

Feed the dough through the cutter from the top, rolling smoothly, like a paper shredder. Catch the cut strands that come out the bottom with your other hand. Separate the strands with your fingers and dust generously with flour to keep from sticking, then loosely pile them together into a neat bundle. Cover the bundle loosely with plastic wrap.

RECIPE CONTINUES

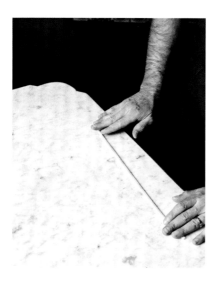

Repeat with a second piece of dough, making two bundles of thick strands.

Form the fusilli: Gently press the end of one strand of pasta onto the lower edge of a large clean work surface and hold it in place with your nondominant hand. Using the fingers of your dominant hand, roll the other end of the strand into a rounded tip, so that as you roll the strand across the board, the pasta will become rounded on all sides. Use the palm of your dominant hand to roll up the strand diagonally across the surface, twisting the strand into a spiral tube while still keeping the other end of the strand clamped down with your nondominant hand. (It can help to twist the rolled end a couple of times to get the spiral going.) Use gentle pressure with your dominant hand to guide the strand upward into a tight, even coil, without pulling or pressing it, which will cause the strand to break. Lightly roll your palm over any slack spots that haven't twisted evenly.

Pick up both ends of the strand and move them to the top of the work surface, pressing down on the ends gently to keep them in place. Flour the fusilli and repeat with the remaining strands. Allow the fusilli to sit for 20 minutes before cooking so the twist can set.

Repeat the rolling process with the remaining two quarters of dough. The rolled out dough can be kept in the refrigerator for up to 4 days before cooking.

When ready to cook, cut the strands into 3- to 4-inch pieces.

To cook, bring 4 quarts water and ½ cup kosher salt to a boil over high heat. Add the fusilli and cook for 45 to 60 seconds. Drain, combine with sauce, and serve.

Capunti

MAKES 4 TO 6 SERVINGS

Similar to cavatelli, capunti is a peapod-shaped pasta from Puglia, the heel of Italy's boot. It's a rustic, chewy pasta with grooves from your fingertips that are excellent for catching sauce; we like to pair it with everything from hearty ragus to simple tomato sauce or butter and cheese.

———

Southern-Style Eggless Pasta (page 134)
"00" or all-purpose flour, for dusting

Make the dough as directed. If it has been refrigerated, let it come to room temperature before rolling and cutting. Cut the dough in quarters and work with one piece at a time, keeping the other pieces wrapped tightly in plastic. Set aside at room temperature.

Using your hands and a clean work surface, roll the dough into a log about 1 inch thick. Cut the log in half crosswise and, working gently with your fingertips, apply pressure from the middle of the log and push outward to roll each half into a thinner log, about ½ inch thick.

Cut each log sharply on the bias into 2- to 3-inch pieces. The cut pieces should resemble tiny baguettes, angled at both ends.

Push the middle of each piece of pasta down with your three middle fingers, gently but with enough pressure to make a distinct indentation. In one fluid motion, with your fingers still pressed into the dough, quickly drag the pasta backward 1 to 2 inches toward the palm of your hand, curling it slightly into a peapod shape.

Set aside on a plate or sheet pan and gently dust with "00" or all-purpose flour.

Repeat with the remaining dough. Allow the capunti to dry for at least 15 to 20 minutes before cooking. (The pasta can be kept in the refrigerator for up to 4 days before cooking.)

To cook, bring 4 quarts water and ½ cup kosher salt to a boil over high heat. Add the capunti and cook for 1 minute. Drain, combine with sauce, and serve.

Orecchiette

This unique "little ear" shape is another pasta specific to Puglia. A few years ago, we visited Bari, a town that seems to consist almost entirely of old Italian ladies making orecchiette together, sitting around little wooden tables and pressing the dough into small ear-shaped pieces. (We're kidding, but we did see a lot of nonnas making pasta.) All you need to make orecchiette is a butter knife and a thumb, and it's quick work once you get the hang of it. The finished pasta has a lot of structure and texture on its own, making it ideal for cupping pestos and ragus, or, as is traditional, broccoli rabe and crumbled Italian sausage.

———

Southern-Style Eggless Pasta (page 134)

"00" or all-purpose flour, for dusting

Make the dough as directed. If it has been refrigerated, let it come to room temperature before rolling and cutting. Cut the dough in quarters and work with one piece at a time, keeping the other pieces wrapped tightly in plastic. Set aside at room temperature.

Using your hands and a clean work surface, roll the dough into a log about 1 inch thick. Cut the log in half crosswise. Working gently with your fingertips, apply pressure from the middle of the log and push outward to roll each half into a thinner log, about ½ inch thick.

Cut each log into ¾-inch pieces and gently press them into flat discs with your fingertips.

Dust a butter knife with flour and press it into the top of one of the discs at a 45-degree angle. Quickly and firmly drag the knife toward you along the cutting board, so that the dough curls up completely, wrapping itself around the knife. Pick up the curl and pop it inside out with your thumb, creating the little ear shape.

Set aside on a plate or sheet pan and gently dust with flour.

Repeat with the remaining dough. Allow the orecchiette to dry for at least 15 to 20 minutes before cooking. (The rolled and cut dough can be kept in the refrigerator for up to 4 days before cooking.)

To cook, bring 4 quarts water and ½ cup kosher salt to a boil over high heat. Add the orecchiette and cook until tender, 45 to 60 seconds. Drain, combine with sauce, and serve.

Fusilli & Scampi, New Orleans Style

SERVES 6

The last time we went to New Orleans, we became mildly obsessed with a local specialty known as barbecue shrimp, reportedly invented in the 1950s at the storied Uptown Italian-Creole seafood restaurant Pascal's Manale. It has nothing to do with barbecue or grilling. Instead, head-on shrimp are sautéed in an insanely rich Worcestershire-spiked butter sauce, and the name is only a reference to the reddish tint of the sauce in the finished dish. The first time we tried it, we liked it so much we immediately ordered a second round, and when we got home, we set about making our own version.

We used shrimp scampi—the Italian-American staple of shrimp with butter, white wine, and garlic—as our base, then amped it up with a layer of piquant seasoning, as well as citrus juice and scallions for freshness. There is a significant amount of butter involved here, but that's the only way to achieve the velvet-smooth texture of the original. If you'd like, you can use just one stick (as opposed to the one-and-a-half sticks as called for) to finish the sauce. We make it with fusilli, which pairs well with the texture of the shrimp, and whose crevices help catch the sauce better than a flat, smooth pasta.

---

1 pound jumbo (21/25 count) shrimp (preferably wild-caught), peeled and deveined

2 tablespoons sugar

1 tablespoon onion powder

1½ teaspoons dried oregano (ideally home-dried, page 301)

1 teaspoon smoked paprika (preferably Spanish pimentón)

½ teaspoon cayenne pepper

2½ teaspoons kosher salt, plus more for the pasta water

1½ teaspoons freshly ground black pepper

½ teaspoon Worcestershire sauce

1 cup (2 sticks) unsalted butter, cut into cubes

3 bay leaves

6 garlic cloves, thinly sliced

½ cup dry white wine, such as Pinot Grigio

1½ cups chicken stock, unsalted store-bought or homemade (page 299)

Fusilli (page 135) or 1 pound store-bought dried fusilli

¾ cup finely grated Parmigiano-Reggiano cheese

½ cup fresh lemon juice (about 2 large lemons)

¾ cup thinly sliced scallions (4 to 6 scallions)

Slice each shrimp horizontally in half, butterflying it from top to tail. In a medium bowl, mix together the sugar, onion powder, oregano, smoked paprika, cayenne, salt, and black pepper. Add the shrimp to the spice mixture along with the Worcestershire sauce and toss to coat. Set aside.

In a large pot, heat 4 tablespoons of the butter and the bay leaves over medium-high heat until the butter is melted and the bay leaves are aromatic, 1 to 2 minutes. Add the garlic. Stir and cook until the garlic is slightly golden, about 2 minutes. Add the wine and cook until dry, 3 to 4 minutes. Add the chicken stock and bring to a simmer. Cook until the volume is reduced by half, about 2 minutes.

In another large pot, bring 4 quarts water and ½ cup kosher salt to a boil over high heat. Add the fusilli and cook until just cooked through and slightly chewy, 45 to 60 seconds for fresh or according to the package directions for dried. Drain the pasta and add it to the pot of chicken stock and wine mixture.

Increase the heat under the pot with the pasta mixture to medium-high. Add the marinated shrimp and stir to combine. Add the remaining 1½ sticks of butter, the parmesan, lemon juice, and about ½ cup of the scallions. Stir very vigorously and continually, until all of the butter has melted and the shrimp has cooked through, about 2 minutes. The spices from the shrimp marinade will turn the sauce a light pink hue, and the sauce should become emulsified, thickened, and creamy.

Discard the bay leaves, then spoon the pasta into individual bowls or a platter. Top with the remaining ¼ cup of scallions. Serve immediately. Leftovers keep, tightly covered in the refrigerator, for up to 2 days. Reheat over low heat, stirring in 3 to 4 tablespoons of water or stock to loosen the sauce and re-emulsify if necessary.

Orecchiette with Chickpeas, Turmeric & Dandelion Greens

SERVES 4 TO 6

This is a hearty, vegetable-based pasta dish in the spirit of *pasta e ceci*, a Roman stew of pasta and chickpeas with a million different variations (some are more soupy, some have tomatoes, some involve bitter greens, etc.). No matter who's making it, though, the two staple ingredients remain the same.

Chickpeas show up often in Italian cuisine, all across the country, where they're combined with pasta, or made into regional specialties that range from porridge to fritters to focaccia. Here, they provide textural contrast and a nutty flavor, while dandelion greens add depth, and the turmeric supplies a pleasantly bitter earthy note to complement the greens.

A splash of heavy cream rounds out the flavors, while lemon juice brightens up everything. If you can't find dandelion greens, feel free to use another hearty green, such as lacinato kale or mature spinach; you can also add a cup or so of crumbled Italian sausage to make a nonvegetarian version.

½ cup extra-virgin olive oil

4 garlic cloves, grated on a Microplane

4 cups diced yellow onions (about 2 medium onions)

4 teaspoons kosher salt, plus more for the pasta water

¼ teaspoon freshly ground black pepper

1 teaspoon crushed Calabrian chiles in oil

1 teaspoon sugar

2 teaspoons ground turmeric

2 teaspoons tomato paste

½ pound dandelion greens, lacinato kale, or spinach, stemmed and cut into 1-inch pieces

1 (15.5-ounce) can chickpeas, drained and rinsed

½ cup heavy cream

Orecchiette (page 138) or 1 pound store-bought dried orecchiette

½ cup finely grated Parmigiano-Reggiano cheese

1 tablespoon fresh lemon juice

In a large heavy-bottomed pot, heat the olive oil over medium heat. Add the garlic and cook until soft and aromatic, 1 to 2 minutes. Add the onions, salt, black pepper, Calabrian chiles, and sugar and increase the heat to medium-high. Cook until the onions are soft but haven't taken on any color, 2 to 3 minutes. Add the turmeric and tomato paste and cook until the onions are translucent, another 2 to 3 minutes. If anything sticks on the bottom of the pot, add a tablespoon of water and scrape it off with a wooden spoon or silicone spatula.

Add the dandelion greens and cook until the greens are very soft and tender, 6 to 8 minutes. Add the chickpeas and heavy cream and cook for an additional minute, then remove from the heat and set aside.

In another large pot, bring 4 quarts water and ½ cup kosher salt to a boil over high heat. Add the orecchiette and cook until just cooked through and slightly chewy, 45 to 60 seconds for fresh or according to the package directions for dried. Drain and return the pasta back to the cooking pot. Add the sauce and stir in the parmesan and lemon juice.

Serve immediately in individual bowls or family style. Leftovers keep, tightly covered in the refrigerator, for up to 3 days.

Capunti with Clams, Capocollo & Potato

SERVES 4 TO 6

Think of this as a sort of amped-up version of linguine and clams, with the addition of golden roasted potatoes and spicy-smoky pork. It's a dish all about textural contrast—the soft, chewy pasta with springy clams, crispy potatoes, and little nubs of capocollo combine in a deeply satisfying way. The finished product feels almost summery, with the white wine and lemon juice lightening it up. We like to serve clams in their shell with peapod-shaped capunti pasta for a rustic-feeling and visually striking effect.

———

NOTE: If you can't find capocollo (see page 20), substitute a smoky ham, or even andouille sausage, which mimics the spicy-smoky-garlicky flavors in the sauce.

Place the clams in a bowl of cold water and let sit for 20 to 30 minutes to purge any sand from the clams. If any shells are open, lightly tap them on the side of the bowl. If they do not close in response to tapping, discard them, as this means they are dead. Rinse the clams with cold water and drain them in a colander.

Preheat the oven to 425°F.

Fill a large bowl with cold water. Cut the potatoes into ¼-inch cubes (you should have about 3 cups) and immediately submerge in the water. Let soak in the water for 15 to 30 minutes (this will yield a crispier final product). Drain the potatoes and lay them onto a baking sheet lined with paper towels. Place another layer of paper towels on top and press down to remove as much moisture from the potatoes as possible.

Shake the potatoes off the paper towels onto the baking sheet. Toss with 1 teaspoon of the paprika and the granulated garlic, coating them evenly. Add ¼ cup of the olive oil and toss well to coat. Bake until golden and crispy, 20 to 22 minutes, stirring them midway through. Season with ¼ teaspoon of the salt and set aside.

24 Manila or 18 small littleneck clams

1 pound Yukon Gold potatoes (about 2 medium potatoes)

2 teaspoons sweet paprika (preferably Hungarian)

½ teaspoon granulated garlic

½ cup extra-virgin olive oil

1¼ teaspoons kosher salt, plus more for the pasta water

½ pound capocollo (see Note), cut into ¼-inch dice

1 tablespoon grated garlic (using a Microplane, 3 to 4 cloves)

¼ teaspoon freshly ground black pepper

2 teaspoons dried oregano (ideally home-dried, page 301)

½ cup finely diced celery (about 2 ribs)

1 cup finely diced yellow onion (about ½ onion)

½ cup finely diced Italian frying pepper (aka cubanelle)

¾ cup dry white wine, such as Pinot Grigio

1 cup chicken stock, unsalted store-bought or homemade (page 299)

Capunti (page 137) or 1 pound store-bought dried short pasta, such as penne

½ cup (1 stick) unsalted butter

¼ cup fresh lemon juice (about 1 large lemon)

3 tablespoons roughly chopped parsley

RECIPE CONTINUES

In a large pot, heat the remaining ¼ cup olive oil over medium-high heat. Add the capocollo and cook, stirring often, until fat renders from the meat, about 6 minutes. Add the grated garlic, pepper, oregano, the remaining 1 teaspoon paprika and 1 teaspoon salt. Stir to combine and cook until the garlic is lightly toasted, about 1 minute. Add the celery, onion, and frying peppers and cook until the vegetables are translucent, stirring often, 7 to 8 minutes.

Add the clams and white wine to the pot and cover with a lid. Let cook until all of the clams have opened, 5 to 7 minutes, depending on the size of the clams. Remove the lid, stir the contents of the pot well, and add the chicken stock. Remove from the heat.

Meanwhile, in another large pot, bring 4 quarts water and ½ cup kosher salt to a boil over high heat. Add the pasta and cook until slightly chewy but not gummy, 45 to 60 seconds for fresh or according to the package directions for dried. Drain, then transfer the pasta into the pot with the clam mixture. Bring the pasta and sauce to a boil over medium-high heat. Add the butter, lemon juice, and parsley and stir vigorously to combine. In 3 to 5 minutes, the sauce will become creamy and coat the pasta.

Spoon the pasta into individual bowls or a platter. Top with the crispy potatoes. Serve immediately. This dish is best made and eaten day-of.

Northern-Style Egg Yolk Pasta

MAKES ABOUT 1 POUND DOUGH OR EIGHT 12 × 7-INCH SHEETS

Egg pastas are found all over Italy, but they're particularly associated with Emilia-Romagna, a wealthier region in north-central Italy that historically had access to premium ingredients like eggs. These pastas are richer and more supple than their eggless counterparts.

Our dough recipe calls for both egg yolks and a whole egg—the yolk adds color and richness, while the white adds structure. You should use a minimum of 7 and up to 9 yolks, adding them one at a time, to reach the desired shaggy, crumbly texture. We give this range because there are so many variables in pasta making, from the humidity and temperature of the room to the size of the eggs. A common mistake when making pasta dough is to expect to immediately see a moist ball of dough. You should err on the side of drier at first, knowing that the dough will hydrate and become smoother as it rests. Play around with the amount of egg yolks until you find what works for you.

As for the flours, it's worth seeking out Italian "00" and durum flours here. Durum flour is the finely ground powder left over from milling durum wheat. It's high in protein and gluten, and creates pasta with a stretchy texture and a slightly nutty flavor. Italian "00" flour is very finely ground soft wheat flour, which is low in protein and makes for soft, supple pasta. For durum flour, we like either King Arthur (sold as "Durum Flour") or Caputo (sold as Semola di Grano Duro Rimacinata and available online). For "00," we also like Caputo Pasta Fresca e Gnocchi Farina di Grano Tenero Tipo "00," available on Amazon. It's possible to substitute regular all-purpose flour for either flour, but it will be more difficult to sheet thinly, and won't have as rich of a flavor.

We sheet our egg pastas to the thinnest or second-thinnest setting on the machine—it's such a luxurious recipe that we want to keep it feeling light. Here, we're providing instructions for one simply cut, sheeted pasta, and two short hand-folded options, though there are countless shapes you can make once you have the basic dough recipe down. This recipe will make enough dough for about eight 12 × 7-inch sheets of pasta. If you are making lasagna, leave the pasta in large sheets and refer to the detailed lasagna instructions in the Lasagnas & Baked Pastas chapter beginning on page 167.

Special equipment

Pasta maker or stand mixer with the pasta attachment

1 cup durum flour

1 cup "00" flour, plus more for dusting

1 large egg

7 to 9 large egg yolks

NOTE: Fresh pasta can be frozen for up to 1 month after it's been cut or rolled out into the desired shape. We recommend dusting the shaped pasta liberally with "00" or all-purpose flour, then arranging it on a sheet pan and quick-freezing to harden it up for 20 to 30 minutes. This ensures that the shapes freeze individually and don't stick together. Once the pasta is frozen, you can remove it from the sheet pan and store in a zip-top plastic bag or plastic container. Fresh pasta sheets for lasagna also freeze well when dusted liberally with "00" or all-purpose flour and stacked gently in a zip-top bag.

To mix with a stand mixer: In a stand mixer with the paddle, mix the durum and "00" flours together with the whole egg on medium speed until incorporated, about 1 minute. Add the egg yolks, one at a time, mixing to incorporate after each addition, 3 to 4 minutes total. Stop after adding 7 yolks and determine whether you need to add 1 or 2 more. The dough should look shaggy and somewhat crumbly at this point, and just come together and hold its shape when squeezed in your hand; it won't form a smooth ball. It should feel dry to the touch, and not sticky. The dough will hydrate and become smooth as it rests.

To mix by hand: Mound the two flours on a clean countertop and mix together with a fork until incorporated. Make a 4- to 6-inch well in the center of the flour, add 7 egg yolks to the well, then with a fork, making 2-inch circles with your hand, slowly make your way around the well in a circular pattern, incorporating the flour into the yolks little by little, about 2 minutes. Add the whole egg to the well,

RECIPE CONTINUES

and repeat the same process, until all of the egg has been incorporated into the dough, about another 2 minutes. Assess whether more moisture is needed to bring the dough together, then add up to 2 more egg yolks, incorporating in the same way. Using a bench scraper, scoop any remaining flour and press it into the wet dough. Knead for 8 to 10 minutes until smooth but not sticky.

Transfer the dough to a clean surface (ideally wood or plastic, not marble, which can chill the dough). Wrap the dough tightly in plastic and rest at room temperature for 30 minutes to relax the gluten and make it easier to roll. Pasta dough can be made and refrigerated up to 2 days before rolling and cutting it into specific shapes. Bring it to room temperature before using.

Cut the dough into quarters and work with one piece at a time, keeping the other pieces wrapped in plastic. Set aside at room temperature.

With the palm of your hand, press the dough evenly on all sides into an oval shape about ¼ inch thick, to feed it into the machine.

Adjust the pasta maker or attachment to its thickest setting and feed the dough through, rolling it smoothly with the crank. Fold the rolled dough in half crosswise, matching end to end, and gently press both sides together with your hands to seal it.

Leave the maker or attachment on the thickest setting and reinsert the dough, folded end first, rolling it through again smoothly with the crank. The dough should be about 12 inches long, as wide as your maker (probably 6 to 7 inches), and about as thick as two nickels.

Repeat the folding, pressing, and rolling process two more times on the same setting, until the dough is a neat rectangular shape. It should feel smooth and supple, and not sticky. (If it is, or it is humid out, sprinkle with a little "00" or all-purpose flour.) Do not fold the dough after this pass.

Adjust the setting on the maker or attachment to one level thinner, then smoothly roll the dough through again. Continue adjusting the setting to one level thinner, and passing the dough through each setting once, until the maker is on its thinnest setting (if using a stand mixer attachment this should be setting #5). You should have a long, thin sheet about 24 inches long and as thick as a dime. Cut the sheet in half to yield two 12-inch sheets.

Repeat with the remaining pieces of the dough. You will have eight 12 × 7-inch sheets. The pasta is now ready to be used or stored as sheets or cut into specific shapes (see the Variations that follow). Once the pasta has been rolled and cut, it can be kept in the refrigerator for up to 4 days before cooking.

Fazzoletti

MAKES 6 TO 8 SERVINGS

Fazzoletti di seta, the Italian name for this pasta, translates to "silk handkerchief," and it's a fitting name for these wide, silky sheets. This is a rustic pasta often seen in Liguria, where it's served with another local invention, pesto. You don't need a cutter to make this elegant, simple shape as you cut it by hand after rolling.

NOTE: For extra color and flavor, you can add ½ cup of chopped herbs (chives, parsley, and dill all work well) during the folding process. To do so, follow the instructions for Northern-Style Egg Yolk Pasta, rolling the pasta to the second-thinnest setting. Lightly brush the surface of the sheeted dough with water, sprinkle the herbs across half of the surface, then fold the other side over like a sandwich. Pass the dough through again on the same setting, then adjust it to the thinnest setting and pass it through a final time.

Northern-Style Egg Yolk Pasta (page 147)
"00" or all-purpose flour, for dusting

Make the pasta, roll into sheets, and cut as directed. Dust the 12-inch sheets with flour and cut in half into 6-inch squares. Stack the sheets on top of one another with a layer of flour in between until ready to cook.

To cook, bring 4 quarts water and ½ cup kosher salt to a boil over high heat. Add the fazzoletti and cook for 45 to 60 seconds. Drain, combine with sauce, and serve.

Sorpresine

MAKES 6 TO 8 SERVINGS

Sorpresine means "little surprises" in Italian, and the twist here is that this pasta, though it resembles something like a tortellini, is unfilled. Its fortune cookie–esque shape looks complicated but is achieved by simply folding opposite ends together. As a more delicate shape, these pair best with a slightly lighter sauce, such as shellfish in a light wine and butter sauce, or with pesto, as opposed to a meaty ragu.

NOTE: If you want to get really fancy here, when making the pasta dough, you can add color and flavor by mixing in 1 tablespoon plus 1 teaspoon tomato powder and 1½ teaspoons smoked paprika (preferably Spanish pimentón), as pictured in the Sorpresine with Mussels, Guajillo, Cilantro & Lime recipe on page 152.

Northern-Style Egg Yolk Pasta (page 147)
"00" or all-purpose flour, for dusting

Make the pasta and roll into sheets as directed. Liberally dust each sheet with flour and stack them on top of one another. Gently cover the stack with plastic wrap while you work with each piece to keep it from drying out.

Cut each 12-inch sheet of pasta lengthwise into strips 2 inches wide. Then cut each strip crosswise into 2-inch squares.

Hold each square like a diamond in the palm of one hand. Using your other thumb and index finger, fold the top corner of the diamond into the bottom corner, and pinch just the corners together to seal the point.

Hold the pointed end together with your dominant thumb and forefinger, and gently press the middle of the pouch toward the pointed ends with the index finger of your other hand. Use your nondominant thumb and index finger to gently pull the remaining corners toward each other in the opposite direction, pinching them together into another point facing the other way. The finished shape should resemble an unfilled tortellini. Set aside on a plate or sheet pan and gently dust with flour.

Allow the sorpresine to dry for 15 to 20 minutes before cooking.

To cook, bring 4 quarts water and ½ cup kosher salt to a boil over high heat. Add the sorpresine and cook for 1 minute. Drain, combine with sauce, and serve.

Farfalle

MAKES 4 SERVINGS

In Italian, *farfalle* refers both to "bow-ties" and "butterflies"; equally poetic in their own rights. You can make these using round or square cutouts, and if you have a cutter with a fluted edge, now is the time to break it out. But a biscuit cutter or even an overturned wineglass will work just as well. While some farfalle recipes call for simply scrunching up the dough and pressing the center together once, we prefer to make a series of individual creases, then joining them together to help the farfalle keep a more distinct shape. Just be sure to press firmly in the middle to ensure the "bow" stays intact.

Northern-Style Egg Yolk Pasta (page 147)

"00" or all-purpose flour, for dusting

Make the pasta and roll into sheets as directed, and cut as directed. Liberally dust each sheet with flour and stack them on top of one another. Gently cover the stack with plastic wrap while you work with each piece to keep it from drying out.

Working with one 12-inch sheet at a time, use a 2¼-inch ring cutter or water glass to cut the sheet into rounds. Discard the excess dough and/or cut the scraps into another shape to cook later.

Find the center of the round and pinch it together with your thumb and index finger to make a crease in the middle. Make two more small creases on either side of the first crease, like accordion folds. Gather all of the creases and the opposite edges of the round in between your thumb and index finger and firmly press them together in the middle. Set aside on a plate or sheet pan and gently dust with flour while you cut the remaining sheets.

Repeat with the remaining sheets. You should have about 75 farfalle. Allow the farfalle to dry for 15 to 20 minutes before cooking.

To cook, bring 4 quarts water and ½ cup kosher salt to a boil over high heat. Add the farfalle and cook for 1 minute 30 seconds. Drain, combine with sauce, and serve.

Sorpresine with Mussels, Guajillo, Cilantro & Lime

SERVES 6

The loose inspiration for this recipe was our favorite summertime drink, the michelada, a brilliant Mexican invention involving, in its simplest form, beer flavored with chile, lime, and salt. Drinking one is both refreshing and complex, and insanely satisfying on a hot day. We wanted to capture that combination of flavors and sensations in pasta form; thus this light, citrusy, fresh-feeling recipe was born.

This flavor profile pairs really well with shellfish, and we've chosen to use mussels along with sorpresine here, because the pasta shape itself resembles a mussel. There's a fair bit of cilantro in this recipe, too, for more freshness, but we don't just scatter it on raw at the end. Although a lot of fresh herbs have a soft, fleeting flavor that gets lost in heat, cilantro takes on a different and delicious flavor when cooked, and especially when paired with lime and chile. We add a bit of sugar at the end to bring out the smokiness of the chiles (guajillo have a mild, raisin-y flavor, though if you're spice-sensitive, remove the seeds before adding them), and the beer adds a bit of bitterness and umami to round everything out.

Don't be alarmed by the combination of shellfish and cheese here—we swear it really works. Yes, some people have strong opinions on this topic, but you know how we feel about "rules" in general. Enjoy this on hot days with a crisp beer in hand.

———

Place the mussels in a bowl of cold water with 1 tablespoon of the salt and let sit for 20 to 30 minutes to purge any sand from them. Rinse the mussels with cold water, scrubbing them gently to remove any barnacles or mud, and drain in a colander. If any shells are open, lightly tap them on the side of the bowl. If they do not close in response to tapping, discard them, as this means they are dead. Remove any beards from the mussels by grabbing the beard between your thumb and forefinger and briskly tugging it toward the hinge of the shell.

Break up the guajillo chiles into 3 to 4 small pieces with your hands and place them in a blender along with the chicken stock. Process on high speed for 1 to 1½ minutes until the stock turns bright red in color.

1½ pounds mussels

1 tablespoon plus 1 teaspoon kosher salt, plus more for the pasta water

3 dried guajillo chiles, or substitute ancho or pasilla

3 cups chicken stock, unsalted store-bought or homemade (page 299)

½ cup extra-virgin olive oil

8 large garlic cloves, thinly sliced

1¼ teaspoons dried oregano (ideally home-dried, page 301)

¼ cup chopped fresh cilantro leaves (about 8 sprigs), plus handful of picked cilantro leaves (4 to 5 sprigs) for serving

1 cup lager beer, such as Peroni

Sorpresine (page 150) or 1 pound store-bought dried short pasta, such as medium shells

½ cup (1 stick) unsalted butter

¼ cup finely grated Parmigiano-Reggiano cheese

Grated zest of 1 lime

¼ cup fresh lime juice (about 2 large limes)

1 teaspoon sugar

½ cup Crispy Garlic Bread Crumbs (page 299)

RECIPE CONTINUES

(If you prefer less spice, remove the seeds from the chiles prior to processing. If you prefer things spicy, leave them in.) Drain the mixture through a fine-mesh sieve into a bowl and set aside.

In a large pot, heat the oil over medium-high heat. Add the garlic, oregano, cilantro, and remaining 1 teaspoon salt and cook, stirring often, until the garlic is very lightly toasted and fragrant, about 4 minutes. Add the mussels and beer and cover the pot with a lid. Cook over medium-high heat until the mussels open, about 4 minutes, discarding any that don't open. Using a slotted spoon, remove the mussels from the pot and set aside. Leave the beer mixture in the pot.

Add the chile/stock mixture to the mussel cooking liquid and stir well. Continue to cook over medium-high, simmering briskly and stirring often until the volume is reduced by two-thirds, 10 to 12 minutes.

In another large pot, bring 4 quarts water and ½ cup kosher salt to a boil over high heat. Add the pasta and cook 1 minute for fresh or according to the package directions for dried. Drain and transfer the pasta to the pot with the stock mixture. Return the mussels to the pot.

Bring back to a boil over medium-high heat, then add the butter, parmesan, lime zest, lime juice, and sugar, stirring to combine and emulsify. The sauce should coat the pasta in a rich, creamy layer.

Spoon the pasta into individual bowls or onto a platter. Top with bread crumbs and fresh cilantro leaves. Serve immediately. This dish is best made and eaten day-of.

Farfalle with White Vodka Sauce

SERVES 4 TO 6

Vodka sauce is always popular, but ours ups the ante by removing the tomatoes entirely, making a sauce that tastes like a sophisticated version of Alfredo. We originally developed it for an off-menu pasta special that came topped with caviar (vodka and caviar, get it?), but even without the luxurious touch, this sauce feels like a treat. It gets its flavor from a lot of onions and shallots, similar in style to a French soubise (a béchamel or heavy cream sauce with the addition of pureed slow-cooked onions), which add both body and flavor when they're pureed into a silky sauce. And in lieu of heavy cream, we use crème fraîche, which has a more complex, tangy flavor.

And vodka, of course. There are lots of theories about how vodka came to be used in Italian cooking—our favorite is the tale of a Roman chef who allegedly invented "sauce alla vodka" in the '80s at the behest of a vodka company who wanted to popularize the liquor in Italy, which may or may not be true—but origin story aside, the spirit definitely helps the ingredients emulsify into a smooth sauce.

We like to pair our white vodka sauce with farfalle for its fun shape, and its little creased pockets that can soak in and hold the sauce. It's just as good with any short, tubular pasta like penne or rigatoni as well.

¾ cup (1½ sticks) unsalted butter

2½ cups thinly sliced yellow onions (about 2 medium)

1½ cups thinly sliced shallots (3 to 4 medium)

1 tablespoon plus 2 teaspoons kosher salt, plus more for the pasta water

¼ teaspoon ground white pepper

½ cup vodka

1 cup vegetable stock or unsalted chicken stock, store-bought or homemade (page 299)

1 cup crème fraîche

½ cup finely grated Parmigiano-Reggiano cheese

Farfalle (page 151) or 1 pound store-bought dried farfalle

In a medium pot, melt 8 tablespoons (1 stick) of the butter over medium heat. Add the onions, shallots, salt, and white pepper and stir well to combine. Cook, stirring often, until the onions release their liquid and wilt, 10 to 12 minutes.

Add the vodka, increase the heat to high, and continue to cook, stirring often, until the alcohol is evaporated, about 4 minutes. Add the stock and continue to cook, stirring often, until the onions are very translucent and soft and the liquid is fully evaporated, another 7 to 9 minutes.

Carefully transfer the onion mixture to a blender along with the crème fraîche and parmesan. Open the steam vent in the blender lid and cover the opening with a towel to avoid hot splatter and blend on high until very smooth, about 3 minutes.

In a large pot, bring 4 quarts water and ½ cup kosher salt to a boil over high heat. Add the farfalle and cook the fresh pasta until the ends are soft and the middle is just cooked through, about 1 minute 30 seconds; for dried, cook according to the package directions. Drain and return to the cooking pot. Add the pureed sauce from the blender and heat over medium-high until the sauce bubbles; it should thicken and coat the pasta in an even layer. Add the remaining 4 tablespoons butter and stir until melted and velvety.

Serve immediately in individual bowls or family style. Leftover pasta keeps, tightly covered in the refrigerator, for up to 3 days. Reheat over low heat, stirring in 1 to 2 tablespoons of water or stock to loosen the sauce if necessary.

Fazzoletti with Pesto Bianco

SERVES 6 TO 8

Pesto bianco (white pesto) is a mash-up of our own creation, combining elements of *spaghetti al limone* from the Amalfi coast (one of Angie's dad's favorite recipes) with traditional Ligurian green pesto. We nixed the basil from the classic and used lemon instead, making for a bright, citrusy pesto that's fantastic on any type of rich egg-based pasta.

———

NOTE: We like using homemade fazzoletti (page 149), but if you don't have time or don't want to make your own, seek out the "fresh" lasagna sheets in the refrigerated section of the grocery store and cut them at home.

1 cup pine nuts (4 ounces)

½ cup finely grated Parmigiano-Reggiano cheese

1½ teaspoons kosher salt, plus more for the pasta water

¼ teaspoon sugar

1 garlic clove, grated on a Microplane

Pinch of ground white pepper

Grated zest of 2 lemons

1 tablespoon fresh lemon juice

¼ cup extra-virgin olive oil

Fazzoletti, homemade (page 149) or store-bought (see Note)

4 tablespoons (½ stick) unsalted butter, cubed

In a food processor, combine the pine nuts, parmesan, salt, sugar, garlic, white pepper, zest of 1 lemon, and lemon juice and pulse until the nuts are broken into a coarse paste. Slowly drizzle in the olive oil, while pulsing briefly until the pesto just comes together. Don't overprocess olive oil or it will become bitter.

In a large pot, bring 4 quarts water and ½ cup kosher salt to a boil over high heat.

In another pot, whisk the pesto together with 1 cup of water over high heat until creamy and bubbling, about 1 minute, then turn off the heat.

Add the pasta to the boiling water and cook until toothsome, 30 to 45 seconds for homemade or according to the package directions for the store-bought. Drain the pasta and place it into the pesto with the butter. Increase the heat to high and stir continually, until all of the butter has melted and the pesto has generously coated the pasta in a light, creamy sauce, about 3 minutes.

Serve immediately in individual bowls or family style. Garnish with the remaining lemon zest. Leftovers keep, tightly covered in the refrigerator, for up to 3 days. Reheat gently over medium-low heat, adding a few tablespoons of water as needed to loosen the sauce.

Polenta Gnocchi with Rosemary, Honey & Toasted Sesame

SERVES 4 TO 6

Gnocchi are typically made with potato and/or cheese, but this one utilizes polenta in the dough, an idea loosely inspired by *gnocchi alla romana*, which is gnocchi made with semolina flour. It's a rich side glazed with a buttery, rosemary-scented sauce. We add toasted sesame seeds for nuttiness and aroma, and rely on an agrodolce-like combo of honey and lemon juice to help cut some of the richer flavors.

Polenta is often served with osso buco or other roasted meats, and polenta gnocchi are also ideal for this purpose. We often serve this as a side dish at cold-weather holiday gatherings, where it's a rib-sticking success.

NOTE: If you have "00" flour, use that in lieu of the all-purpose.

Make the gnocchi: In a medium pot, combine the milk and 1¼ cups water and bring to a boil over medium-high heat. While whisking, slowly pour in the polenta in a steady stream, then immediately reduce the heat to low. (The polenta will bubble and splatter as it comes to a boil, so be careful here and turn the heat to low as soon as you add the polenta.) Continue cooking over low heat, whisking continually, until the polenta has thickened, 2 to 3 minutes. It should be pasty and thick, resembling spackle.

Spread the polenta in an even layer across a large plate and loosely cover with plastic wrap. Place in the refrigerator until completely chilled, about 30 minutes.

Once chilled, transfer the polenta to a food processor or a stand mixer with the paddle. The polenta will be a solid mass. Mix on medium speed until smooth, about 3 minutes. Add the egg, parmesan, salt, pepper, sugar, and lemon zest and mix on medium for 30 to 45 seconds, until fully incorporated. Add ¼ cup of the flour and mix or process for 30 to 45 seconds to fully incorporate. Scrape down the bowl if needed to ensure that all ingredients are fully mixed together. You should have a sticky, pasty dough.

Gnocchi

½ cup whole milk

½ cup instant polenta

1 large egg

⅓ cup finely grated Parmigiano-Reggiano cheese

2 teaspoons kosher salt, plus more for the pasta water

¼ teaspoon freshly ground black pepper

1 teaspoon sugar

Grated zest of 1 lemon

¼ cup all-purpose flour (see Note), plus more for the work surface

Sauce

3 tablespoons honey

2 tablespoons fresh lemon juice

1 teaspoon kosher salt

1 teaspoon sesame oil

½ cup (1 stick) unsalted butter, cubed

1 sprig rosemary, leaves picked

For serving

2 tablespoons finely grated Parmigiano-Reggiano cheese

1 tablespoon toasted sesame seeds

RECIPE CONTINUES

Liberally flour a clean work surface. Using a large spoon, scoop out half of the gnocchi dough and place it on the work surface. Dust the top with more flour. Roll into a log about ½ inch thick, as evenly as possible. Repeat the process with the remaining gnocchi dough, dusting with more flour as needed. It's important to have a well-floured work surface to create smooth dumplings. Using a bench scraper or a chef's knife, cut across the logs to create gnocchi about 1½ to 2 inches long. You should get 40 to 45 gnocchi. As the gnocchi are cut, transfer them to a lightly floured large plate and place in the refrigerator, uncovered, allowing them to sit for at least 30 minutes or up to overnight before cooking.

In a large pot, bring 4 quarts water and ½ cup kosher salt to a boil over high heat.

Meanwhile, make the sauce: In a small bowl, whisk together the honey, lemon juice, salt, sesame oil, and 1 tablespoon water. Set aside.

In a large sauté pan or large pot, heat 4 tablespoons of the butter over medium-high heat until melted and large, foamy bubbles start to appear, 2 to 3 minutes. Swirl the pan to ensure even cooking. The butter will make loud sputtering noises, then the bubbles will dissipate and the noise will subside—this is when you should notice the white milk solids in the butter turning deep golden brown in color. As soon as the butter starts to brown, add the rosemary. The rosemary will fry and bubble vigorously. Fry for 10 seconds, then pour in the honey–lemon juice mixture and stir. Add in the remaining 4 tablespoons butter and whisk vigorously to create a creamy sauce. Once the butter is melted and the sauce is thickened (large bubbles will appear on the surface and the sauce will resemble a thick glaze), remove from the heat.

Drop the gnocchi into the pot of boiling water and cook until they float, about 1 minute. Drain into a colander, then carefully pour the gnocchi from the colander into the pot of honey sauce. Turn the heat to high and bring the sauce to a boil with the gnocchi in it, gently moving it around until the gnocchi are just coated, about 1 minute.

To serve: Arrange the gnocchi on a platter or individual plates. Top with the parmesan and toasted sesame seeds and serve immediately. Leftovers will keep, tightly covered in the refrigerator, for up to 3 days. Reheat over low heat, stirring in 1 to 2 tablespoons of water to loosen the sauce if necessary.

cooking together in the DoN Angie kitcheN

Potato Gnocchi with Chive & Dill in Taleggio Cream Sauce

SERVES 4 TO 6

This is an impressive-looking dish that's easier to pull off than it might seem. The gnocchi themselves are quite light, thanks in part to the potato starch, which helps create a lighter, fluffier pasta than those made with all flour, and acts as a binder so the pasta maintains its structural integrity. We like using Taleggio in the sauce, but this recipe is flexible—try it with Gorgonzola, sharp Cheddar, or smoked Gouda; the freshness of the herbs will lighten it up regardless.

Eat this on its own as a luxurious lunch, or serve it alongside grilled meats. It's pretty as part of a holiday spread, and remember that even if some of your gnocchi are a little lumpy or misshapen, they'll still taste great.

Preheat the oven to 400°F. Set a wire rack in a sheet pan.

Make the gnocchi: Prick the potatoes with a fork and place on the rack in the pan. Transfer to the oven and bake until tender, about 1 hour. Remove the potatoes from the oven and let cool enough to handle. Peel the potatoes and pass through a ricer or food mill (if you don't have either you can press the cooked potato through a fine-mesh sieve with the back of a spoon). You should have about 2 packed cups of riced potato.

In a stand mixer with the paddle, combine the potato, potato starch, salt, granulated onion, black pepper, parmesan, and flour and mix on low speed until combined, about 1 minute. Add the dill, chives, and egg. Paddle again on low until combined, about 1 minute. (If you do not have a stand mixer, this step can be done by hand.)

Liberally flour a clean work surface. Using a large spoon, scoop out one quarter of gnocchi dough and dust the top liberally with more flour. Using both hands, roll the dough into a rope about 12 inches long and 1 inch in diameter. Repeat the process with the rest of the dough, flouring each. Using a bench scraper or a chef's knife, cut across the rope into 1-inch lengths to make individual gnocchi.

Gnocchi

1½ pounds russet potatoes (about 3 medium potatoes)

1 tablespoon potato starch

2 teaspoons kosher salt, plus more for the pasta water

2 teaspoons granulated onion

½ teaspoon freshly ground black pepper

⅔ cup finely grated Parmigiano-Reggiano cheese

½ cup "00" or all-purpose flour, plus more for the work surface

¼ cup finely chopped dill (about 6 sprigs)

¼ cup finely chopped chives (about 1 small bunch)

1 large egg

Sauce

3 tablespoons unsalted butter

¼ cup finely chopped garlic (about 7 cloves)

2 teaspoons kosher salt

½ teaspoon freshly ground black pepper

2 cups crème fraîche

1 cup heavy cream

3 ounces Taleggio, Gorgonzola, sharp Cheddar, or smoked Gouda cheese

2 tablespoons finely grated Parmigiano-Reggiano cheese

For serving

Dill fronds, picked from 4 to 5 sprigs

Freshly ground black pepper

RECIPE CONTINUES

You should get 50 to 55 gnocchi. Place the gnocchi on a lightly floured baking sheet in the refrigerator, cover loosely with plastic wrap, and let chill for at least 1 hour or up to 12 hours before cooking.

Make the sauce: In a medium pot, melt the butter over medium-high heat. Add the garlic, salt, and black pepper. Cook until the garlic is lightly toasted and fragrant, about 2 minutes. Add the crème fraîche and cream and stir well to combine. Reduce the heat to medium-low and cook until the volume of the liquid is reduced by two-thirds and large bubbles appear, about 5 minutes. Whisk in the Taleggio and parmesan until melted. Remove from the heat and set aside until ready to use.

In a large pot, bring 4 quarts water and ½ cup kosher salt to a boil over high heat. Working in batches to avoid overcrowding, carefully drop the gnocchi into the water. Cook until the gnocchi float, 1½ to 2 minutes. Scoop out the cooked gnocchi with a slotted spoon or mesh strainer and drop them into the sauce. Bring the sauce up to a simmer over medium-low heat after adding the gnocchi. Cook, until the sauce is slightly reduced, stirring gently to just coat the gnocchi, about 1 minute.

To serve: Spoon the gnocchi onto a serving platter or individual bowls. Top with dill fronds and freshly ground pepper. This dish is best made and eaten day-of.

Ricotta Gnudi with Peanuts, Cilantro & Roasted Grapes

SERVES 4 TO 6

Gnudi are sometimes called "naked ravioli" because they're like the filling without the pasta. The traditional method is a multiday affair involving rolling the cheese in semolina flour and resting it several times, in order to create a thin "skin," which allows you to cook the ricotta dumpling without it melting in hot water. We developed a technique that cuts the prep time way down, and makes an even lighter, more delicate exterior. The tricks: Chill the dough completely before shaping, and be very liberal with flouring their tops and the baking sheet they rest on.

The flavors here were inspired by a dessert Angie loves at a Taiwanese restaurant in Brooklyn that serves a savory fried doughnut with vanilla ice cream, cilantro, and peanuts. We took a note from that flavor combination and added roasted grapes in a nod to the classic pairing of peanut butter and jelly. Ricotta generally pairs well with toasted nuts, though you could swap hazelnuts or walnuts for peanuts here for a more typically Italian flavor.

NOTE: It's crucial to drain the ricotta overnight, as removing any excess moisture helps make a sturdier dumpling that won't fall apart.

Make the gnudi: In a stand mixer with the paddle, mix the ricotta, pecorino, sugar, salt, pepper, coriander, egg yolk, and flour on medium speed. The ricotta should look visibly thicker, smoother, sturdier, and slightly yellower. Place in the refrigerator to chill completely, about 1 hour. (The gnudi mixture can be made and held in the refrigerator for up to 2 days.)

Liberally flour a clean work surface. Using a large spoon, scoop one-third of the gnudi mixture onto the surface and dust the top liberally with more flour. Using both hands, roll the dough into a rope about 15 inches long and 1 inch in diameter. Repeat the process with the rest of the dough to make 3 ropes.

Line a sheet pan with parchment paper and dust liberally with flour. Using a bench scraper or a chef's knife, cut across the rope in 1-inch lengths to make individual gnudi. You should get 12 to 14 pieces per

Gnudi

2 cups whole-milk ricotta cheese, packed and drained overnight (see page 19)

¼ cup finely grated pecorino cheese (preferably Pecorino Toscano)

1 tablespoon sugar

1½ teaspoons kosher salt, plus more for the pasta water

¼ teaspoon freshly ground black pepper

½ teaspoon ground coriander

1 large egg yolk

¼ cup plus 1 tablespoon "00" or all-purpose flour, plus more for the work surface

Roasted grapes

3 tablespoons honey

1 tablespoon balsamic vinegar

2 cups seedless red grapes (about ⅔ pound)

1 tablespoon extra-virgin olive oil

¼ teaspoon kosher salt

Sauce

½ cup (1 stick) unsalted butter

2 tablespoons finely chopped shallots (about ½ medium shallot)

1 tablespoon finely chopped cilantro stems (about 4 sprigs, leaves reserved)

⅓ cup chopped roasted unsalted peanuts

1 tablespoon fresh lime juice

¼ teaspoon kosher salt

For serving

¼ cup finely grated pecorino cheese (preferably Pecorino Toscano)

15 cilantro leaves (from about 4 sprigs)

RECIPE CONTINUES

rope. Gently roll each of the gnudi between the palms of your hands to form balls. Place the gnudi on the lined and floured sheet pan. Top the gnudi with more flour. You should get 42 to 44 gnudi. Gently shake the baking sheet, rolling the gnudi around in the flour, to ensure that each one is coated thoroughly. This step is important for creating round, smooth gnudi and for forming the exterior "shell" that keeps them together while cooking.

Refrigerate for at least 30 minutes to chill before cooking. (Gnudi keep, uncooked and loosely covered in the refrigerator, for up to 2 days.)

Prepare the roasted grapes: Preheat the oven to 450°F.

In a large bowl, stir together the honey and balsamic vinegar until well combined. Set aside. Place the grapes in a small baking dish. Drizzle with the olive oil and season with the salt, then stir the grapes around to evenly coat them with the oil and salt. Bake until they start to wrinkle and release their liquid, about 30 minutes. Immediately transfer the hot grapes and the liquid they release into the bowl with the honey-vinegar mixture and gently toss to coat. Set aside.

In a large pot, bring 4 quarts water and ½ cup kosher salt to a boil over high heat to cook the gnudi.

Meanwhile, make the sauce: In a large sauté pan, heat the butter over medium-high heat until melted and large, foamy bubbles start to appear, 2 to 3 minutes. Swirl the pan to ensure even cooking. The butter will make loud sputtering noises, then the bubbles will dissipate and the noise will subside—this is when you should notice the white milk solids in the butter turning deep golden brown in color. As soon as the butter starts to brown, add the shallot, cilantro stems, peanuts, lime juice, and salt and stir well to combine. Remove from the heat.

Drop the gnudi into the boiling salted water. Cook until set and slightly shiny on the outside, 1½ minutes, then carefully scoop out with a spider or slotted spoon and drop them into the peanut sauce.

Set the pan of sauce and gnudi over medium-high and cook until bubbles appear, about 2 minutes. Swirl the pan to gently coat the gnudi with the sauce, about 1 minute.

To serve: Spoon the gnudi onto a platter or individual plates. Carefully spoon the roasted grapes onto the platter or plates among the gnudi, evenly dispersing them throughout and drizzling their liquid around evenly. Top with pecorino and cilantro leaves and serve. This dish is best made and served day-of.

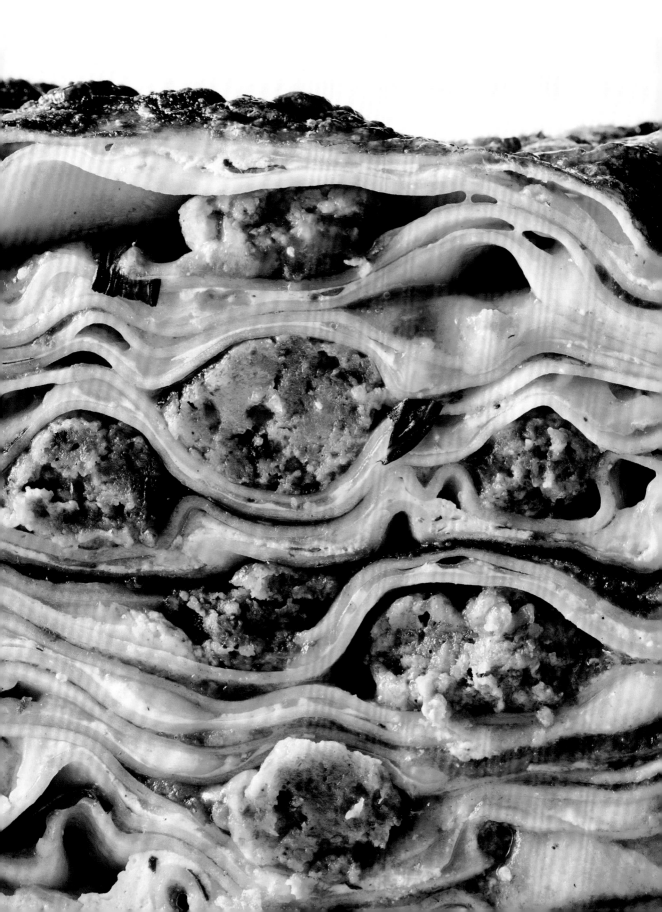

Lasagnas & Baked Pastas

Lasagnas and baked pastas are their own distinct subcategory under the larger pasta umbrella. Although some versions of these dishes do exist in traditional Italian cuisine, red-sauce classics like baked ziti, and great towering stacks of molten cheese-and-tomato lasagna are really an Italian-American invention, perfected by generations of immigrant home cooks.

It makes sense, given the humble roots of the cuisine, as lasagnas and baked pastas are hearty, comforting, large-format dishes that can feed a whole family, and often need only a single pot to execute. They can be made with economical ingredients and still taste very satisfying, and the leftovers usually are, too.

As you might have guessed by now, we like to think outside the box when it comes to what flavors and textures to build into a lasagna or baked pasta, with some nontraditional results. Here, you'll find a "white" baked ziti with zucchini and provolone; a lasagna inspired by scalloped potatoes; shells stuffed with clams and pancetta in addition to spinach and ricotta. And, of course, we'll show you how to make our much-requested Don Angie "pinwheel" lasagna, a showstopper of a dish that's worth the effort it takes to make its many moving parts. We've also included a vegetarian version as well, that's something of a cross between lasagna and eggplant parm. All of our lasagna recipes call for using fresh pasta sheets from the recipe on page 147, but we provide instructions for using store-bought sheets as well.

Scalloped Potato Lasagna Bianca

SERVES 8 TO 10

This "white" baked pasta is the unholy union of lasagna and scalloped potatoes—a fancy golden casserole with delicate fresh pasta sheets, rich firm potatoes, and a creamy white sauce. It's not very traditional to put potatoes into lasagna, but the textural contrast here works.

Potatoes pair famously well with sour cream and onions, so we chose to use crème fraîche and chives for a more modern twist. Definitely seek out waxy Yukon Golds here, as russets will become too starchy and fall apart. This is a great side for holiday entertaining or any other cool-weather celebration—it's rich and a little decadent, yet versatile enough to pair with almost anything.

───────

NOTE: We use a full cup of kosher salt to season the pasta cooking water in this and other lasagna recipes because the pasta sheets are plunged into an unseasoned ice bath after cooking, which removes much of the seasoning.

Make the sauce: In a large heavy-bottomed pot or Dutch oven, melt the butter over medium-high heat. Add the garlic, salt, and pepper. Cook, stirring continually, until the garlic sizzles and becomes fragrant, about 2 minutes. Add the onion and bay leaves. Reduce the heat to medium-high and cook, stirring continually, until the onions are translucent and cooked through, about 10 minutes.

Add the flour and stir well to combine. Reduce the heat to medium and continue to cook, stirring often, until the flour is lightly toasted, about 3 minutes. Add 2 cups of the milk and the crème fraîche. Cook, stirring often with a silicone spatula and continually scraping down the sides as needed, until the sauce thickens enough to coat the back of a spoon, about 5 minutes. Remove from the heat, stir well, and remove the bay leaves. Add the parmesan and whisk well to combine.

Sauce

½ cup (1 stick) unsalted butter

2 tablespoons garlic, grated on a Microplane (6 to 8 cloves)

1 tablespoon plus 1 teaspoon kosher salt

1 teaspoon freshly ground black pepper

3 cups thinly sliced yellow onion, cut from root to stem (about 1 medium)

3 bay leaves

½ cup all-purpose or Wondra flour (see page 18)

2 cups whole milk, plus up to ¼ cup more as needed

1 cup crème fraîche

2 cups finely grated Parmigiano-Reggiano cheese

To assemble

1 cup kosher salt (see Note)

Northern-Style Egg Yolk Pasta (page 147) or 8 store-bought fresh pasta sheets (12 × 7 inches)

2½ pounds Yukon Gold potatoes, washed and scrubbed (about 5 medium potatoes)

2¼ cups shredded whole-milk mozzarella cheese

¼ cup finely grated Parmigiano-Reggiano cheese

⅓ cup chopped chives (about 2 small bunches)

RECIPE CONTINUES

Allow the sauce to cool to room temperature, about 30 minutes. The sauce should be thick, but smooth and loose enough to spread across the lasagna. If the sauce thickens too much and becomes pasty, add up to an additional ¼ cup whole milk to loosen it. You should have about 4½ cups of sauce.

To assemble: In a large pot, bring 4 quarts water and the kosher salt to a boil over high heat. Meanwhile, set up an ice bath in a large bowl. Line a sheet pan with parchment paper.

Working with one sheet at a time, place a pasta sheet in the boiling water for 15 seconds, then immediately remove and chill in the ice bath for 15 seconds. Transfer to the lined sheet pan and pat dry with a paper towel. Cover with another layer of parchment paper and repeat with the remaining pasta, creating a stack of sheets, each patted dry and each layer separated by parchment. Set aside. (Keep the pasta water on the stove.)

Fill a large bowl with cold water. Line a baking sheet with paper towels. Slice the potatoes on a mandoline ⅛ inch thick and immediately immerse in the water. Bring the pasta cooking water back up to a boil over high heat. Working in batches to avoid overcrowding, cook the potatoes in the boiling water until slightly translucent and cooked through but not mushy or crumbly, 6 to 8 minutes. Carefully remove them with a slotted spoon or spider and place on the lined baking sheet. Dab the potatoes with paper towels as needed to ensure they are dry. Spread out as much as possible and let cool to room temperature.

Preheat the oven to 400°F. Spray a 9 × 13-inch baking dish with nonstick cooking spray.

Place two lasagna sheets in the bottom of the dish, overlapping in the center by about 1 inch, and trim the sides of the sheets if necessary to create one flat, even layer. Top with 1 cup of the sauce, spreading as evenly as possible with a rubber spatula. Shingle about one-quarter of the cooked potato slices on top, packing them tightly together, slightly overlapping, to cover the entire surface in an even layer. Sprinkle ¾ cup of the mozzarella evenly over the top.

Repeat this layering process 2 more times. Top the final layer with the remaining 2 sheets of pasta, 1 cup sauce, and the potatoes, followed by the parmesan.

Cover the pan with foil, tightly attaching the foil to the edges of the dish but being careful not to press it down on the top of the lasagna, or the cheese will stick. Place in the oven and cook for 40 minutes. Remove the foil, switch to the broil setting, and cook until the potatoes are golden brown, 3 to 4 minutes. Remove from the oven and let rest for 20 minutes before slicing into squares and serving.

Top with the chives. Serve immediately. Leftovers keep, refrigerated, for up to 4 days.

Lasagna Verde with Pistachio Pesto

SERVES 6 TO 8

Lasagna verde pops up around Bologna, but it's usually made with green pasta sheets dyed with spinach. This recipe incorporates the green color via a less complicated process, thanks to a pistachio and herb pesto that lends a vibrant forest hue to the final dish. (It's important to blanch the herbs before pureeing them to help them retain their color.) The flavor here is nice and fresh, and the overall effect is a lasagna on the lighter side, with a good amount of textural contrast from the many layers of pasta. If you're looking to bolster this with a heartier component, try adding sautéed vegetables, such as zucchini, kale, or spinach.

NOTE: We use a full cup of kosher salt to season the pasta cooking water in this and other lasagna recipes because the pasta sheets are plunged into an unseasoned ice bath after cooking, which removes much of the seasoning.

Make the pesto: Bring a medium pot with 4 cups of water to a boil over high heat. Meanwhile, fill a small bowl with ice water and set aside.

Quickly submerge the basil, parsley, and chives in the boiling water, then, using a small fine-mesh sieve, scoop them immediately into the ice water until completely cool. Drain, then use a clean, dry kitchen towel to wring all of the water from the herbs. It's important to get these herbs as dry as possible at this point—any excess water in the final product will cause the pesto to turn brown.

In a blender, combine the blanched herbs, pistachios, pepper flakes, parmesan, and salt. Blend on high just until smooth, about 10 seconds, then add the oil and lemon juice and blend until the mixture forms a smooth, thick paste, about 30 seconds, pausing to scrape the sides of the blender with a rubber spatula as needed. You should have about 2 cups of pesto. Set aside. Pesto can be made up to 2 days in advance and kept, tightly covered, in the refrigerator.

Pesto

2 cups (3 ounces) tightly packed basil leaves

2 cups (3 ounces) tightly packed flat-leaf parsley leaves

½ cup (½ ounce) roughly chopped chives

½ cup pistachios

Pinch of crushed red pepper flakes

½ cup finely grated Parmigiano-Reggiano cheese

1 tablespoon kosher salt

¾ cup neutral oil, such as vegetable

3 tablespoons fresh lemon juice

To assemble

1 cup kosher salt (see Note)

2 recipes Northern-Style Egg Yolk Pasta (page 147) or 16 store-bought fresh pasta sheets (12 × 7 inches)

2 cups shredded whole-milk mozzarella cheese

2 cups Besciamella (page 302)

2 cups finely grated Parmigiano-Reggiano cheese, plus more for garnish

Freshly ground black pepper

To assemble: Bring a large pot with 4 quarts water and the kosher salt to a boil over high heat. Meanwhile, set up an ice bath in a large bowl. Line a sheet pan with parchment paper.

Working with one sheet at a time, place a pasta sheet in the boiling water for 15 seconds, then immediately remove and chill in the ice bath for 15 seconds. Transfer to the lined sheet pan and pat dry with a paper towel. Cover with another layer of parchment paper and repeat with the remaining pasta, creating a stack of sheets, each patted dry and each layer separated by parchment. Set aside.

Preheat the oven to 400°F. Lightly spray a 9 × 13-inch baking dish with nonstick cooking spray.

Place two lasagna sheets in the bottom of the dish, overlapping in the center by about 1 inch, and trim the sides of the sheets if necessary to create one flat, even layer. Spread with ⅓ cup of the pesto and sprinkle ½ cup of the mozzarella on top. Add 2 more sheets of pasta (trimming sheets as necessary to form an even single layer), then spread ½ cup of besciamella, followed by ½ cup of parmesan. Repeat the layering in this order 3 more times (2 sheets of pasta topped with pesto and mozzarella, then 2 sheets of pasta topped with besciamella and parmesan) for a total of 8 pasta layers, with the final layer being pasta, ½ cup of besciamella, and ½ cup of parmesan. You may have some leftover pesto, which can be reserved for another use (i.e., pasta). (The lasagna can be frozen at this point, tightly covered in plastic wrap, for up to 3 months; thaw it in the refrigerator before baking.)

Cover with foil, tightly attaching the foil to the edges of the dish but being careful not to press it down on the top of the lasagna, or the cheese will stick. Bake for 15 minutes. Uncover, then bake until the top is golden brown and the center is set, 20 to 25 minutes.

Allow the lasagna to cool in the pan for 15 minutes before cutting into squares and serving. Garnish each serving with freshly ground black pepper and a sprinkling of parmesan. Leftovers keep, tightly covered in the refrigerator, for up to 4 days.

Scott's mother with family on her first Holy Communion

Don Angie Pinwheel Lasagna

MAKES 16 PINWHEELS (SERVES 8 TO 10)

We came up with this recipe while brainstorming how to make a pasta dish for two, and landed on lasagna because it's the ultimate crowd-pleaser, the king of all baked pastas, the most impressive thing we could think of. We are not ashamed to admit that the idea for presenting it this way came from a photo of baked cinnamon buns in a pan, though we later learned that there is in fact a classic, pinwheel-shaped pasta dish that exists in Italy, called *rotolo*.

We wanted to make this version taste like classic lasagna, and pulled in all the flavors of a true lasagna Bolognese—fresh pasta, besciamella, Bolognese sauce—and added some Italian-American twists of our own (i.e., mozzarella, tomato sauce, sweet Italian sausage). In its finished form, this is the perfect amalgamation of regional Italian and Italian-American cuisine, with a unique presentation that's helped make this one of our most-requested dishes at the restaurant.

It's perfect for sharing, because each person gets a pinwheel, and the whole top is crispy, so every bite is perfect. And because the pasta is rolled around the filling, instead of stacked and compacted, it feels lighter than most lasagnas. Diehard regional Italian connoisseurs will say this isn't a "real" lasagna, in the traditional sense, but nothing we do is, and we don't claim it to be. This is just us doing our thing.

———

NOTES: If you can, we recommend making the components in advance as they need to be chilled before assembling—the Bolognese sauce and besciamella can be done up to 2 days ahead, and the tomato sauce a day early. If you don't have the time or desire to roll your own fresh pasta sheets, you can also use fresh store-bought ones. The rolls come together quickly once all of that is done, but they can be messy, and are easier to handle when chilled thoroughly before slicing. The logs themselves can also be frozen, preslicing, for you to bust out a truly impressive dinner at the drop of a hat.

We use a full cup of kosher salt to season the pasta cooking water in this and other lasagna recipes because the pasta sheets are plunged into an unseasoned ice bath after cooking, which removes much of the seasoning.

Kosher salt, for the pasta water (see Note)

Northern-Style Egg Yolk Pasta (page 147) or 8 store-bought fresh pasta sheets (12 × 7 inches)

1 cup plus 3 tablespoons Besciamella (page 302), chilled

4 cups shredded whole-milk mozzarella cheese

1 cup finely grated Parmigiano-Reggiano cheese

4 cups Italian Sausage Bolognese (page 114), chilled

2 cups 10-Minute San Marzano Tomato Sauce (page 95), chilled

½ cup robiolina cheese (see page 19) or whipped cream cheese

2 tablespoons roughly chopped parsley

3 tablespoons extra-virgin olive oil, for finishing

RECIPE CONTINUES

In a large pot, bring 4 quarts water and 1 cup kosher salt to a boil over high heat. Meanwhile, set up an ice bath in a large bowl. Line a sheet pan with parchment paper.

Working with one sheet at a time, place a pasta sheet in the boiling water for 15 seconds, then immediately remove and chill in the ice bath for 15 seconds. Transfer to the lined sheet pan and pat dry with a paper towel. Cover with another layer of parchment paper and repeat with the remaining pasta, creating a stack of sheets, each patted dry and each layer separated by parchment.

On a clean countertop, lay out one pasta sheet with a short side facing you (the sheet should look like a portrait shot). Spread ¼ cup of the besciamella in a thin layer evenly across the sheet. Sprinkle 1 cup of the mozzarella and ¼ cup of parmesan over the besciamella.

Place another sheet of pasta on top. Spread 1 cup of the Bolognese evenly across the second pasta sheet, leaving a 2-inch border uncovered at the top short edge. Spoon 2 teaspoons of the besciamella onto the uncovered edge (this will act like your "glue" to seal the roll closed).

Starting at the bottom, roll up the layered pasta into a thick log (like a jelly roll). Transfer to a small sheet pan seam-side down. Place in the refrigerator to chill for at least 1 and up to 2 hours, which will firm it up and make it easier to slice.

Repeat the process with the remaining pasta sheets to make a total of 4 rolls, transferring to the refrigerator as you finish each roll. (The rolls can be tightly wrapped in plastic at this point and refrigerated for up to 2 days, or frozen for up to 3 months, before cooking. If frozen, thaw in the refrigerator before slicing.)

Preheat the oven to 400°F.

Transfer the rolls to a cutting board. Using a serrated knife, slice each log in half crosswise, then slice each half in half to give you 4 slices per roll, each about 1¾ inches thick.

Ladle all of the tomato sauce into a 9 × 13-inch baking dish, covering the entire bottom of the dish. Arrange the lasagna pinwheels cut-side down in the baking dish, 4 pinwheels across in one direction and 4 across in the other. (All 16 pieces should fit in one layer, gently staggered to fit.)

Bake until the pasta edges are golden brown, 20 to 25 minutes. Remove the baking dish from the oven and add tablespoon-sized dollops of robiolina in between the pinwheels in a random pattern. Return to the oven and bake until the robiolina is warm and melted, an additional 2 to 3 minutes. Top with chopped parsley and olive oil.

Serve immediately. Leftovers keep, refrigerated, for up to 4 days.

Eggplant Parm Pinwheel Lasagna

MAKES 16 PINWHEELS (SERVES 8 TO 10)

For the vegetarian version of the Don Angie Pinwheel Lasagna (page 175), we turn to eggplant, which lends a hearty, almost meaty texture to the sauce. (It also shares a flavor profile with the Layered Eggplant Parm on page 213, a perennial crowd-pleaser.) This lasagna comes together a little faster than the meat one, since you don't have to make a Bolognese sauce, though you can still make the besciamella and tomato sauce in advance to break things up a bit.

———

NOTES: If the eggplant is too wide to fit on the mandoline whole, halve it lengthwise and slice each half into long strips ⅛ inch thick.

We use a full cup of kosher salt to season the pasta cooking water in this and other lasagna recipes because the pasta sheets are plunged into an unseasoned ice bath after cooking, which removes much of the seasoning.

Make the eggplant mixture: Set up a breading station in three wide bowls: In one bowl, beat the eggs. Spread the flour in a second bowl. Spread the bread crumbs in a third. Set the bowls in a row in this order: flour, eggs, bread crumbs. Dredge the eggplant slices, one at a time, dipping each slice first into the flour and shaking off the excess, then in the egg and allowing the excess to drip off, then pressing it into the bread crumb mixture to evenly coat both sides. Set aside on a baking sheet until ready to use.

In a large sauté pan, heat ½ cup of the olive oil over medium-high heat. Working in batches to avoid overcrowding, gently fry the eggplants in the oil, flipping once, until golden brown, about 30 seconds per side. Remove from the pan and set aside onto a plate lined with paper towels, seasoning lightly with salt while still hot. Repeat with the remaining eggplant, replenishing the pan with olive oil as needed. Continue stacking and seasoning the fried eggplant slices with a fresh paper towel in between the layers. Let cool completely.

Eggplant mixture

5 large eggs

1 cup all-purpose flour

2 cups Italian seasoned bread crumbs, store-bought or homemade (page 298)

1 medium Italian eggplant (¾ to 1 pound), peeled and sliced lengthwise ⅛ inch thick on a mandoline

1 cup extra-virgin olive oil

Kosher salt

¼ cup roughly chopped basil (about 10 medium leaves)

1 cup finely grated pecorino cheese (preferably Pecorino Toscano)

1½ cups 10-Minute San Marzano Tomato Sauce (page 95)

⅓ cup Oven-Dried Tomatoes (page 302), or store-bought oil-packed sun-dried tomatoes, drained and chopped (optional)

To assemble

Kosher salt, for the pasta water (see Note)

Northern-Style Egg Yolk Pasta (page 147) or 8 store-bought fresh pasta sheets (12 × 7 inches)

1 cup plus 3 tablespoons Besciamella (page 302), chilled

4 cups shredded whole-milk mozzarella cheese

1 cup finely grated Parmigiano-Reggiano cheese

2 cups 10-Minute San Marzano Tomato Sauce (page 95), chilled

½ cup robiolina cheese (see page 19) or whipped cream cheese

10 basil leaves, for garnish

3 tablespoons extra-virgin olive oil, for finishing

Once cool, finely dice the eggplant into ¼-inch pieces. Toss in a medium bowl with chopped basil, 1 teaspoon salt, the pecorino, tomato sauce, and oven-dried tomatoes (if using). Set aside.

Assemble the rolls (see page 176 for step-by-step photos): In a large pot, bring 4 quarts water and 1 cup kosher salt to a boil over high heat. Meanwhile, set up an ice bath in a large bowl. Line a sheet pan with parchment paper.

Working with one sheet at a time, place a pasta sheet in the boiling water for 15 seconds, then immediately remove and chill in the ice bath for 15 seconds. Transfer to the lined sheet pan and pat dry with a paper towel. Cover with another layer of parchment paper and repeat with the remaining pasta, creating a stack of sheets, each patted dry and each layer separated by parchment. Set aside.

On a clean countertop, lay out one pasta sheet in front of you with a short side facing you (the sheet should look like a portrait shot). Spread ¼ cup of the besciamella in a thin layer evenly across the sheet. Sprinkle 1 cup of mozzarella and ¼ cup parmesan over the besciamella.

Place another sheet of pasta on top. Spread 1 cup of the eggplant mixture evenly across the second pasta sheet, leaving a 2-inch border uncovered at the top short edge. Spoon 2 teaspoons of the besciamella onto the uncovered edge (this will act like your "glue" to seal the roll closed).

Starting at the bottom edge, roll up the layered pasta into a thick log (like a jelly roll). Transfer to a small sheet pan seam-side down. Place in the refrigerator to chill for at least 1 and up to 2 hours, which will firm it up and make it easier to slice.

Repeat the process with the remaining pasta sheets to make a total of 4 rolls, transferring to the refrigerator as you finish each roll. (The rolls can be tightly wrapped in plastic at this point and refrigerated for up to 2 days, or frozen for up to 3 months, before cooking. If frozen, thaw in the refrigerator before slicing.)

Preheat the oven to 400°F.

Transfer the rolls to a cutting board. Using a serrated knife, slice each log in half crosswise, then slice each half in half to give you 4 slices per roll, each about 1¾ inches thick.

Ladle the tomato sauce into a 9 × 13-inch baking dish, covering the entire bottom of the dish. Arrange the lasagna pinwheels cut-side down in the baking dish, 4 pinwheels across in one direction and 4 across in the other. (It should fit all 16 pieces in one layer, gently staggered to fit.)

Bake until the pasta edges are golden brown, about 20 minutes. Remove the baking dish from the oven and add tablespoon-sized dollops of robiolina in between the pinwheels in a random pattern. Return to the oven and bake until the robiolina is warm and melted, an additional 2 to 3 minutes. Top with basil leaves and olive oil.

Serve immediately. Leftovers keep, refrigerated, for up to 4 days.

Grandma Addario's Lasagna with Tiny Meatballs

SERVES 6 TO 8

Here we have a classic Italian-American lasagna for the purists, rife with sauce, ricotta, and melty "muzzarell." Scott's grandmother made lasagna for all occasions, and the tiny meatballs were her signature move. It takes a bit of extra time and labor, but the end result is that much more special for it. We didn't tweak Grandma Addario's version all that much, but we did lighten it up a bit with our 10-minute San Marzano Tomato Sauce instead of the long-simmered Sunday gravy she liked to use. Serve this with the Broccoli Salad with Oregano Vinaigrette, Olives & Crispy Shallots (page 73), or just a simple green salad. *See photo on pages 166–167.*

———

NOTE: We use a full cup of kosher salt to season the pasta cooking water in this and other lasagna recipes because the pasta sheets are plunged into an unseasoned ice bath after cooking, which removes much of the seasoning.

½ recipe Classic Meatballs mixture (page 193), unformed and uncooked

2½ cups whole-milk ricotta cheese

2 large eggs

1 teaspoon kosher salt, plus more for the pasta water (see Note)

1 teaspoon freshly ground black pepper

2 tablespoons roughly chopped parsley

2 recipes Northern-Style Egg Yolk Pasta (page 147) or 16 store-bought fresh pasta sheets (12 × 7 inches)

2½ cups 10-Minute San Marzano Tomato Sauce (page 95)

2 cups shredded whole-milk mozzarella cheese

2 cups finely grated Parmigiano-Reggiano cheese

15 basil leaves

Preheat the oven to 400°F. Line a sheet pan with parchment paper and spray with nonstick cooking spray.

Form the ground meat mixture into 48 to 54 teaspoon-sized meatballs and place them on the lined pan. Bake until browned and firm, about 10 minutes, rotating the pan from front to back halfway through.

In a medium bowl, whisk together the ricotta, eggs, salt, pepper, and parsley until combined.

In a large pot, bring 4 quarts water and 1 cup kosher salt to a boil over high heat. Meanwhile, set up an ice bath in a large bowl. Line a sheet pan with parchment paper.

Working with one sheet at a time, place pasta in the boiling water for 15 seconds, then immediately remove and chill in the ice bath for 15 seconds. Transfer to the lined sheet pan and pat dry with a paper towel. Cover with another layer of parchment paper and repeat with the remaining pasta, creating a stack of sheets, each patted dry and each layer separated by parchment. Set aside.

Spray a 9 × 13-inch baking dish with nonstick cooking spray. Spread ½ cup of the tomato sauce across the bottom of the dish in an even layer. Place two lasagna sheets in the bottom of the dish, overlapping in the center by about 1 inch, and trim the sides of the sheets if necessary to create one flat, even layer. Spread ½ cup of the ricotta mixture and sprinkle ½ cup of the mozzarella on top. Add another layer of pasta (2 sheets, trimmed), then spread ½ cup of tomato sauce, ½ cup of grated Parmesan, 16 to 18 of the tiny meatballs, and 5 pieces of torn basil on top.

Repeat the layering (2 sheets of pasta covered with ricotta and mozzarella, then 2 sheets of pasta covered with tomato sauce, grated parmesan, meatballs, and basil) in this order 2 more times. Add 2 more sheets of pasta, ricotta, mozzarella, followed by 2 final sheets of pasta, tomato, and parmesan. You should have a total of 8 pasta layers.

Cover with foil, being careful not to press it down on the top of the lasagna, or the sauce and cheese will stick. Bake for 15 minutes. Uncover and bake until the top is golden brown and the center is set, 20 to 25 minutes.

Allow the lasagna to cool in the pan for 10 minutes before cutting into squares and serving. Leftovers keep, tightly covered in the refrigerator, for up to 4 days, or in the freezer for up to three months.

Stuffed Shells with Clams, Spinach & Pancetta

SERVES 6 TO 8

Pasta shells are typically stuffed with ricotta and spinach, but since their shape reminds us of the sea, we wanted to turn this dish on its head by combining it with two other seafood classics: linguine and clams, and clams casino. The resulting dish is unique and incredibly tasty, lighter than the original stuffed shells but just as satisfying. The filling takes a cue from casino-style, in which clams are topped with bread crumbs and bacon, though here we turn to greens, pancetta, bread crumbs, and some cheese to bind it all together. Serve this alongside Broccoli Salad with Oregano Vinaigrette, Olives & Crispy Shallots (page 73), Chrysanthemum Caesar (page 75), or the Grilled Romano Bean Salad (page 76), or add it to the menu for a Feast of the Seven Fishes dinner, if that's on your holiday agenda.

———

Make the filling: Place the clams in a bowl of cold water and let sit for 20 to 30 minutes in order to purge any sand from them. If any shells are open, lightly tap them on the side of the bowl. If they do not close in response to tapping, discard them, as this means they are dead. Rinse the clams with cold water and drain them in a colander.

Place the cleaned clams in a medium saucepan along with the wine. Cover, bring to a simmer over medium-high heat, and cook until the clams have opened and released liquid, about 3 minutes. Remove from the heat. Strain the liquid through a fine-mesh sieve to remove any grit, reserving the liquid. You should have about 1 cup clam broth. Set the clams aside to cool.

When the clams are cool enough to handle, remove them from their shells, discarding the shells. Roughly chop the clams so that no piece is larger than a dime. You should have about ½ cup chopped clams.

In a large pot, cook the pancetta over medium heat, stirring often, until its fat has rendered and the meat is browned, about 3 minutes. Add the garlic, anchovy, oregano, pepper flakes, and scallion whites and stir to combine for another 3 minutes. If anything sticks, add 1 tablespoon of water to release it from the bottom of the pot. Add the scallion greens and

Filling

2 pounds littleneck clams

½ cup dry white wine, such as Pinot Grigio

¼ pound pancetta or bacon, finely chopped

4 garlic cloves, grated on a Microplane

1 anchovy fillet, finely chopped

2 teaspoons dried oregano (ideally home-dried, page 301)

¼ teaspoon crushed red pepper flakes

½ cup thinly sliced scallion whites (10 to 12 scallions)

1 cup thinly sliced scallion greens (10 to 12 scallions)

4 cups packed roughly chopped stemmed spinach (from about 6 ounces)

½ cup finely grated Parmigiano-Reggiano cheese

½ cup whole-milk ricotta cheese

½ cup shredded whole-milk mozzarella cheese

1 teaspoon kosher salt

¼ cup Italian seasoned bread crumbs, store-bought or homemade (page 298)

Grated zest of 1 lemon

Pasta

⅓ cup kosher salt

20 jumbo pasta shells (about half of a 12-ounce box)

2 tablespoons olive oil

Sauce

4 tablespoons (½ stick) unsalted butter

2 tablespoons all-purpose or Wondra flour (see page 18)

1 cup whole milk

½ cup heavy cream

¾ teaspoon kosher salt

To assemble

¼ cup finely grated Parmigiano-Reggiano cheese

Juice of 1 lemon

¼ cup Crispy Garlic Bread Crumbs (optional; page 299)

RECIPE CONTINUES

spinach, stir well, and cook until the greens have wilted and the mixture is dry, another 3 minutes. Remove the mixture from the pot and set aside to cool.

In a large bowl, mix together the cooled spinach mixture, chopped clams, parmesan, ricotta, mozzarella, salt, bread crumbs, and lemon zest until well combined. Place this mixture in the refrigerator to chill.

Cook the pasta: In a large pot, bring 4 quarts water and the kosher salt to a boil over high heat. Add the shells and cook to al dente according to the package directions. Drain, then lightly toss with olive oil and set aside on a baking pan lined with parchment to cool to avoid sticking.

Make the sauce: In a medium pot, melt the butter over medium heat. Stir in the flour and cook until the flour has lost its raw taste, about 2 minutes. Add the reserved clam broth, milk, heavy cream, and salt. Whisk over medium-low heat until the sauce is slightly thickened and coats the back of a spoon, 1 to 2 minutes. Set aside.

Preheat the oven to 375°F.

Assemble the dish: Spray a 9 × 13-inch baking dish with nonstick cooking spray. Stuff each pasta shell with the clam mixture and place the stuffed pasta in a snug even layer in the baking dish, stuffed-side up. Once all the shells are in the dish, carefully pour the sauce over them, covering them evenly, using all of the sauce.

Top with the parmesan. Bake until the sauce is bubbling and the tops of the shells are golden brown, about 35 minutes. Remove from the oven and squeeze the lemon over the top. Top with the crispy garlic bread crumbs, if using.

Serve immediately. This dish is best made and eaten day-of.

Baked Ziti Nerano with Zucchini & Provolone

SERVES 6 TO 8

This white baked ziti, with zucchini and provolone, is based on *spaghetti alla nerano*, a dish from the town of Nerano on the Sorrento peninsula. That particular specialty—which happens to be one of Scott's favorite pasta dishes—is made with fried zucchini and Provolone del Monaco, a stringy semihard local cheese. It's nearly impossible to find that particular cheese outside of that one town, so we use a combination of soft provolone—the mild kind you get at the deli counter, that melts like mozzarella—and hard provolone, which has a much sharper, more pungent taste and less-gooey texture. Combine that with soft onions, melted zucchini, and crispy garlic bread crumbs on top, and you have a recipe for a hearty, satisfying vegetarian main. Eat with a simple green salad with a nice acidic dressing for balance.

In a large pot, bring 4 quarts water and the kosher salt to a boil over high heat. Add the ziti and cook until al dente, 6 to 7 minutes. Drain well, toss with olive oil, return to the empty pot, and set aside.

Make the zucchini mixture: Halve the zucchini lengthwise, then cut crosswise into ¼-inch-thick half-moons. Set aside.

In a medium pot, melt the butter over medium heat. Add the grated garlic and thyme and cook until the garlic is soft and aromatic, 2 to 3 minutes. Add the onions, salt, and pepper. Cook, stirring occasionally, until the onions are soft and translucent, about 15 minutes. Add the zucchini and cook, stirring occasionally, until tender and cooked through, about 5 minutes.

Preheat the oven to 400°F.

Make the sauce: In a medium sauté pan, melt the butter over medium heat. Add the flour, stirring often with a wooden spoon or silicone spatula, ensuring nothing sticks to the pan, until the flour is lightly toasted and loses its raw taste, 2 to 3 minutes. Whisk in the milk and simmer until the sauce thickens, about 1 minute. Reduce the heat to medium-low. Whisk in

Ziti

¾ cup kosher salt, for the pasta water

1 pound dried ziti

2 tablespoons extra-virgin olive oil

Zucchini

2 pounds zucchini (about 3 medium)

½ cup (1 stick) unsalted butter

6 garlic cloves, grated on a Microplane

1 tablespoon chopped thyme (10 to 12 sprigs)

2 medium yellow onions, sliced into thin half-moons

1 tablespoon kosher salt

1½ teaspoons freshly ground black pepper

Sauce

4 tablespoons (½ stick) unsalted butter

2 tablespoons all-purpose or Wondra flour (see page 18)

½ cup whole milk

1 teaspoon kosher salt

½ cup labneh or whole-milk Greek yogurt

½ cup crème fraîche

2 cups coarsely grated sharp hard provolone cheese (8 ounces)

To assemble

3 cups coarsely grated mild soft provolone cheese (12 ounces)

1 cup Crispy Garlic Bread Crumbs (optional; page 299)

the salt, labneh, crème fraîche, and sharp provolone and continue cooking, whisking often, until the sauce is melted and smooth. Remove from the heat.

Assemble the pasta: To the pot of cooked ziti, add the onion-zucchini mixture, sauce, and mild provolone and mix until well combined. Transfer to a 9 × 13-inch baking dish and bake until the sauce is bubbling and the pasta is golden brown around the top edges, 25 to 30 minutes, rotating the dish from front to back halfway through. Remove from the oven and sprinkle with garlic bread crumbs, if using.

Serve hot, straight out of the baking dish. Leftovers keep, tightly covered in the refrigerator, for up to 4 days, or in the freezer for up to 3 months, and can be eaten hot or cold.

Semolina Crepe Manicotti

MAKES 10 TO 14 MANICOTTI (SERVES 4 TO 6)

Manicotti suffers from a reputation as being heavy, which can be true when it's made with dried pasta shells and overstuffed with cheese. But this is a light, delicate version made with thin durum flour crepes (we use durum because it has a pasta-like flavor), which always impresses guests. Scott's mother used to make crepe manicotti when he was a kid, and he developed this recipe based on that memory.

NOTE: The crepe batter needs to be mixed very well and should look very thin, just slightly thicker than water. Allow it to rest for at least 30 minutes in the refrigerator before using. The first crepe is usually a little messy, and it might tear, but don't stress about it—you'll get better as you go.

Make the crepes: In a blender, combine both flours, the eggs, milk, melted butter, and salt and blend on high until very smooth, about 30 seconds. Transfer the batter to a large bowl and whisk in the chopped basil. Chill in the refrigerator for at least 30 minutes.

Meanwhile, make the filling: In a stand mixer with the paddle, mix the ricotta, parmesan, pecorino, salt, pepper, and egg on medium speed until well combined, about 30 seconds. (This step can also be done by hand with a whisk and a large bowl.) Chill in the refrigerator while you make the crepes.

To assemble: Line a plate with parchment or a paper towel. Heat an 8½-inch nonstick sauté pan over medium heat. Spray it lightly with nonstick cooking spray and wipe out any extra residue. Gently rewhisk the batter, then, using a ladle or a ¼-cup dry measure, pour about 3 tablespoons of batter into the pan and tilt it around to cover the entire surface with the batter—you're making a crepe here, so aim for one thin layer. Cook until just set on one side, 30 to 45 seconds, then use a thin spatula (or an offset spatula) to flip and cook the other side until lightly browned, 30 to 45 seconds. Set the crepe aside on the lined plate and repeat with the remaining batter, spraying and wiping out the pan each time and

Crepes

1 cup durum flour

½ cup "00" flour

3 large eggs

1⅓ cups whole milk

4 tablespoons (½ stick) unsalted butter, melted and cooled

1 teaspoon kosher salt

2 tablespoons finely chopped basil

Filling

2 cups whole-milk ricotta cheese

½ cup finely grated Parmigiano-Reggiano cheese

½ cup finely grated pecorino cheese (preferably Pecorino Toscano)

1½ teaspoons kosher salt

¼ teaspoon freshly ground black pepper

1 large egg

To assemble

1½ cups 10-Minute San Marzano Tomato Sauce (page 95)

¼ cup finely grated pecorino cheese (preferably Pecorino Toscano)

12 basil leaves, for garnish

stacking the crepes with fresh paper in between. You should get 10 to 14 crepes.

Preheat the oven to 375°F.

Pour half of the tomato sauce into a 9 × 13-inch baking dish and spread it in an even layer on the bottom.

Working with one at a time, place a crepe on a clean work surface. Add about ¼ cup of the chilled filling in the center and spread it gently with a spoon. Roll the crepe up like a cigar, leaving the ends open, and place it, seam-side down, in the prepared baking dish.

Continue stuffing and rolling more crepes, keeping them in a single layer in the baking dish. Pour the remaining sauce on top and sprinkle with the pecorino. Bake until the edges are just golden brown and bubbling, 20 to 25 minutes.

Let cool for 10 minutes before serving with a spatula to scoop out crepes and their sauce. Leftovers keep, tightly covered in the refrigerator, for up to 3 days.

Sausage-Stuffed Rigatoni with Peppers & Onions

SERVES 6 TO 8

When Angie saw stuffed rigatoni for the first time in Scott's hometown, she was thoroughly intrigued. It seemed that ricotta-stuffed rigatoni, smothered in tomato sauce, appeared on the menu of nearly every central Jersey red-sauce joint. In our version, instead of stuffing them with just cheese, we use a mixture of ricotta and sausage, which naturally made us think about another classic Italian-American combination: sausage and peppers. Forget the griddled sausage and peppers at the San Gennaro street fair, though—this is done in the red-sauce tradition, by cooking onions and peppers in a thin, tangy tomato sauce that smells like the Italian-American grandma's house of your dreams.

———

NOTE: Piping the rigatoni with the sausage filling might seem fussy, but it takes just a few minutes (and is a fun activity with kids).

Make the sauce: In a heavy-bottomed medium pot, heat the olive oil over medium heat. Add the garlic, pepper flakes, salt, black pepper, oregano, and fennel seeds and cook until the garlic is lightly toasted, about 1 minute. Add the onion and bell peppers, stirring every few minutes, and cook until completely soft, about 20 minutes. If the vegetables start to stick or burn, add 1 to 2 tablespoons of water to the pan.

Add the crushed tomatoes and fill the tomato can with the same amount of water (or a scant 2 cups, in case you're using a can bigger than 15 ounces), adding that as well. Simmer for 10 minutes to allow the flavors to meld, then remove from the heat. Transfer to a large bowl and refrigerate for 30 minutes to cool the sauce.

Cook the rigatoni: In a large pot, bring 4 quarts water and the kosher salt to a boil over high heat. Add the rigatoni and cook for 10 minutes (they should be slightly undercooked). Drain, toss with the olive oil, and set aside to cool.

Make the filling and assemble: In a food processor, process the sausage, ricotta, eggs, ½ cup of the pecorino, and the salt for a full minute, until smooth and well combined (it should resemble a thick paste).

Sauce

¼ cup extra-virgin olive oil

4 garlic cloves, grated on a Microplane

¼ teaspoon crushed red pepper flakes

1 tablespoon kosher salt

¼ teaspoon freshly ground black pepper

½ teaspoon dried oregano (ideally home-dried, page 301)

½ teaspoon fennel seeds

1 medium yellow onion, sliced into ¼-inch half-moons

1 large green bell pepper, cut into 1 × ¼-inch strips

2 large red bell peppers, cut into 1 × ¼-inch strips

1 (15-ounce) can crushed tomatoes

Rigatoni

½ cup kosher salt

1 pound dried rigatoni (no. 24)

2 tablespoons extra-virgin olive oil

Filling & assembly

1 pound sweet Italian sausage, casings removed

1 cup whole-milk ricotta cheese

2 large eggs

2½ cups finely grated pecorino cheese (preferably Pecorino Toscano)

2½ teaspoons kosher salt

Transfer the mixture to a piping bag or a zip-top bag with the corner cut off. Carefully fill each rigatoni with the sausage mixture from one end, squeezing the mixture all the way through to the other end. Repeat until all of the rigatoni are filled.

Preheat the oven to 400°F.

Transfer the stuffed rigatoni to the bowl of chilled sauce. Add 1¾ cups of the pecorino and, using a rubber spatula, gently fold everything to combine. Transfer to a 9 × 13-inch baking dish and top with the remaining ¼ cup pecorino.

Bake the pasta until its ends are browned and crispy, and the tomato is bubbling, about 40 minutes.

Rest on a cooling rack for 15 minutes before serving. Leftovers keep, tightly covered in the refrigerator, for up to 5 days.

Is there a more quintessential Italian-American dish than spaghetti and meatballs? We think not. Sure, meatballs exist in Italy, but in truth, they're more of an Italian-American thing, burned into our consciousness along with red-checkered tablecloths and straw-covered Chianti bottles. That's amore and all, and though we'd never diss the original, we wanted to showcase a broad spectrum of meatballs in this chapter, some more traditional than others.

We use all different kinds of meats, including cured meats, along with seafood, vegetables, and grains in our meatballs. We came up with shrimp parm meatballs in honor of one of Scott's favorite red-sauce dishes, and spiced lamb meatballs with currants and almonds in a nod to the Arab influence in Sicily. We have a couple of vegetarian "meatballs," one with broccoli and farro and another made with eggplant, both of which taste just as hearty and satisfying as any meaty version; and veal piccata meatballs smothered in a caper and lemon-laced sauce inspired by Swedish meatballs with gravy.

All of that said, we of course have a classic version, inspired by both of our grandmothers, who spent hours chopping, mixing, and rolling theirs when we were kids. Scott grew up with a steady supply of Sunday gravy loaded with meatballs, sausage, and braciole; while Angie's family served their meatballs in a big bowl along with roasted Italian sausage as a side dish. Our recipe today is the result of a lot of tinkering to reimagine the finished product as the best possible version of itself, and we're very proud of how they turned out. Eat them as is, or break them up and stir them into the Amatriciana with Braised Pork Shoulder (page 107), or the Leftover Spaghetti & Meatball Frittata (page 131).

You've got options, lots of options, when it comes to meatballs. If you'd like to serve them as a stand-alone dish, all of these recipes have a suggested dressing or sauce, or they can be slapped on a sandwich, salad, or pasta. We also like to make mini meatballs and serve them as cocktail bites, along with some antipasti from pages 24–69. With the diversity of styles and flavors in this chapter, the world is your meatball.

Classic Meatballs

MAKES ABOUT 26 MEATBALLS

Scott developed this recipe as a fusion of both of our grandmas' beloved meatball recipes, and it is one of the inventions of which we are most proud. We put a lot of thought into each component, and think it shows (or rather, tastes) in the finished product.

Typically, Italian grandmothers use bread crumbs as a binder, but we use the slightly more sophisticated technique of making a *panade*—really just a fancy way of saying soaking bread in milk—which adds moisture and richness all at once. And instead of using raw garlic, which never fully cooks in the meatball, we use a puree of roasted garlic, which adds a deep, caramelized flavor. Similarly, we use onion puree in lieu of diced onion, so a soft oniony flavor imbues every bite. *See photo on pages 190–191.*

———

SERVING NOTE: These are as classic as they get. Serve with the 10-Minute San Marzano Tomato Sauce (page 95) or your favorite tomato sauce alongside pasta, on a sandwich, or with a side from the Vegetable chapter (beginning on page 239), sprinkled with parmesan. For the ultimate Sunday gravy, add 6 to 8 cooked meatballs to the pork Amatriciana recipe (for more details see page 108); these are also the same meatballs called for in the Leftover Spaghetti & Meatball Frittata on page 131 and Grandma Addario's Lasagna with Tiny Meatballs on page 180.

2½ cups nickel-sized chunks bread, crusts removed (from about half an Italian-style loaf or small baguette)

1 cup whole milk

1 large yellow onion, coarsely chopped

¾ pound ground beef

¾ pound ground veal

⅓ cup Roasted Garlic Puree (page 300)

1 cup finely grated pecorino cheese (preferably Pecorino Toscano)

1 cup finely grated Parmigiano-Reggiano cheese

1 tablespoon plus 1 teaspoon kosher salt

1½ teaspoons freshly ground black pepper

1½ cups roughly chopped parsley

2 large eggs

Preheat the oven to 425°F. Line a baking sheet with parchment paper and spray the paper with nonstick cooking spray.

In a medium bowl, combine the bread and milk and soak until the bread is thoroughly saturated, about 15 minutes. Squeeze the bread in a clean kitchen towel to wring out as much milk as possible and discard the liquid. You should have about 1½ cups of wrung bread.

In a food processor, puree the chopped onion until smooth. Place the onion puree in a clean towel and wring it to remove all extra moisture. You should have about 1 cup of wrung onion.

In a large bowl, combine the bread, onion puree, beef, veal, roasted garlic puree, pecorino, parmesan, salt, pepper, parsley, and eggs. Using your hands, gently mix the ingredients together until just combined—don't overmix, or the meatballs will be tough. Form into 2-inch meatballs (about ¼ cup each) and arrange on the lined baking sheet.

Bake the meatballs until browned and firm, and a thermometer poked in the center reads 150°F, about 15 minutes, rotating the sheet from front to back halfway through.

Serve the meatballs immediately, with one of the suggestions in the Serving Note. Leftovers keep, tightly covered in the refrigerator, for up to 3 days, or in the freezer for up to 3 months.

Mortadella & Chicken Meatballs

MAKES ABOUT 28 MEATBALLS

We developed this dish as part of a special-occasion Japanese-inspired pasta omakase menu, feeling inspired by *tsukune*, the juicy ground chicken skewers popular as a drinking snack in izakayas. But it was so delicious that we now make these meatballs all the time, mixing ground chicken (ideally dark meat) and mortadella, the Italian-American version of bologna, which adds an extra dose of fat and flavor.

———

SERVING NOTE: These meatballs are great when rolled into a smaller size and served in chicken broth with pastina and a scattering of fresh green scallions and herbs on top, or in a sandwich with stracchino cheese and pesto.

2 cups nickel-sized chunks bread, crust removed (from about half an Italian-style loaf or small baguette)

1 cup whole milk

½ pound mortadella, roughly chopped

½ pound ground chicken (preferably dark meat)

3 tablespoons Roasted Garlic Puree (page 300)

⅓ cup finely grated Parmigiano-Reggiano cheese

1 tablespoon kosher salt

½ teaspoon freshly ground black pepper

¼ teaspoon cayenne pepper

⅓ cup thinly sliced scallions, whites only (4 to 6 scallions)

1 large egg

Preheat the oven to 400°F. Line a baking sheet with parchment paper and spray the paper with nonstick cooking spray.

In a medium bowl, combine the bread and milk and soak until the bread is thoroughly saturated, about 15 minutes. Squeeze the bread in a clean kitchen towel to wring out as much milk as possible and discard the liquid. You should have about 1¼ cups of wrung bread.

Meanwhile, in a food processor, process the mortadella into small pieces, the same size as the ground chicken.

In a large bowl, combine the chicken, mortadella, bread, roasted garlic puree, parmesan, salt, black pepper, cayenne, scallion whites, and egg and mix by hand until well incorporated. Form into 1½-inch meatballs (about 2 tablespoons each) and place on the lined baking sheet.

Bake the meatballs until golden brown and firm, and a thermometer poked in the center reads 160°F, about 15 minutes.

Serve immediately (and see also Serving Note for more suggestions). Leftovers keep, tightly covered in the refrigerator, for up to 3 days.

Broccoli & Farro Polpette

MAKES ABOUT 30 POLPETTE

If you're looking for a hearty, robust vegetarian meatball, look no further. These broccoli and farro polpette are filling and satisfying, thanks to the combination of umami-heavy cheese and chewy, nutty farro. They're not too far off from arancini, the fried rice balls beloved across Southern Italy.

We like to almost overcook the farro here, making it very soft, which adds a meaty texture and helps to bind everything together with the broccoli. It's similar to our technique of using panade (soaked bread) in meat-based meatballs, to get just the right structure. If you're feeling particularly decadent, these are also excellent deep-fried at 350°F for 1½ to 2 minutes.

_____

SERVING NOTE: These polpette can stand on their own, or serve them in a bowl with the Spicy Fra Diavolo Sauce (page 103) and shaved parmesan on top.

Make the polpette: Place the broccoli in a food processor and process until evenly chopped and about the size of grains of rice. You should have about 4 packed cups of broccoli crumbles.

In a medium sauté pan, heat the oil over medium heat. Add the onion, 1 teaspoon of the salt, the chiles, and oregano and cook, stirring continually until soft, about 5 minutes. Add the processed broccoli and cook, stirring often, until tender, about 4 more minutes. Transfer the broccoli mixture to a medium bowl and refrigerate to cool completely.

In a small pot, bring 3 cups water and 1 teaspoon of the salt to a rolling boil over medium-high heat. Rinse the farro well in cold water, drain, and add to the boiling water. Reduce the heat to medium and cook the farro until very soft and all the water is absorbed, 30 to 35 minutes. Once cooked, spread the farro in a single layer on a sheet pan or large plate to cool completely.

In a large bowl, combine the cooled farro, broccoli mixture, roasted garlic puree, pecorino, parmesan, bread crumbs, mozzarella, 1 teaspoon of the salt, and egg until very well incorporated.

Polpette

1¼ pounds broccoli (about 1 large head), roughly chopped (florets and tender stalk)

2 tablespoons extra-virgin olive oil

1 medium yellow onion, diced

3 teaspoons kosher salt

¼ teaspoon crushed Calabrian chiles in oil

½ teaspoon dried oregano (ideally home-dried, page 301)

1 cup farro

¼ cup Roasted Garlic Puree (page 300)

¼ cup finely grated pecorino cheese (preferably Pecorino Toscano)

1 cup finely grated Parmigiano-Reggiano cheese

⅓ cup Italian seasoned bread crumbs, store-bought or homemade (page 298)

½ cup shredded whole-milk mozzarella cheese

1 large egg, beaten

Lemon wedges, for serving

Coating and frying

1 cup all-purpose flour

1 cup neutral oil, such as vegetable

2 teaspoons kosher salt

Coat and fry the polpette: Spread the flour in a shallow bowl. Scoop the polpette mixture into lightly packed 1½-inch balls (about 2 tablespoons each) and roll each ball gently in the flour. Transfer to a baking sheet.

In a large sauté pan, heat half of the oil over medium-high heat until shimmering. Working in batches to avoid overcrowding, add half of the polpette and cook, turning gently with tongs, until golden brown on all sides, 3 to 5 minutes. Set aside on a plate lined with paper towels and season with 1 teaspoon of the salt. Repeat with fresh oil until all of the polpette are cooked. Transfer to the lined plate and season with the remaining salt.

Serve immediately (see the suggestions in the Serving Note). Leftovers keep, tightly covered in the refrigerator, for up to 3 days. Reheat in the oven at 350°F until warmed through.

Eggplant Polpette

MAKES ABOUT 20 POLPETTE

This take on vegetarian meatballs is based on an eggplant dish typical of Puglia, but we add a few extra elements to enhance their flavor and texture— sun-dried tomatoes, two kinds of cheese, and pine nuts. We also like using Japanese eggplants, which have fewer seeds than Italian, making for a firmer polpette.

SERVING NOTE: These are hearty, savory little bites, ideal for eating at room temperature as a snack, along with some 10-Minute San Marzano Tomato Sauce (page 95) as part of a vegetarian entrée with pasta or rice, or on a sandwich with that same sauce and some Ricotta Infornata (page 307) or melted mozz.

Preheat the oven to 400°F. Line a sheet pan with parchment paper.

Make the polpette: Halve the eggplants lengthwise and drizzle evenly with the olive oil. Place on the lined sheet pan cut-side up. Roast until the eggplant is fully softened and slightly golden brown, about 20 minutes. Once cool enough to handle, scrape the roasted eggplant flesh into a medium bowl, discarding the skin. Place the flesh in a fine-mesh sieve and let drain for 20 minutes. You should have about 2 cups of eggplant.

In a food processor, puree the chopped onion until smooth. Place the onion puree in a clean towel and wring it to remove all extra moisture. You should have about ¼ cup of wrung onion.

Roughly chop the roasted eggplant and place in a medium bowl. Add the onion, pine nuts, parsley, garlic puree, dried tomatoes, egg, bread crumbs, pecorino, parmesan, salt, and pepper and mix with your hands until well incorporated. Chill in the refrigerator for 20 minutes.

Roll the eggplant mixture into 1½-inch balls (about 2 tablespoons each) and arrange on a sheet pan. Return to the refrigerator for another 20 minutes.

Polpette

2 pounds Japanese eggplants (about 3 large)

¾ cup extra-virgin olive oil

½ yellow onion, coarsely chopped

¼ cup pine nuts, lightly toasted

2 tablespoons flat-leaf parsley, finely chopped

¼ cup Roasted Garlic Puree (page 300)

¼ cup Oven-Dried Tomatoes (optional; page 302), or store-bought oil-packed sun-dried tomatoes, drained and finely chopped

1 large egg

1 cup Italian seasoned bread crumbs, store-bought or homemade (page 298)

½ cup finely grated pecorino cheese (preferably Pecorino Toscano)

¼ cup finely grated Parmigiano-Reggiano cheese

2 teaspoons kosher salt

¼ teaspoon freshly ground black pepper

Breading and frying

1 cup all-purpose flour

3 large eggs, beaten

1 cup Italian seasoned bread crumbs, store-bought or homemade (page 298)

Neutral oil, such as vegetable, for deep-frying (about 6 cups)

Kosher salt

Bread the polpette: Set up three bowls for dredging, one with the flour, one with the eggs, and one with the bread crumbs. Working with one ball at a time, roll in the flour to coat evenly and shake off the excess. Dip the ball in the eggs, allowing the excess to drip off. Roll again in the bread crumbs to coat evenly, shaking off the excess. Set aside on the sheet pan and repeat until all of the polpette have been dredged. (The polpette can be held like this for up to 2 days in the refrigerator, and fried just before serving.)

Fry the polpette: Pour 3 or 4 inches oil into a large heavy-bottomed pot or Dutch oven and heat over medium-high heat until it reaches about 325°F.

Working in batches to avoid overcrowding, fry the polpette until golden brown and crispy, 2 to 3 minutes. Drain on paper towels and season with salt while still warm. Repeat the process with the remaining polpette, making sure the oil comes back up to temperature before frying the next batch.

Serve as is or as part of one of the suggestions in the Serving Note.

Leftover polpette will keep, tightly covered in the refrigerator, for up to 4 days. Reheat in a 400°F oven for about 10 minutes before serving.

Veal Piccata Meatballs

MAKES ABOUT 28 MEATBALLS

Veal piccata, with its buttery lemon-caper sauce, is one of those classic Italian-American dishes—and when we say classic, we mean we're not sure we've ever seen it in Italy. Our idea here was to flavor the meatballs themselves with a good amount of lemon and capers, then serve them in a rich gravy—almost like what you find on Swedish meatballs—made with butter, flour, mustard, garlic, and yet more lemon and capers. Save this for a cold night when you're craving comfort food hard. Or don't—these are frankly delicious anytime.

SERVING NOTE: Serve these meatballs with an egg-based pasta, such as pappardelle or farfalle (page 151), or really any starch, including a nice hunk of crusty bread. They're rich and saucy, though the creamy gravy is nicely balanced by the acidity of the lemon and the brininess of the capers. (It's also worth noting here that you don't *have* to make the sauce—the meatballs are plenty flavorful on their own.)

Meatballs

1½ cups nickel-sized chunks bread, crusts removed (from about one-third of an Italian-style loaf or a small baguette)

1 cup buttermilk

1 pound ground veal

⅓ cup Roasted Garlic Puree (page 300)

¼ cup coarsely chopped flat-leaf parsley

½ cup brine-packed capers, rinsed and drained

1 cup finely grated Parmigiano-Reggiano cheese

2½ teaspoons kosher salt

1½ teaspoons freshly ground black pepper

1 large egg

Grated zest of 2 lemons

Sauce

¾ cup (1½ sticks) unsalted butter

6 garlic cloves, finely chopped

½ cup all-purpose flour

3 cups chicken stock, unsalted store-bought or homemade (page 299)

¼ cup brine-packed capers, rinsed, drained, and roughly chopped

2½ teaspoons kosher salt

1 teaspoon freshly ground black pepper

1 cup heavy cream

Grated zest of 1 lemon

1½ tablespoons fresh lemon juice

2 teaspoons Dijon mustard

Make the meatballs: In a medium bowl, combine the bread and buttermilk and soak until the bread is thoroughly saturated, about 15 minutes. Squeeze the bread in a clean kitchen towel to wring out as much milk as possible and discard the liquid. You should have about 1 cup of wrung bread.

Preheat the oven to 475°F. Line a baking sheet with parchment paper and spray with nonstick cooking spray.

In a large bowl, combine the bread, veal, roasted garlic puree, parsley, capers, parmesan, salt, pepper, egg, and lemon zest. Using your hands, gently mix the ingredients together until just combined—don't overmix, or the meatballs will be tough. Scoop into 1½-inch meatballs (about 2 tablespoons each) and place on the lined baking sheet.

Bake until the meatballs are golden brown on the outside, and a thermometer inserted reads 150°F, about 10 minutes.

Make the sauce: In a large pot, heat the butter over medium-high heat. Add the garlic and cook until lightly browned, 2 to 3 minutes. Whisk in the flour and continue whisking and cooking over medium heat until lightly toasted and golden, 3 to 5 minutes.

Whisk in the chicken stock, capers, salt, pepper, and cream. Bring to a simmer over medium heat and cook, stirring occasionally, until the sauce thickens enough to coat the back of a spoon, 3 to 5 minutes. Whisk in the lemon zest, lemon juice, and mustard. Remove from the heat. You should have about 4 cups of sauce.

Add the cooked meatballs to the sauce and serve, with plenty of sauce on each portion (these should be saucy!). Meatballs and sauce keep, tightly covered in the refrigerator, for up to 3 days.

Pork Meatballs with Caramelized Fennel

MAKES ABOUT 28 MEATBALLS

We've made various attempts at sausage-flavored meatballs, but they usually fall flat in the texture department, as sausage tends to be coarse and fatty, so the resulting meatball often feels quite dense. Here, we take the idea behind our classic meatball recipe—using bread soaked in milk for lightness—and combine it with flavors typically used to season Italian pork sausage, including fennel seed, black pepper, and pepper flakes. The result *tastes* like sausage, but has a tender texture, the way a great meatball should.

───────

SERVING NOTE: These are great on their own, in sandwich form, or atop a simple buttered pasta, but to really drive home that fennel flavor, opt in to the caramelized fennel topping, which adds a double layer of anise-y delight.

Preheat the oven to 425°F. Line a baking sheet with parchment paper and spray with nonstick cooking spray.

Make the meatballs: In a medium bowl, combine the bread and milk and soak until the bread is thoroughly saturated, about 15 minutes. Squeeze the bread in a clean kitchen towel to wring out as much milk as possible and discard the liquid. You should have about 1½ cups of wrung bread.

In a food processor, puree the chopped onion until smooth. Place the onion puree in a clean towel and wring it to remove all of the extra moisture. You should have about 1 cup of wrung onion.

In a large bowl, combine the bread, onion puree, pork, roasted garlic puree, parmesan, salt, black pepper, pepper flakes, ground fennel, chopped fennel fronds, and eggs. Using your hands, gently mix the ingredients together until just combined—don't overmix, or the meatballs will be tough. Form into 1½-inch meatballs (about 2 tablespoons each) and place on the lined baking sheet.

Bake until the meatballs are browned and firm, and a thermometer inserted reads 160°F, 15 to 17 minutes, rotating the sheet from front to back halfway through.

Meatballs

2½ cups nickel-sized chunks bread, crusts removed (from about half an Italian-style loaf or small baguette)

1 cup whole milk

1 large yellow onion, coarsely chopped

1½ pounds ground pork

⅓ cup Roasted Garlic Puree (page 300)

2 cup finely grated Parmigiano-Reggiano cheese

1 tablespoon plus 1½ teaspoons kosher salt

1½ teaspoons freshly ground black pepper

¼ teaspoon crushed red pepper flakes

1 tablespoon ground fennel

¼ cup roughly chopped fennel fronds

2 large eggs

Caramelized fennel (optional)

½ cup extra-virgin olive oil

4 medium fennel bulbs, halved, cored, and thinly sliced lengthwise

½ teaspoon crushed red pepper flakes

2 teaspoons fennel seeds

1 tablespoon plus 1 teaspoon kosher salt

1 cup rice vinegar

1 cup honey

¼ cup fresh lemon juice (about 1 large lemon)

Make the caramelized fennel (if using): In a large pot, heat the olive oil over high heat. Add the fresh fennel, reduce the heat to medium-high, and cook, stirring often, until the fennel starts to wilt and turn brown, 4 to 5 minutes.

Add the pepper flakes, fennel seeds, and salt and continue to cook, stirring often, for another minute. Add the vinegar and honey and stir well to combine. Increase the heat to high and cook, stirring often, until the liquid is reduced enough to coat the back of a spoon and large bubbles appear at the surface, 7 to 10 minutes. The mixture should be thick and glaze-like.

Remove from the heat, add the lemon juice and stir well to combine. Set aside until the meatballs are ready. You should have 3½ to 4 cups of fennel.

Serve the meatballs immediately, as is or topped with the caramelized fennel. Leftovers keep, tightly covered in the refrigerator, for up to 3 days.

Chicken & 'Nduja Meatballs

MAKES ABOUT 28 MEATBALLS

Scott loves spicy food, and wanted to make an *arrabbiata*-style meatball for snacking (arrabbiata, meaning "angry," is a common mouth-burning preparation at Italian-American joints). 'Nduja, a rich, spicy spreadable salami from Calabria, provides plenty of heat, so it made sense to pair it with chicken, a lean, mild meat that soaks up and balances out stronger flavors.

If you can find 'nduja, definitely use it (it's often available at Italian delis or online, though we have seen it start to pop up at Whole Foods as well), but if not, cured Spanish-style chorizo makes a good substitute. If you're using chorizo, remove the casing and grind it in the food processor into pieces about the size of a grain of rice, and cut the amount of salt you add in half.

SERVING NOTE: Serve these as is, on a sandwich, or stick a toothpick in them as an app, with or without the simple herbed yogurt to cut the heat.

Preheat the oven to 400°F. Line a baking sheet with parchment paper or silicone baking mat and spray with nonstick cooking spray.

Make the polpette: In a medium bowl, combine the bread and milk and soak until the bread is thoroughly saturated, about 15 minutes. Squeeze the bread in a clean kitchen towel to wring out as much milk as possible and discard the liquid. You should have about 2 cups of wrung bread.

In a large bowl, combine the bread, 'nduja, chicken, oregano, roasted garlic puree, parmesan, salt, and egg. Using your hands, gently mix the ingredients together until just combined—don't overmix, or the meatballs will be tough. Form into 1½-inch meatballs (about 2 tablespoons each) and place on the lined baking sheet.

Bake until the meatballs are golden brown and a thermometer inserted into the center reads 160°F, 20 to 25 minutes.

Polpette

3 cups nickel-sized chunks Italian bread, crusts removed (from about three-quarters of one Italian-style loaf or small baguette)

1 cup whole milk

¼ pound 'nduja (or cured chorizo, ground in a food processor)

¾ pound ground chicken

2 teaspoons dried oregano (ideally home-dried, page 301)

2 tablespoons Roasted Garlic Puree (page 300)

⅓ cup finely grated Parmigiano-Reggiano cheese

1 tablespoon kosher salt

1 large egg

Herbed yogurt (optional)

2 cups labneh or whole-milk Greek yogurt

1 garlic clove, grated on a Microplane

1 teaspoon dried oregano (ideally home-dried, page 301)

1 tablespoon plus 1 teaspoon sugar

2 teaspoons kosher salt

1 tablespoon chopped cilantro

1 tablespoon fresh lemon juice

For serving (optional)

2 sprigs cilantro, leaves picked

¼ cup thinly sliced scallions, whites only (1 to 2 scallions)

Make the herbed yogurt (if using): In a small bowl, whisk together the labneh, garlic, oregano, sugar, salt, cilantro, and lemon juice.

To serve: Arrange the meatballs on a serving platter. If using yogurt sauce, drizzle over the meatballs and sprinkle the top with cilantro and scallion whites. Leftover meatballs will keep, tightly covered in the refrigerator, for up to 3 days.

Spiced Lamb Meatballs with Currants, Almonds & Feta

MAKES ABOUT 28 MEATBALLS

Inspired by the Italian islands of Sicily and Sardinia, these lamb meatballs are perfect for summer. In Sicily, it's common to find meatballs with pine nuts and raisins (a holdover from the island's centuries of Arab rule), so we used that as a starting point, then thought about more classic pairings: lamb and mint, lamb and anchovies. The result is a lighter lamb meatball studded with currants, chopped almonds, and feta and served with a tangy-fresh mint salsa verde made with anchovies. And while feta isn't traditionally Italian, we took some liberties here, pairing it with another Italian sheep's milk cheese (pecorino, that is). These are super flavorful and pair best with a simple starch, such as the Fazzoletti with Pesto Bianco (page 156).

Make the meatballs: In a medium bowl, combine the bread and milk and soak until the bread is thoroughly saturated, about 15 minutes. Squeeze the bread in a clean kitchen towel to wring out as much milk as possible and discard the liquid. You should have about 1½ cups of wrung bread.

In a food processor, puree the chopped onion until smooth. Place the onion puree in a clean towel and wring it to remove all of the extra moisture. You should have about 1 cup of wrung onion.

In a large bowl, combine the bread, onion puree, lamb, roasted garlic puree, pecorino, feta, currants, almonds, coriander, cumin, dried mint, salt, pepper, and eggs. Using your hands, gently mix the ingredients together until just combined—don't overmix, or the meatballs will be tough. Refrigerate for at least 1 hour before rolling.

Preheat the oven to 425°F. Line a baking sheet with parchment paper and spray with nonstick cooking spray.

Form the mixture into 1½-inch meatballs (about 2 tablespoons each) and place on the lined baking sheet.

Bake until the meatballs are browned and firm and a thermometer inserted reads 150°F, about 15 minutes, rotating the sheet from front to back halfway through.

Meatballs

2½ cups nickel-sized chunks bread, crusts removed (from about half an Italian-style loaf or small baguette)

1 cup whole milk

1 large yellow onion, coarsely chopped

1½ pounds ground lamb

⅓ cup Roasted Garlic Puree (page 300)

½ cup finely grated pecorino cheese (preferably Pecorino Toscano)

1 cup crumbled feta cheese (about 5 ounces)

½ cup dried currants, roughly chopped

¼ cup finely chopped toasted almonds

2 teaspoons ground coriander

1 teaspoon ground cumin

1 tablespoon dried mint (ideally home-dried, page 301)

2 tablespoons plus 2 teaspoons kosher salt

1½ teaspoons freshly ground black pepper

2 large eggs

10 mint leaves, for garnish

Mint salsa verde (optional)

2 anchovy fillets, finely chopped

½ cup chopped brine-packed capers (rinsed before chopping)

2 garlic cloves, grated on a Microplane

1 cup packed mint leaves, finely chopped

1 cup extra-virgin olive oil

Grated zest of 1 lemon

¼ cup fresh lemon juice

1 tablespoon sugar

Make the salsa verde (if using): In a small bowl, stir together the anchovies, capers, garlic, chopped fresh mint, olive oil, lemon zest, lemon juice, and sugar.

To serve, arrange the meatballs on a platter and serve hot, drizzled with salsa verde (if using) and garnished with fresh mint leaves.

Leftovers keep, tightly covered in the refrigerator, for up to 3 days.

Sardine Polpette

MAKES ABOUT 12 POLPETTE

When Scott was a kid, his grandfather used to serve him sardine sandwiches with ketchup and onions. He didn't care much for the combination, but he ate it anyway, out of love for anything his grandfather did or made. Though we'll leave the sardines and ketchup combo for another day, we wanted to pay homage to the tiny fish with these delicious fritters. Sardine polpette are typical in Sicily, where they're usually made with fresh fish. If you have access to the fresh stuff, great, but if not, the tinned version works just as well, and makes this a perfect back-pocket lunch or light dinner. You can also make these, minus the cucumber salad, as an appetizer, and serve them with the Lemon Aioli (page 306) for dipping.

———

NOTE: We like to use Wild Planet wild sardines in extra-virgin olive oil, though any wild-caught sardine in olive oil will do.

Make the polpette: Remove any bones from the fish with your fingers or a fork. Place in a medium bowl and break up into small flakes with a fork. Add the labneh, roasted garlic puree, onion powder, panko, lemon zest, Calabrian chiles, sumac, and salt and stir well to combine.

Using a spoon, gently scoop and roll the mixture into 1½-inch meatballs (about 2 tablespoons each). In a small bowl, combine the flour and potato starch. Roll each meatball in the starch to evenly coat and transfer to a large plate.

Pour 3 to 4 inches oil into a large heavy-bottomed pot or Dutch oven and heat over medium-high heat to about 360°F. Line a sheet pan with paper towels.

Meanwhile, make the cucumber salad (if using): Toss the cucumbers with the creamy Italian dressing.

Working in batches to avoid overcrowding, fry the sardine meatballs until deeply golden brown and crispy, stirring occasionally, 2 to 3 minutes.

Polpette

2 (4.4-ounce) tins sardines in olive oil (see Note), drained (about 1 cup fish)

5 tablespoons labneh or whole-milk Greek yogurt

2 teaspoons Roasted Garlic Puree (page 300)

1 teaspoon onion powder

¼ cup panko bread crumbs

Grated zest of 1 lemon

1½ teaspoons crushed Calabrian chiles in oil

1 teaspoon ground sumac

1 teaspoon kosher salt, plus more for seasoning

½ cup all-purpose flour

2 tablespoons potato starch

Neutral oil, such as vegetable, for deep-frying (about 6 cups)

Cucumber salad (optional)

2 cucumbers, thinly sliced (preferably English but any will do)

1 cup Creamy Italian Dressing (page 305)

3 tablespoons roughly chopped dill

Carefully remove with a slotted spoon and set on the paper towels. Season the meatballs with salt while still warm.

Serve immediately, as is or alongside the cucumber salad, garnished with dill. This dish is best made and eaten day-of.

Shrimp Parm Meatballs

MAKES ABOUT 20 MEATBALLS

Shrimp parm breaks the alleged Italian "rule" about not mixing seafood and dairy, but it's Scott's guilty pleasure, and one that he actually doesn't feel so guilty about after all.

Making regular shrimp parm is kind of a pain—you have to clean, bread, and fry each shrimp individually before assembling the rest of the dish. Putting it into meatball form is both a little more sophisticated, and a little more fun. The key here is to mix the shrimp with cream, cheese, and bread crumbs, then bind the whole thing together with egg whites, which makes for a lighter finished product. If you just use shrimp, you'll wind up with a dense, rubbery ball—no thanks.

———

SERVING NOTE: Serve these as is, with the buttery tomato sauce spooned over the top, or put them on a sandwich or over pasta.

Make the meatballs: Preheat the oven to 400°F. Line a baking sheet with parchment paper and spray with nonstick cooking spray.

Roughly chop the shrimp into ¼-inch pieces. Place in a food processor with the salt, oregano, granulated onion, granulated garlic, black pepper, tomato paste, mozzarella, parmesan, and bread crumbs. Pulse 8 to 10 times, until the mixture resembles a chunky paste and all the ingredients are evenly incorporated. Add the heavy cream and egg whites. Pulse to incorporate, about 5 times. Transfer the mixture to a medium bowl and refrigerate for 30 minutes to 1 hour to chill.

Roll the mixture into 1½-inch meatballs (about 2 tablespoons each). Place them on the lined baking sheet.

Bake until firm and lightly toasted, about 10 minutes.

Meanwhile, make the sauce: In a medium saucepan, melt 2 tablespoons of the butter over medium heat. Add the garlic, pepper flakes, salt, and oregano. Cook, stirring continually, until the garlic is aromatic and very light golden brown, about 3 minutes. Add the crushed tomatoes and cook, stirring often, for 3 minutes to meld the flavors and slightly reduce the

Meatballs

1 pound medium (41/50 count) shrimp (preferably wild-caught), peeled and deveined

2½ teaspoons kosher salt

2 teaspoons dried oregano (ideally home-dried, page 301)

2 tablespoons granulated onion

2 tablespoons granulated garlic

¼ teaspoon freshly ground black pepper

3 tablespoons tomato paste

½ cup shredded whole-milk mozzarella cheese

½ cup grated Parmigiano-Reggiano cheese

½ cup Italian seasoned bread crumbs, store-bought or homemade (page 298)

¼ cup heavy cream

2 large egg whites

Sauce

½ cup (1 stick) cold unsalted butter, cubed

1 tablespoon garlic, grated on a Microplane (3 to 4 cloves)

Pinch of crushed red pepper flakes

1½ teaspoons kosher salt

1 teaspoon dried oregano (ideally home-dried, page 301)

1¾ cups canned crushed tomatoes (14 ounces)

⅓ cup dry white wine

½ teaspoon sugar

2 tablespoons chopped basil (7 to 8 leaves)

For serving

2 tablespoons finely grated Parmigiano-Reggiano cheese

12 to 15 small basil leaves, for garnish

1 lemon, cut into wedges

sauce. Add the wine and increase the heat to medium-high. Stir continually, cooking until all of the liquid evaporates, about 3 minutes. Remove from the heat and whisk in the remaining 6 tablespoons butter, 1 tablespoon at a time, until incorporated. Add the sugar and chopped basil. You should have about 2 cups of sauce.

To serve: Place the shrimp balls on individual plates or a platter and spoon the sauce over the top. Sprinkle with the parmesan and garnish with basil leaves. Add a squeeze of fresh lemon over the top. Serve immediately. This dish is best made and eaten day-of.

A lot of Italian-American restaurants offer a standard menu for main courses—chicken, fish, veal, and so on, prepared in the style of the usual suspects—alla Parmigiana, Milanese, maybe piccata or diavolo if you're lucky. We love a staple, but we like to think about our food a little differently, so in this chapter, we tried to offer a variety of entrées, each with a distinct point of view.

That means a few things that seem like standbys—chicken scarpariello and veal Milanese, for example are done our way, which means using Anaheim chiles and pickled deli peppers in the former, and seasoned cheese spread, smoky speck, and mustardy mizuna salad in the latter. And it means a few completely true-to-us creations, like the Campari and orange-flavored baby back ribs on page 229, inspired by our love of Chinese-American takeout. We're also perpetually interested in coming up with creative new vegetarian mains, like the Savoy cabbage seared in brown butter and draped with Parmesan and mozzarella, or the polenta baked with rich San Marzano tomato sauce in lieu of milk.

This chapter also runs the gamut in terms of technique, featuring dishes that are baked, grilled, pan-fried, braised, and more. Most of the recipes can be made year-round as few rely on heavily seasonal ingredients. There are a couple—the Easter Pie comes to mind—that we serve at specific times of the year (ahem . . . Easter), but absolutely nothing says you can't make it in, say, November. Cut loose and feel free to mix and match these recipes with different antipasti (pages 24–69) and vegetable dishes (pages 240–57). And don't worry about making too much food—that's part of the spirit of Italian-American cooking.

Layered Eggplant Parm

SERVES 6 TO 8

Eggplant parm is one of those dishes that every Italian-American family makes differently. We know people who roast the eggplant instead of breading it; or who just slather one big, thick piece of eggplant with sauce and call it a day. Our families both make it the same way, in a style similar to lasagna, with multiple thin layers of eggplant, sauce, and cheese. We prefer it like this, partially out of tradition, and more important, because the texture of many fried layers of eggplant is better than the texture of one thick, spongy layer of eggplant.

Scott is a firm believer in peeling off the tough skin of the eggplant, though Angie is less convinced that it matters, as long as your eggplant is paper thin; try both and see which you prefer. You can serve this bubbling hot as a vegetarian main, put a slab of it onto a sandwich, or, do as we do, and eat it cold.

———

NOTE: If the eggplant is too wide to fit on the mandoline whole, halve it lengthwise and slice each half into long strips ⅛ inch thick.

Prepare the eggplant: In a shallow bowl, combine the bread crumbs, oregano, 2 teaspoons kosher salt, 1 teaspoon black pepper, the parmesan, and pecorino. Place the flour in another shallow bowl and the beaten eggs in a third bowl. Season the beaten eggs with 1 teaspoon kosher salt and 1 teaspoon black pepper.

Working one slice at a time, dredge the eggplant in the flour to coat both sides, shaking off any excess. Dip the eggplant in the egg, allowing the excess to drip off. Coat the eggplant in the bread crumbs, pressing evenly to coat, then shake off any excess. Place the breaded eggplant on a sheet pan and set aside.

Line a second sheet pan with paper towels. In a large heavy-bottomed sauté pan, heat ⅔ cup of the olive oil over medium-high heat. Working in batches to avoid overcrowding, cook the eggplant slices, turning once, until golden brown, about 5 minutes. Transfer to the paper towels. Season generously with salt. Repeat with the remaining slices, wiping out the skillet and adding the remaining oil as needed. Allow the eggplant to cool to room temperature.

Eggplant

3 cups Italian seasoned bread crumbs, store-bought or homemade (page 298)

2 teaspoons dried oregano (ideally home-dried, page 301)

3 teaspoons kosher salt, plus more for seasoning

2 teaspoons ground black pepper

¾ cup finely grated Parmigiano-Reggiano cheese

½ cup finely grated pecorino cheese (preferably Pecorino Toscano)

1½ cups all-purpose flour

5 large eggs, beaten

2 pounds Italian eggplant (2 to 3 medium eggplants), peeled and sliced lengthwise ⅛ inch thick on a mandoline

1⅓ cups extra-virgin olive oil

To assemble

3 cups finely grated Parmigiano-Reggiano cheese

1 cup finely grated pecorino cheese (preferably Pecorino Toscano)

5½ cups 10-Minute San Marzano Tomato Sauce (page 95)

20 basil leaves, large leaves roughly torn

4 cups shredded whole-milk mozzarella cheese

2 cups Oven-Dried Tomatoes (page 302), or store-bought oil-packed sun-dried tomatoes, drained and roughly chopped (optional)

RECIPE CONTINUES

To assemble: Preheat the oven to 350°F.

In a medium bowl, combine the parmesan and pecorino cheeses. Spread 1½ cups of the tomato sauce on the bottom of a 9 × 13-inch baking dish. Top the sauce with a single layer of the breaded eggplants. Drizzle another 1 cup of tomato sauce evenly across the top of the eggplants. Sprinkle 1 cup of the parmesan-pecorino mixture in an even layer across the top. Place another layer of breaded eggplants on top of the cheese, repeating with another layer of the tomato sauce and cheese mixture on top.

On top of this layer, arrange 10 of the basil leaves and sprinkle with 2 cups of the shredded mozzarella. Repeat with another layer of eggplant, tomato sauce, parmesan-pecorino mixture, and half of the dried tomatoes (if using). Add a fourth and final layer of the eggplant, tomato sauce, parmesan-pecorino mixture, and the remaining dried tomatoes (if using). Top with the remaining 10 basil leaves and 2 cups mozzarella.

Cover with foil, ensuring the foil doesn't touch the cheese (or else it will stick) and bake for 45 minutes. Remove the foil and bake until the cheese on top is golden brown and bubbling, another 10 minutes. Let rest for 30 minutes before slicing.

Parm can be served hot, at room temperature, or cold. Leftovers keep, tightly covered in the refrigerator, for up to 3 days, or frozen for up to 3 months. If frozen, thaw in the refrigerator before baking.

Polenta Rossa with Eggs & Roasted Tomatoes

SERVES 4 TO 6

The backstory here is simple: We just thought it would be cool to cook polenta with tomato instead of milk, to give it a unique color and flavor. And we were right! Eat this baked polenta for breakfast or brunch, or for dinner, rounded out with toasted bread and olive oil, or a simple green salad. Mixing in the cheese before it goes in the oven keeps the polenta soft as it bakes, making for one luxurious casserole.

———

Preheat the oven to 425°F.

Place a colander over a medium bowl and pour the canned tomatoes into it. Carefully remove 4 tomatoes, gently break them into halves lengthwise, and place in a small baking dish. Add ½ teaspoon of the salt, the sugar, and 2 tablespoons of the olive oil to the tomatoes in the baking dish and gently toss. Roast in the oven until lightly browned and slightly caramelized, about 30 minutes. (When done, remove the baking dish but leave the oven on and reduce the temperature to 350°F.)

Meanwhile, place the remaining tomatoes and all the remaining liquid in the blender. Blend on high until pureed. You should have 2 to 2½ cups. Add enough stock to make a total of 5½ cups of liquid. Set aside.

In a medium pot, heat the remaining ¼ cup olive oil over medium-high heat. Add the garlic, oregano, ¼ teaspoon of the black pepper, and the remaining 1 tablespoon plus 1½ teaspoons salt and cook until the garlic is lightly toasted, 1 to 2 minutes. Add the pureed tomato mixture and stir to combine, cooking until the liquid reaches a boil, 1 to 2 minutes.

Slowly pour in the polenta, whisking continually to avoid lumps. It will bubble and splatter, so work carefully. Reduce the heat to medium-low and continue to cook, stirring continually, until the mixture thickens, 2 to 3 minutes. Whisk in the mozzarella, butter, and ½ cup of the parmesan. Mix well to combine, until the cheese has melted. Remove from the heat.

1 (28-ounce) can whole tomatoes (preferably San Marzano DOP)

1 tablespoon plus 2 teaspoons kosher salt

1 teaspoon sugar

¼ cup plus 2 tablespoons extra-virgin olive oil, plus more for drizzling

3 to 4 cups vegetable stock or unsalted chicken stock, store-bought or homemade (page 299)

2 tablespoons finely chopped garlic

¼ teaspoon dried oregano (ideally home-dried, page 301)

½ teaspoon freshly ground black pepper

1¼ cups (8 ounces) instant polenta

1 cup shredded whole-milk mozzarella cheese

½ cup (1 stick) unsalted butter, cubed

1 cup finely grated Parmigiano-Reggiano cheese

4 to 6 large eggs

½ teaspoon flaky finishing salt, such as Maldon (optional)

10 basil leaves, large leaves roughly torn

Spray a 9 × 13-inch baking dish with nonstick cooking spray. Pour in the polenta. Arrange the roasted tomatoes across the surface of the polenta. Let cool slightly, about 10 minutes.

Using a large spoon, create 4 to 6 deep divots on the top of the polenta (the number of divots will depend on the number of eggs), equally spaced out. Crack an egg into each of the divots. Top the dish with the remaining ½ cup parmesan.

Transfer to the oven and bake until the egg whites have set but the yolk is still runny, 18 to 20 minutes. Remove from the oven and drizzle with a generous amount of olive oil, the flaky salt, and the remaining ¼ teaspoon black pepper. Top with the torn basil leaves.

Serve immediately. Leftovers keep, tightly sealed in the refrigerator, for 1 to 2 days. Leftovers can be reheated, tightly covered with plastic wrap, in the microwave, or covered with foil in a low oven.

Savoy Cabbage with Browned Butter, Tomato & Mozz

SERVES 4 TO 6

Think of this hearty vegetarian main as a cross between cabbage parm and stuffed cabbage. Cabbage and butter are a perfect combination—browning the butter here brings out its nutty flavor, while caramelizing the cabbage to a deep golden brown in said butter adds incredible depth to the dish. This is a substantial dish on its own, and can be served alongside a simple green salad to round out a meal.

———

Preheat the oven to 400°F.

Remove any damaged outer leaves and cut the cabbage in half, cutting directly through the middle of the core in order to keep the halves intact. Cut each half through the core again. Cut each quarter through the core one final time to yield 8 even wedges.

Heat a large cast-iron or heavy-bottomed skillet over medium heat. Working in batches to avoid overcrowding, place 4 of the wedges and 8 tablespoons (1 stick) of the butter. As the butter melts, add ½ teaspoon of the salt to the butter. With a large spoon begin basting the cabbage with the melted butter. Continually baste and cook until the butter browns, has a nutty smell, and the cabbage is dark golden brown, about 5 minutes. If the butter begins to smoke or smells burnt, reduce the heat. Remove the cabbage and place it in a 9 × 13-inch baking dish, seared-side up. Pour the butter out of the pan into a large bowl and set aside.

Wipe out the pan and repeat the browning and searing process with the remaining butter, cabbage, and salt. Place the second batch of cabbage in the baking dish and pour the butter from the pan into the bowl with the reserved butter.

Add the tomato sauce to the bowl with the butter and whisk until incorporated. Carefully pour all of the tomato-butter sauce around the cabbage. Top the cabbage with all of the mozzarella and ½ cup of the parmesan.

1½- to 2-pound head Savoy cabbage

1 cup (2 sticks) unsalted butter

1 teaspoon kosher salt

4 cups 10-Minute San Marzano Tomato Sauce (page 95)

1 cup shredded whole-milk mozzarella cheese

1 cup finely grated Parmigiano-Reggiano cheese

½ cup Crispy Garlic Bread Crumbs (page 299)

¼ cup extra-virgin olive oil

¼ cup roughly chopped parsley

Roast until the cheese is melted and golden and the sauce is bubbling, about 5 minutes. Remove from the oven and top with the remaining ½ cup parmesan, the bread crumbs, olive oil, and parsley.

Serve directly out of the baking dish. Leftovers keep, tightly covered in the refrigerator, for up to 3 days.

Sesame-Seared Fish with Sicilian Red Pesto

SERVES 4

Here's a versatile fish recipe that's hearty in flavor but light on the palate. Scott likes to say it has the muscle memory of fried fish minus the actual deep-frying. *Pesto rosso* (red pesto) is also known as *pesto alla trapanese*, hailing from Trapani on the west coast of Sicily. It utilizes umami-forward Sicilian ingredients (dried tomatoes, oil-cured olives, toasted almonds) to make a rich pesto with a depth of flavor. The sesame pairs well with the tomato in the pesto—think about how delicious it is to dunk sesame-crusted Italian bread into tomato sauce, and you have the right idea.

———

NOTE: We call for blitzing the panko in the food processor to make it smaller and more even in size, which helps make a crispier crust. Feel free to use whatever thin-cut fillets look freshest at the market (we suggest several options); just be sure the fillets are a uniform thickness so they cook evenly.

3 large egg whites

4 teaspoons cornstarch

½ cup toasted sesame seeds

1 cup panko bread crumbs, pulsed for 30 seconds in a food processor until finely ground

4 skin-on fillets (4 to 4½ ounces each, ½ inch thick), such as branzino, sea bass, or flounder, or other mild whitefish

Kosher salt

4 tablespoons neutral oil, such as vegetable

4 tablespoons extra-virgin olive oil

1 cup Red Pesto (recipe follows)

10 basil leaves, large leaves roughly torn

Preheat the oven to 350°F.

In a small bowl, whisk together the egg whites and cornstarch until well incorporated and foamy. In a separate bowl, mix the toasted sesame seeds and processed panko crumbs.

Season each side of the fish fillets with ¼ teaspoon kosher salt. Working one at a time, dip each fillet, skin-side only (if no skin, just dip one side of the fish), into the egg white mixture. Allow the excess egg to drip off, then press the eggy side of the fish into the sesame breading. Transfer to a large plate, breading-side up, and repeat with the remaining fish.

Heat a large nonstick sauté pan over medium heat. Add 2 tablespoons of the neutral oil along with 2 tablespoons of the olive oil. Carefully place 2 fish fillets in the pan, breading-side down, and cook until the breading is golden brown, 1 to 2 minutes. Remove and place, breading-side up, in a baking dish. Repeat the process with fresh oil and the remaining fish.

Place the baking dish in the oven and roast until the fish is just cooked through and firm to the touch, 4 to 6 minutes.

To serve, spoon 1 cup of the red pesto on and around the fish, dispersing it evenly across all fillets. Scatter basil leaves across the surface and serve immediately, with any remaining pesto on the side. This dish is best made and eaten day-of.

Red Pesto

MAKES ABOUT 1½ CUPS

½ cup roughly chopped dry-pack sun-dried tomatoes

¼ cup roughly chopped toasted blanched almonds

2 garlic cloves, grated on a Microplane

1 teaspoon sugar

½ teaspoon kosher salt

Pinch of crushed red pepper flakes

1 cup extra-virgin olive oil

1 tablespoon fresh lemon juice

2 tablespoons thinly sliced pitted oil-cured black olives

6 basil leaves, chopped

In a food processor, combine the sun-dried tomatoes, almonds, garlic, sugar, salt, and pepper flakes. Pulse until a paste forms, about 1 minute. Transfer to a small bowl and whisk in the olive oil, lemon juice, black olives, and chopped basil. Pesto can be stored in the refrigerator for up to 3 days.

Chicken Milanese with Fresh Fennel, Herbs, Honey & Mustard

SERVES 4

You see veal or chicken Milanese on every Italian-American restaurant menu, and this is a particularly American version, loosely inspired by the always stylish combo of chicken tenders with honey mustard. To class it up a bit, we turn to mustard powder and turmeric, which add a vibrant golden hue to the breading; there's also fennel seed to tie the flavor back to the fennel salad on top. The cool, herby salad is a good contrast to the hot, crispy chicken—this dish is really all about textural and temperature contrast. It comes together quickly, for what we think is a peppier, brighter take on a classic. *See photo on pages 224–225.*

———

Fill a medium bowl with ice and water. Cut the fennel bulb in half and remove the core at the base. With a chef's knife or on a mandoline, very thinly slice the fennel. Add to the ice bath and soak for 10 minutes to crisp up. Drain and dry thoroughly with a salad spinner or on paper towels.

Meanwhile, prepare the chicken: Working with one at a time, place a chicken breast in a freezer bag and pound with a meat mallet or tenderizer until evenly pounded to about ¼ inch thick.

Set up a breading station in three shallow bowls: In one bowl, whisk together the panko, paprika, granulated garlic, oregano, mustard powder, turmeric, fennel seeds, black pepper, 2 teaspoons of the salt, and the parmesan. In a second bowl, whisk together the flour and potato starch. In a third bowl, whisk the eggs, lemon zest, and remaining 1 teaspoon salt. Set up the bowls in a row in this order: flour, egg, panko.

Working with one piece at a time, dredge the chicken in flour to coat both sides, shaking off the excess. Dip the chicken in the egg, allowing the excess to drip off. Coat the chicken in the panko mixture, carefully pressing the breading to the chicken so it adheres evenly. Set the breaded chicken aside.

Salad

1 large fennel bulb

15 oil-cured olives, pitted and roughly chopped

5 sprigs dill, fronds picked from stems

12 basil leaves, roughly torn

¾ cup thinly sliced scallions (4 to 6 scallions)

⅓ cup Cured Lemons (page 306)

½ cup Honey-Mustard Dressing (recipe follows)

¼ cup finely grated Parmigiano-Reggiano cheese

Chicken

4 boneless, skinless chicken breasts (6 ounces each)

1½ cups panko bread crumbs

1 teaspoon sweet paprika (preferably Hungarian)

2 teaspoons granulated garlic

2 teaspoons dried oregano (ideally home-dried, page 301)

2 teaspoons mustard powder

½ teaspoon ground turmeric

2 teaspoons fennel seeds

1 teaspoon freshly ground black pepper

3 teaspoons kosher salt

½ cup finely grated Parmigiano-Reggiano cheese

½ cup all-purpose flour

1 tablespoon potato starch

3 large eggs

Grated zest of 1 lemon

½ cup extra-virgin olive oil

In a large sauté pan, heat the olive oil over medium-high heat. Add the breaded chicken breasts, one by one, flipping once, until golden brown on both sides, 2 to 3 minutes total. Remove the chicken from the pan and place on a plate lined with paper towels. Blot the top of the chicken with another paper towel.

Once all of the chicken is cooked, assemble the salad: In a large bowl, toss together the fennel, olives, dill, basil, scallions, cured lemons, and dressing.

To serve, place the cooked chicken on individual plates and top with the dressed salad. Sprinkle the parmesan over the salad. Leftover chicken and leftover salad keep, stored tightly in the refrigerator, for up to 3 days.

Honey-Mustard Dressing

MAKES ABOUT 1¼ CUPS

⅓ cup rice vinegar

1 tablespoon plus 1 teaspoon Dijon mustard

¼ cup honey

1 teaspoon freshly ground black pepper

½ teaspoon dried oregano (ideally home-dried, page 301)

1 teaspoon kosher salt

2 garlic cloves, grated on a Microplane

1 tablespoon fresh lemon juice

1 teaspoon sriracha sauce

⅓ cup extra-virgin olive oil

In a small bowl, whisk together the rice vinegar, Dijon mustard, honey, black pepper, oregano, salt, garlic, lemon juice, sriracha, and olive oil. The dressing keeps, tightly covered in the refrigerator, for up to 4 days.

Clockwise from top left:

Steak al Limone 235

Chicken Milanese with Fresh
  Fennel, Herbs, Honey & Mustard
  222

Saltimbocca-Style Fennel with
  Prosciutto & Fontina 257

Mushrooms in Gorgonzola Cream
  Sauce 253

Charred Broccoli with Pecorino
  & Toasted Sesame 249

Eggplant Agrodolce with Spiced
  Pignoli Brittle 254

Chicken Parm

SERVES 6

Chicken parm is the ultimate crowd-pleaser of the parm world. Who cares if it's an entirely American invention? We challenge you to find someone who doesn't like the combination of breaded chicken, tangy tomato sauce, and gooey melted cheese. (Sorry, vegetarians.)

We set out to make the best possible version of this classic, perfecting the handful of qualms we tend to have with the original. We add a touch of potato starch to the chicken breading to help keep it extra crisp; chicken parms all too often dissolve into mush under the weight of all that sauce and cheese. We urge you to cook the chicken in a cast-iron skillet, if possible—cast-iron conducts heat more evenly and therefore creates a perfectly craggy, crispy crust. And we use a combination of cheeses here—parm, pecorino, and mozz—that we think strikes the perfect balance of tangy, salty, and creamy.

This parm is great served hot or cold, and though some people pair chicken parm with pasta, we prefer eating it with a salad with an acidic dressing to help cut through all the richness. *See photos on page 210–211.*

Set up a breading station in three shallow bowls: In one bowl, combine the bread crumbs, potato starch, parmesan, pecorino, oregano, granulated garlic, and 1 teaspoon each of the salt and pepper. In a second bowl, season the beaten eggs with a pinch of salt and pepper. Place the flour in the third bowl. Arrange the bowls in a row in this order: flour, egg, bread crumbs.

Prepare the chicken: Working with one at a time, place a chicken breast in a freezer bag and pound with a meat mallet or tenderizer until evenly pounded to about ¼ inch thick. Cut each chicken breast in half crosswise. Season with salt and pepper.

Working with one piece at a time, dredge the chicken in flour to coat both sides, shaking off the excess. Dip the chicken in the egg, allowing the excess to drip off. Coat the chicken in the breading mixture, carefully pressing the breading to the chicken so it adheres evenly. Set the breaded chicken aside.

In a large Dutch oven or cast-iron pan, heat the olive oil and vegetable oil together over medium-high heat.

Breading

2 cups Italian seasoned bread crumbs, store-bought or homemade (page 298)

¼ cup potato starch

½ cup finely grated Parmigiano-Reggiano cheese

¼ cup finely grated pecorino cheese (preferably Pecorino Toscano)

4 teaspoons dried oregano (ideally home-dried, page 301)

1 tablespoon granulated garlic

1 teaspoon kosher salt, plus more for seasoning the eggs

1 teaspoon freshly ground black pepper, plus more for seasoning the eggs

2 large eggs, beaten

½ cup all-purpose flour

Chicken

3 boneless, skinless chicken breasts (about 2 pounds total)

Kosher salt and freshly ground black pepper

1 cup extra-virgin olive oil

½ cup neutral oil such as vegetable

To assemble

1½ cups shredded whole-milk mozzarella cheese

1½ cups finely grated Parmigiano-Reggiano cheese

½ cup finely grated pecorino cheese (preferably Pecorino Toscano)

4 cups 10-Minute San Marzano Tomato Sauce (page 95)

15 basil leaves, large leaves roughly torn

Working in batches to avoid overcrowding, add half of the chicken and cook, turning once, until golden brown on both sides, 3 to 5 minutes. Set aside in a 9 × 13-inch baking dish. Season with salt. Repeat with the remaining chicken.

To assemble: Set the oven to broil.

In a medium bowl, mix together the mozzarella, parmesan, and pecorino. Cover the chicken with the tomato sauce, distributing the sauce evenly. Top with the cheese mixture, dispersing evenly over the chicken. Place the chicken in the oven and broil until the sauce is bubbling and the cheese is melted, 4 to 5 minutes.

Garnish with basil and serve immediately. Leftovers keep, tightly covered in the refrigerator, for up to 3 days.

Chicken Scarpariello with Sweet & Sour Vinegar Peppers

SERVES 6

A one-pot wonder, this sweet-and-sour braised chicken with sausage and peppers packs a flavorful punch with minimal effort. Scarpariello is a true Italian-American dish, in that we've never seen it in Italy. The name translates to "shoemaker's chicken," allegedly because even the family of a poor shoemaker could cobble together the ingredients to make it. Recipes typically call for bell peppers and vinegar, but we use Anaheim or poblano chiles, which are spicier and have a more concentrated pepper flavor, along with pickled deli peppers for brightness and acidity, and a touch of heat and garlicky flavor from sriracha sauce. It's perfect for a cold day, served alongside crusty Italian bread, or a simple pasta like penne with butter.

---

1 pound sweet Italian sausage, casings removed

6 bone-in, skin-on chicken thighs (about 8 ounces each)

2 teaspoons kosher salt

1 teaspoon freshly ground black pepper

3 tablespoons vegetable oil

2 Anaheim or poblano chiles, seeded and cut into ¼-inch strips

6 garlic cloves, finely chopped

1 teaspoon dried oregano (ideally home-dried, page 301)

1 teaspoon fennel seeds

4 sweet pickled cherry peppers (such as B&G), seeded and chopped

1 cup sweet pickled cherry pepper liquid

2 tablespoons rice vinegar

2 cups chicken stock, unsalted store-bought or homemade (page 299)

2 tablespoons sriracha sauce

2 tablespoons honey

1 tablespoon sugar

2 tablespoons unsalted butter

2 teaspoons fresh lemon juice

Roll the sausage into meatballs the size of golf balls and set aside. Season the chicken thighs with the salt and pepper.

In a large heavy-bottomed pot or Dutch oven, heat the vegetable oil over high heat until almost smoking. Add the chicken in a single layer, skin-side down, to sear (working in batches if necessary to avoid overcrowding). Reduce the heat to medium-high and cook the chicken until evenly golden brown and crispy, 8 to 10 minutes. Do not flip. Remove the chicken from the pot and set aside. Do not wash the pot.

Return the pot to medium-high heat and add the sausage meatballs to sear on all sides until evenly golden brown, about 5 minutes. Remove the sausage from the pot and set aside with the chicken. Do not wash the pot.

Return the pot to medium heat and add the Anaheim chiles and cook until soft, 2 to 3 minutes, scraping up any browned bits on the bottom. Add the garlic, oregano, and fennel seeds and cook until the garlic is golden, about 1 minute. Stir in the pickled deli peppers, pepper pickling liquid, rice vinegar, chicken stock, sriracha, honey, and sugar. Bring to a simmer over medium-high heat and cook until the volume is reduced by two-thirds, about 10 minutes.

Add the chicken, skin-side up, and any accumulated juices to the pot. The sauce should come about halfway up the sides of the chicken. Simmer for 12 minutes, stirring the sauce occasionally but leaving the chicken skin-side up.

Nestle in the meatballs around the chicken. Cover, reduce the heat to medium-low, and cook until a thermometer inserted into the thickest part of a chicken thigh reads 160°F and the sauce has thickened to a loose, glossy glaze (you should be able to draw a line along the bottom of the pot with your spoon), another 10 minutes.

Stir in the butter and lemon juice. Serve immediately. Leftovers keep, tightly covered in the refrigerator, for up to 3 days.

Campari & Orange Sticky Ribs

SERVES 4 TO 6

If these sticky red-stained ribs remind you of Chinese-American takeout, then we've done our job, though we've added our own twist in the form of a Campari-infused glaze. Herbaceous Campari and orange are a classic pairing, and we find that the bitterness and aromatic nature of the liqueur goes well with pork. It's a subtle way of adding aromatics, though we bump up the flavor with ginger and garlic, too.

Eat these with your fingers—they're sticky-sweet and messy. We like serving them with the Cacio e Pepe Pastina (page 124) in the winter, and the caprese salad on page 87 with grilled stone fruit in lieu of the persimmons in the summer.

———

Make the ribs: Preheat the oven to 300°F. Line a sheet pan with foil.

Clean the ribs by rinsing them with cold water and patting them dry. Using a clean, dry kitchen towel, remove the membrane on the underside of the racks by pulling gently. It should come off in one piece.

In a small bowl, stir together the olive oil, garlic, ground ginger, orange zest, salt, and pepper. Rub the ribs all over with the spice mixture and place them meaty-side up on the lined sheet pan. Cover tightly with foil, place in the oven, and bake for 2 hours.

Meanwhile, prepare the sauce: In a large pot, heat the oil over medium-high heat. Add the garlic, fresh ginger, and salt and cook, stirring continually with a wooden spoon, until the garlic is fragrant and just turning pale gold, 2 to 3 minutes. Add the Campari, orange juice, vinegar, sugar, honey, and red food coloring (if using) and stir well to combine. Bring to a boil over medium-high heat, then reduce the heat to low and keep the sauce at a simmer, stirring often, until its volume reduces by three-quarters, 35 to 45 minutes. Large bubbles should appear, and the sauce should be thick enough to coat the back of a spoon.

Stir in the lemon juice. You should have 1½ to 2 cups of thick, sticky sauce. Set aside somewhere warm.

Ribs

2 racks baby back ribs (3 to 4 pounds total)

¼ cup extra-virgin olive oil

4 garlic cloves, grated on a Microplane

2 teaspoons ground ginger

Grated zest of 1 orange

3 tablespoons kosher salt

2 teaspoons freshly ground black pepper

Sauce

2 tablespoons neutral oil, such as vegetable

1 head garlic, peeled and finely chopped

1 tablespoon finely chopped peeled fresh ginger

2 tablespoons kosher salt

1½ cups Campari

1 cup orange juice (strained of pulp)

1 cup rice vinegar

1 cup sugar

1 cup honey

3 drops red food coloring (optional)

2 tablespoons fresh lemon juice

1 orange, sliced into half-moons, for garnish

Remove the ribs from the oven and check for doneness—a cake tester or tip of a sharp knife should slide in easily. If not, return to the oven for another 10 to 20 minutes, until tender.

Allow the ribs to rest, still covered, until cool enough to handle. Cut between the bones into individual pieces and transfer to a large bowl. Carefully pour the warm Campari glaze over the ribs and toss carefully to coat. (If the glaze has cooled and thickened too much to toss, reheat it over medium-low heat, stirring continually, until heated through, 2 to 3 minutes.)

To serve, place the ribs on a platter and top with sliced oranges. Leftover ribs keep, covered in the refrigerator, for up to 3 days.

Pork Chop alla Pizzaiola

SERVES 4

Alla pizzaiola, meaning "in the style of the pizza maker," is a preparation usually done with steak that involves broiling tomato sauce and cheese on top of the meat, like a pizza. We jazzed it up a bit, swapping out beef for pork, and making a coarse tomato/pickled pepper sauce that caramelizes as it cooks, infusing a delicious sweet-and-sour flavor into every bite. We top the whole thing with a pesto-marinated provolone, which melts into perfect herby, creamy dollops against the punchy tomato-pepper sauce.

Serve these chops with Roasted Potatoes Oreganata (page 251), Broccoli Rabe & Provolone Gratin (page 250), or a classic mac and cheese.

---

4 boneless pork chops, 1 inch thick (about 7 ounces each)

1 cup chopped seeded sweet pickled cherry peppers, such as B&G

4 plum tomatoes (about 1 pound), seeded and roughly chopped

4 garlic cloves, grated on a Microplane

¼ cup rice vinegar

3 tablespoons sugar

1 tablespoon kosher salt

1 teaspoon dried oregano (ideally home-dried, page 301)

½ cup extra-virgin olive oil

1 cup Pesto-Marinated Provolone (page 40)

12 basil leaves

Trim the excess fat from each chop if necessary. Place each chop between two plastic freezer bags (not inside of the bag, just between two of them). Using a meat mallet or heavy-bottomed skillet, pound each chop to about ½ inch thick. Prick the chops all over with a fork on both sides.

In a food processor, combine the pickled peppers, tomatoes, garlic, vinegar, sugar, salt, and oregano and pulse until combined and slightly chunky, like a salsa. While the machine is running, slowly drizzle in the olive oil to combine. The sauce will become slightly smoother, but should still be chunky—you want to process it only enough to incorporate the oil. You should have about 3 cups of marinade.

Divide the chops between two plastic freezer bags (two chops per bag) and pour half of the marinade into each bag, massaging the meat to ensure even coverage. Set aside in the refrigerator for at least 4 hours, or up to overnight.

Preheat the oven to broil.

Place the pork chops in a baking dish and top with any marinade from the bags. Place under the broiler and cook until the tomatoes have gently browned and a thermometer inserted in the middle of the pork reads 135°F, 12 to 15 minutes.

Remove the chops from the broiler and evenly distribute the pesto-marinated provolone across each chop. Return the baking dish to the broiler for another 2 minutes to melt the cheese.

Transfer the chops to a serving platter and garnish with fresh basil. Serve immediately. Leftovers keep, tightly covered in the refrigerator, for up to 3 days.

Pizza Chiena (Easter Pie)

SERVES 8 TO 10

The majority of the recipes in this book are our updated spins on old classics, but this one is so special we're presenting it exactly as Scott's grandparents made it for decades. It's his most formative cooking memory from childhood: Every Easter, they'd turn their Queens apartment into a miniature Easter pie factory, making 10 or 12 each year, on a wooden board that Scott's grandpa built specifically for rolling out the dough. His grandma cut every single ingredient in the filling with a paring knife, which meant the pies took two days to make, and each year they'd make Scott and his brother their own mini pies with the leftover dough scraps. We wanted to preserve that memory and the tradition that comes with it by keeping this recipe virtually untouched.

Easter pie is known by several names across Italy, including *pizza chiena, pizza rustica,* and *pizza gain.* It's an impressive, stuffed savory pastry typically made with cured meats, egg, and cheese, traditionally enjoyed on Easter, after the meatless season of Lent that precedes the holiday. Every family makes theirs a little differently—some fillings have more eggs or salami, some are made with puff pastry, etc. Scott's grandma's recipe uses raw sausage and cooked ham, simmering them together with water and reserving the flavorful, fat-infused liquid to make the dough.

You don't have to make this for Easter specifically, and you can serve it at any temperature, ideally alongside a simple green salad with an acidic vinaigrette to help cut the richness.

11 large eggs

1½ pounds smoked ham steak

¾ pound sweet Italian sausage

¾ pound spicy Italian sausage

1 teaspoon sweet paprika (preferably Hungarian)

About ½ cup vegetable shortening or lard

3 cups all-purpose flour

1 teaspoon baking powder

2 teaspoons kosher salt

2 cups coarsely grated sharp provolone cheese (about 7 ounces)

3 cups shredded whole-milk mozzarella cheese

½ cup roughly chopped parsley

½ teaspoon freshly ground black pepper

Set up a bowl of ice and water. Place 6 of the eggs in a medium pot and add cold water to cover by 1 inch. Set the pot over medium-high heat and bring to a boil. As soon as the water reaches a boil, remove from the heat. Cover the pot, let sit for 12 minutes, then immediately transfer the eggs to the ice water to cool. Once cool, peel the eggs and cut them lengthwise into quarters, then again into ¼-inch pieces. Transfer to a small bowl and set aside.

In a large pot, combine the ham, sweet and hot sausage, paprika, and 10 cups cold water. With a paring knife, pierce each sausage casing so the fat renders while it cooks. Bring to a boil over medium

Grandma Addario's recipe for Easter Pie

RECIPE CONTINUES

heat, then reduce the heat to maintain a simmer until the sausage is cooked through, about 30 minutes.

Remove from the heat. Using tongs, pull the meat out of the cooking liquid and set aside. Place the cooking liquid (and any fat that has melted into it) in the refrigerator to cool. Once the meat is cool enough to handle, trim all the large fat and sinew from the ham, and remove the casings from the sausages. Cut all of the meat roughly into a ¼-inch dice. You should have about 4 cups of ham and 3 cups of sausage.

Once the cooking liquid has chilled enough for the fat to separate, use a large spoon to skim off as much fat from the top as possible and place in a measuring cup. (Set the cooking broth aside.) Add as much vegetable shortening or lard to the skimmed fat as needed to come to ½ cup total of fat.

In a stand mixer with the paddle, mix the flour, baking powder, and 1 teaspoon of the salt on medium speed until just combined, about 20 seconds. Slowly add the reserved fat mixture, little by little, then add ½ cup of the cooking broth and mix on low speed until well incorporated and the dough looks slightly shaggy and isn't sticky, 1 to 2 minutes.

Transfer the dough to a clean, dry surface and knead with the palms of your hands for 1 minute until well incorporated. The dough should be soft but not sticky, and hold together in one ball. Wrap in plastic wrap and leave out on the countertop to rest for at least 30 minutes or up to 1 hour. You can make the dough in advance and store it, tightly wrapped in plastic, in the refrigerator for up to 2 days, but allow it to come to room temperature before using.

In a large bowl, whisk 4 of the eggs. Add the ham, sausage, hard-boiled eggs, sharp provolone, mozzarella, parsley, pepper, and remaining 1 teaspoon salt and mix to combine.

Preheat the oven to 375°F. Spray a 10-inch springform pan (2 inches deep) with nonstick cooking spray.

Divide the dough in half. On a clean, dry surface, evenly roll out half of the dough into an 18-inch round. Carefully ease the dough into the springform pan, trying not to stretch the dough too much, and gently press it into the corners. Some of the dough should hang over the sides of the pan by ¼ to ½ inch. Add the meat and egg mixture, packing it in firmly but gently.

Roll out the remaining half of the dough into another 18-inch round. In a small bowl, whisk the last egg. With a pastry brush, brush the egg wash on the exposed edges of the bottom piece of dough, the part that's hanging over the pan. Place the second piece of dough on top. Trim the edges of the dough with scissors or a sharp paring knife so there's a ½-inch overhang all around. Gently roll the edge over on itself, the bottom dough over the top, toward the middle of the pan until it's tightly sealed. It should look like a rope and sit inside the edges of the pan (not on top of the rim).

Brush the remaining egg wash over the top of the pie and make four 1-inch slits on top. Bake until the top of the pie is golden brown and the liquid is bubbling out of the slits, 50 to 55 minutes. Let cool for 15 minutes on a wire rack before removing from the pan. Cool for an additional 15 minutes on the rack before cutting.

Serve warm, at room temperature, or chilled, cut into wedges. Leftover pie keeps, tightly covered in the refrigerator, for up to 5 days. The pie also freezes well after cooking, for up to 3 months. Thaw in the refrigerator and reheat in a 350°F oven until hot and crispy.

Steak al Limone

SERVES 4 TO 6

Angie's family always serves grilled steak with lemon wedges—her Uncle Biagio is notorious for requesting "a lotta lemon" at family cookouts—so we decided to double-down on his favorite citrus in both the marinade and the lemon relish that garnishes the steak. We use both juice and zest in the marinade, along with fish sauce to boost umami and depth of flavor. (This one's for you, Uncle B!)

It's best to grill these steaks (ideally outdoors, though a grill pan is an acceptable substitute), so the flames can caramelize the sugar in the marinade and leave you with a slightly sweet, deliciously charred lemony flavor. *See photo on pages 224–225.*

──────

Make the marinade: In a small bowl, whisk together the oregano, salt, sugar, colatura, lemon zest, lemon juice, chiles, garlic, and olive oil. You should have about 2 cups of marinade. If making lemon relish, measure out and set aside 3 tablespoons of the marinade.

Prepare the steaks: Place the steaks in a 1-gallon plastic zip-top bag. Pour the marinade into the bag and move it around, gently massaging the meat to ensure even coverage. Place in the refrigerator to marinate for a minimum of 4 hours or up to overnight.

Take out the steaks, pat with a paper towel to remove any excess marinade, and season liberally with salt and pepper on both sides. Spray each steak on both sides with nonstick cooking spray.

Prepare a grill to medium-high heat.

Add the steak to the grill and cook to medium-rare: 2 minutes on one side, then flip and cook for another 2 minutes. Flip back to the original side and cook for 1½ minutes, then flip for a fourth time and cook for a final 1½ minutes. If there's a thick fatty edge, stand the steak on its side and sear the fat for about 30 seconds to render some of the fat. Transfer to a cutting board and let rest for 4 minutes, then cut across the grain into ¼-inch slices. Sprinkle evenly with flaky sea salt.

Marinade

1 tablespoon dried oregano (ideally home-dried, page 301)

1 tablespoon kosher salt

¼ cup sugar

2½ teaspoons colatura or fish sauce

Grated zest of 6 lemons

1 cup fresh lemon juice (about 4 large lemons)

1 teaspoon crushed Calabrian chiles in oil

2 garlic cloves, grated on a Microplane

1 cup extra-virgin olive oil

Steaks

4 New York strip steaks, about 1 inch thick (10 ounces each)

Kosher salt and freshly ground black pepper

1 tablespoon flaky sea salt, such as Maldon

½ cup Cured Lemons (optional; page 306), roughly chopped, for relish

1 lemon, cut into wedges

If making the lemon relish, in a small bowl, mix the chopped cured lemons with the 3 tablespoons reserved marinade until well combined. Spoon the relish over the steak.

Serve the steaks with lemon wedges. Leftovers keep, tightly covered in the refrigerator, for up to 4 days.

Veal Milanese da Pepi

SERVES 4

Trieste, in the northeast of Italy, holds a special place in our hearts since we honeymooned there. One of the most intriguing aspects of the food there is the influence of the former Austro-Hungarian empire. Case in point: the prevalence of "buffets," casual restaurants serving regional fare that in other parts of Italy might be known as trattorias.

Our favorite buffet, da Pepi, specializes in smoked meats, serving giant piles of the stuff with a dollop of mustard and a generous shaving of fresh horseradish. We wanted to pay homage to Buffet da Pepi and this unique corner of Italy, hence this Milanese-style veal chop coated in seasoned Stracchino cheese spread and thinly sliced speck, a smoked cured meat from northern Italy. We use pickled mustard seeds and fresh mizuna in lieu of mustard, and caraway seeds in the crust to add a rye-like flavor that's vaguely reminiscent of a pastrami sandwich.

This dish packs a flavorful punch without being heavy—the delicate veal is pounded thin and the acid from the pickled mustard seeds, pepperoncini, and lemon juice cuts through the fat from the speck. If veal chops are unavailable, substitute pork.

Make the pickled mustard seeds: In a small pot, bring ⅓ cup water, the salt, vinegar, and sugar to a boil over high heat. Place the mustard seeds in a small heatproof bowl and pour this mixture over them. Set aside to cool for about 30 minutes while you prep the veal.

Prepare the veal: Trim any excess fat from the meat, if necessary. If using chops, place each one in a plastic freezer bag and pound with a meat mallet or tenderizer until evenly pounded to about ¼ inch thick. If using cutlets, which are already pounded, this step is not necessary.

In a food processor, combine the panko, parmesan, caraway seeds, and 1 tablespoon kosher salt and process for 30 seconds until evenly combined and the panko is the consistency of coarse sand.

Pickled mustard seeds

1½ teaspoons kosher salt

½ cup rice vinegar

2 tablespoons plus 1½ teaspoons sugar

¼ cup yellow mustard seeds

Veal

4 boneless veal rib chops or veal cutlets (about 4 ounces each)

4 cups panko bread crumbs

1 cup finely grated Parmigiano-Reggiano cheese

5 tablespoons freshly ground caraway seeds

Kosher salt

5 large eggs

1 cup all-purpose flour

1 cup extra-virgin olive oil, plus more as needed

To assemble

1 cup Seasoned Stracchino Cheese Spread (page 39)

¼ pound speck or prosciutto, thinly sliced

8 pickled pepperoncini peppers, sliced into thin rounds

¼ pound mizuna or arugula

2 tablespoons extra-virgin olive oil

1 tablespoon fresh lemon juice, plus 4 lemon wedges for serving

1 small piece fresh horseradish root (about ¼ pound) or 1 tablespoon prepared horseradish

Set up a dredging station in three shallow bowls: In one bowl, spread out the panko mixture. Beat the eggs in a second bowl. Spread the flour in a third bowl. Set up the bowls in a row in this order: flour, eggs, panko.

Working one piece at a time, dredge the veal in flour to coat both sides, shaking off the excess. Dip the veal in the egg, allowing the excess to drip off. Press it into the panko mixture to evenly coat both sides.

In a large heavy-bottomed sauté pan, heat ½ cup of the olive oil over medium-high heat. Cook one piece of veal at a time, carefully sautéing each side until golden brown, 1 to 1½ minutes per side. Set the veal aside on a plate lined with a paper towel. Season with a pinch of salt on each side. Repeat with the remaining veal, replenishing the oil between batches as necessary.

To assemble: Transfer the veal to serving plates. Spread ¼ cup of the cheese spread on the top of each chop. Drape 3 to 4 slices of speck over the cheese spread, to cover the surface of the meat. Top each with 1 tablespoon drained mustard seeds and about ¼ cup of the sliced pepperoncini, spreading them around evenly across the surface.

Just before serving, dress the mizuna with the olive oil and lemon juice (if using prepared horseradish, mix it in with the olive oil and lemon juice as well) and evenly disperse it across the veal. Grate a generous amount of fresh horseradish over the top with a Microplane (you should not have much leftover, though go lighter if you like things less spicy).

Serve with lemon wedges. This dish is best made and eaten day-of.

Italian Americans love to garden. Scott's grandparents used the tiniest little edge of dirt lining their cement courtyard in Queens to grow great quantities of zucchini, peppers, and tomatoes, coaxing life out of the barest strip of land. They'd can and preserve their harvest every year, busting out sweet beans and bright pickled peppers in the dead of winter.

Angie's family had more space in Ohio, and grew everything—cucumbers, tomatoes, herbs, you name it. Her great-grandfather Antonio had his sprawling backyard garden, but so did many others in the family. Her great-grandmother Gemma always grew a steady supply of cherry tomatoes in the summer, which Angie loved snacking on as a kid, and her other great-grandmother Venora grew tart Concord grapes that begged to be popped from their thick purple skins directly into your mouth. The sweet, earthy scent of a backyard garden in the shimmering heat of summer is forever a memory we try to capture in our recipes today.

The recipes in this chapter are all vegetable-focused, and range from simple sides like spaghetti squash aglio e olio to more complex preparations like a stuffed saltimbocca-style fennel. Most of them are more recent creations, as opposed to time-honored family recipes, and are inspired by our travels to Italy and the flavors we've come to know and love in New York. But even when we veer from tradition, we always bring it back to our roots. The Japanese sweet potato, for example, is a not particularly Italian ingredient that happens to taste delicious with our homemade creamy Italian dressing. This chapter really captures our attitude toward cooking—embracing flavors and ingredients we love from around the world, and respectfully adapting them within the context of our own cuisine.

Spaghetti Squash Aglio e Olio

SERVES 4 TO 6

Here, spaghetti squash stands in for pasta; specifically, the simple-yet-classic aglio e olio preparation, most often prepared with actual spaghetti. Squash is something of a blank canvas, making it the ideal vehicle for soaking up the flavors of olive oil, garlic, red pepper flakes, and lemon. Finished with bread crumbs for texture, it's a quick and easy comforting side for all kinds of mains.

NOTE: It's important not to overcook the squash here—you want it just cooked enough to scrape out into individual spaghetti-like strands without dissolving into mush. Be sure to flip the squash when it comes out of the oven to release its steam; the flesh should still have some crunch that can withstand being sautéed in a pan.

1 spaghetti squash (3 pounds)

2 tablespoons plus ¼ cup extra-virgin olive oil

3 teaspoons kosher salt

Pinch of ground black pepper

3 garlic cloves, grated on a Microplane

1½ teaspoons dried oregano (ideally home-dried, page 301)

½ teaspoon crushed red pepper flakes

4 tablespoons (½ stick) unsalted butter

2 tablespoons fresh lemon juice

¼ cup roughly chopped parsley

¾ cup Crispy Garlic Bread Crumbs (optional; page 299)

Preheat the oven to 425°F.

Carefully cut the squash in half lengthwise and poke the skin all around with a fork. Scrape out the seeds with a large spoon and discard. Transfer to a sheet pan, cut-side up. Drizzle each half with 1 tablespoon of the olive oil, ½ teaspoon salt, and a pinch of black pepper. Rub with your fingers to disperse the seasoning evenly. Flip the squash so they're cut-side down and roast until the squash is tender, 35 to 45 minutes.

Remove from the oven and flip the squash over to cut-side up to release the steam. Let stand until cool enough to handle.

Once cool, use a fork to scrape the interior of the squash to remove the flesh in long, spaghetti-like strings. Scrape all the way down to the rind to get as much squash as possible. Set the strands aside and discard the outer shell.

In a large pot, heat the remaining ¼ cup olive oil over medium heat. Add the garlic, oregano, pepper flakes, and 2 teaspoons salt. Cook, stirring often, until the garlic is fragrant and very lightly toasted, about 2 minutes. Add the squash and stir well to incorporate.

Increase the heat to medium-high and continue cooking the squash until glistening and evenly coated with the garlic-oil mixture, 3 to 4 minutes. Stir in the butter, lemon juice, and parsley and stir well to combine, until the butter is melted, about 1 minute.

Spoon the squash onto a serving platter and top with bread crumbs, if using. Serve immediately. Leftovers keep, tightly covered in the refrigerator, for up to 4 days.

Brussels Sprouts Calabrese with Spicy Colatura Vinaigrette

SERVES 6 TO 8

The combination of citrus, chiles, sugar, and fish sauce is very common in Southeast Asian cuisine, and we love the way it hits on that sweet-sour-salty-umami bull's-eye. Those flavors work well with roasted Brussels sprouts, and we added a few things from our Italian-American pantry (roasted garlic puree, which acts as an emulsifier; crushed Calabrian chiles; and the aforementioned colatura) for good measure. The sprouts come out tangy, spicy, citrusy, and ultimately just very craveable. Note that if you're using Southeast Asian fish sauce in lieu of colatura, you may want to use a spoonful or two less than what this recipe calls for—the best way to know is to taste it for potency before measuring.

Serve these alongside a simple roasted meat—we try to avoid complexly flavored mains with this one, as it has a lot of intense flavors going on already. Any leftover dressing is great on cruciferous vegetables like broccoli or cauliflower.

Preheat the oven to 425°F. Line one or two sheet pans (the Brussels sprouts should be in a single layer) with parchment paper or silicone baking liner(s).

Make the Brussels sprouts: In a large bowl, toss the sprouts with the olive oil and salt to coat evenly. Spread in a single layer on the sheet pan(s). Roast until golden brown, rotating the pan from front to back halfway through, 25 to 30 minutes.

Meanwhile, make the dressing: In the same bowl you seasoned the sprouts in, whisk together the lemon juice, sugar, roasted garlic puree, chiles, sriracha, colatura, olive oil, honey, and salt until incorporated. You should have about 1¼ cups.

Transfer the sprouts to a serving bowl and toss with the dressing and the mint. Garnish with mint leaves.

Serve immediately.

Leftovers keep, tightly covered in the refrigerator, for up to 3 days.

Brussels sprouts

2 pounds Brussels sprouts, halved through the base

6 tablespoons extra-virgin olive oil

2 teaspoons kosher salt

¼ cup chopped mint, plus 10 to 12 picked leaves, for garnish

Dressing

½ cup fresh lemon juice (about 2 large lemons)

6 tablespoons sugar

¼ cup Roasted Garlic Puree (page 300)

1½ teaspoons crushed Calabrian chiles in oil

2 tablespoons sriracha sauce

2 tablespoons colatura or fish sauce

2 tablespoons extra-virgin olive oil

1 tablespoon honey

1 tablespoon kosher salt

Japanese Sweet Potatoes with Creamy Italian Dressing

SERVES 4 TO 6

Sweet potatoes don't need to taste like candy—we prefer this savory version, dusted with a flavorful spice mixture laced with sumac, whose tangy flavor plays off the natural sweetness of the tuber. We serve them dressed in a riff on the American salad bar stalwart, creamy "Italian" dressing—though we've never tasted anything like it in Italy.

Japanese sweet potatoes have a mildly sweet flavor and a starchy, firm texture, as opposed to orange-fleshed sweet potatoes, which get soft and mushy. If you can't find them, sub a waxy type like a Yukon Gold potato. Always start potatoes in cold water and bring them up to hot, because otherwise, the outside will cook faster than the inside—doing it this way ensures more even cooking. And we prefer old-school granulated onion and garlic, as opposed to powdered, because its coarse texture adheres to the potatoes better.

Make the potatoes: In a large pot, combine the potatoes, garlic, and 8 to 10 cups cold water (enough to cover). Add the salt. Bring to a simmer over medium heat and cook until the potatoes are fork-tender, 25 to 30 minutes. Drain the potatoes, discarding the garlic, and set aside until still warm but cool enough to handle.

With a fork, gently break each potato apart into rustic pieces 1½ to 2 inches in size. Add the pieces to a large bowl and toss with the potato starch to evenly coat on all sides. It's important that the potatoes are still warm at this point—the residual heat helps the starch adhere and activates it. This step ensures a very crispy outer coating when you fry the potatoes. Arrange the potatoes in a single layer on a sheet pan or large plate and refrigerate for 45 minutes to 1 hour to chill.

Meanwhile, make the spice mix: In a small bowl, combine the granulated onion, granulated garlic, sumac, salt, sugar, and oregano and whisk together until evenly combined. Set aside.

To finish: Pour 3 to 4 inches oil into a large heavy-bottomed pot or Dutch oven and heat over medium-high heat until it reaches about 360°F.

Potatoes

4 medium Japanese sweet potatoes (about 2 pounds total), scrubbed clean

2 heads garlic, halved horizontally

¼ cup kosher salt

1 cup potato starch

Spice mix

2 tablespoons granulated onion

2 tablespoons granulated garlic

1 tablespoon ground sumac

2 tablespoons kosher salt

2 tablespoons sugar

½ teaspoon dried oregano (ideally home-dried, page 301)

To finish

Neutral oil, such as vegetable, for deep-frying (about 8 cups)

1 cup Creamy Italian Dressing (page 305)

3 tablespoons finely grated Parmigiano-Reggiano cheese

3 tablespoons finely chopped chives

Working in batches to avoid overcrowding, fry half of the potatoes until golden brown and crispy, 3 to 4 minutes. Carefully remove with a slotted spoon and set in a large bowl and toss with half of the spice mixture. Transfer the spiced potatoes to a serving platter. Allow the oil to come back up to temperature and repeat the process with the remaining potatoes, adding them to the platter with the first batch of potatoes.

Drizzle the dressing over the potatoes in a generous coating. Garnish with parmesan and chives.

Serve immediately. This dish is best prepared and eaten day-of.

Sicilian-Style Roasted Cauliflower

SERVES 4 TO 6

For hundreds of years between the ninth and eleventh centuries, Sicily was under Arab rule, the legacy of which is apparent today in the frequent use of ingredients like honey, pistachios, golden raisins, and cinnamon. We nod to that heritage in the flavor profile here, making a vibrantly spiced roasted cauliflower with a briny sweet-and-sour vinaigrette that hits all parts of your palate. The result is a complex, eye-catching dish with a burst of bright color from the turmeric; it pairs best with simple mains, such as grilled meat or fish.

———

Preheat the oven to 450°F. Line one or two sheet pans (the cauliflower should be in a single layer) with parchment paper.

Make the spice mix: In a large bowl, combine the salt, turmeric, paprika, fennel, oregano, cinnamon, granulated garlic, and pepper.

Prepare the cauliflower: Add the olive oil to the spice mix and whisk to combine. Add the cauliflower and toss thoroughly to coat the florets evenly.

Arrange the cauliflower in a single layer on the lined sheet pan(s) and roast until golden brown and fragrant and the thickest part of the floret can be easily pierced with the tip of a paring knife, 12 to 15 minutes.

Remove from the oven and transfer to a serving platter. Gently toss the cauliflower with ½ cup of the vinaigrette.

Serve immediately. Leftovers keep, tightly covered in the refrigerator, for up to 3 days.

Spice mix

2 teaspoons kosher salt

¾ teaspoon ground turmeric

¾ teaspoon sweet paprika (preferably Hungarian)

¾ teaspoon freshly ground fennel seeds

½ teaspoon dried oregano (ideally home-dried, page 301)

¼ teaspoon ground cinnamon

2½ teaspoons granulated garlic

¼ teaspoon freshly ground black pepper

Cauliflower

¼ cup extra-virgin olive oil

2 pounds cauliflower, trimmed into 2-inch florets (about 1 large head)

½ cup Caper-Raisin Vinaigrette (recipe follows)

Caper-Raisin Vinaigrette

MAKES 1½ CUPS

In addition to the cauliflower, you can use this vinaigrette to dress roasted fish, chicken, and potatoes.

———

⅓ cup rice vinegar

⅓ cup honey

1 teaspoon kosher salt

⅔ cup golden raisins

1 tablespoon fresh lemon juice

¼ cup extra-virgin olive oil

2 tablespoons brine-packed capers, rinsed, drained, and roughly chopped

In a small pot, combine the vinegar, honey, salt, raisins, and ¼ cup water. Bring to a boil over medium heat, then reduce the heat to maintain a simmer and cook until the raisins soften and plump up, about 1 minute.

Transfer the mixture to a blender. Add the lemon juice and olive oil and blend on high until combined and smooth, about 1 minute. Add the chopped capers and stir to combine. Leftovers keep for up to 1 week in the refrigerator.

Charred Broccoli with Pecorino & Toasted Sesame

SERVES 4

This dish is pretty simple, but so tasty—when you roast broccoli at high heat, it brings out a caramelized note that pairs perfectly with the roasted flavor of toasted sesame seeds. We've found that it's easier to buy pretoasted sesame than attempting to do it ourselves; they never come out quite the same at home. Sesame is one of our favorite global ingredients—Angie grew up dusting it across Italian breads and grissini in her family's bakery, but it's also common across Asia and the Middle East, which we think is pretty cool.

It's important to evenly coat the broccoli in oil, insulating it on all sides, to ensure it roasts and browns evenly. Because this is a relatively straightforward flavor profile, the broccoli pairs well with tons of main courses and pastas: Try it with the Layered Eggplant Parm (page 213) or the Pork Chop alla Pizzaiola (page 230).

Preheat the oven to 425°F.

In a large bowl, toss the broccoli florets with the olive oil, salt, and pepper, using your hands to ensure that all sides of the broccoli are coated with oil.

Arrange the broccoli in a single layer on a sheet pan (use two pans if necessary) and roast without stirring until the thickest part of the stalk can be easily pierced with the tip of a paring knife, about 20 minutes.

Turn the broiler on. Once hot, place the pan(s) of broccoli under the broiler until the ends of the florets are dark brown and crispy, 2 to 3 minutes.

Remove the pan(s) from the broiler and return the broccoli back to the bowl it was tossed in. Toss with the soffritto and lemon juice to evenly coat.

Top with pecorino and sesame seeds and serve immediately. Leftovers keep, tightly covered in the refrigerator, for up to 3 days.

1½ pounds broccoli (about 1 large head), cut into 2-inch spears (florets and tender stalk)

¼ cup extra-virgin olive oil

1 teaspoon kosher salt

¼ teaspoon freshly ground black pepper

¼ cup Garlic & Chile Soffritto (page 300)

2 tablespoons fresh lemon juice

¼ cup finely grated pecorino cheese (preferably Pecorino Toscano)

2 teaspoons toasted sesame seeds

Broccoli Rabe & Provolone Gratin

SERVES 6

Rich, creamy, cheesy, comfort food—what could be better? We whipped this up for Thanksgiving one year when we wanted an Italian-American alternative to a green bean casserole. Broccoli rabe and provolone go hand-in-hand—the sharpness of the cheese stands up to the bitter greens, and somehow they manage to make each other better. The long cook time on the rabe mellows it out, making for a warm and comforting casserole with classic Italian flavors. Serve this with a festive main course like Chicken Parm (page 226) or Steak al Limone (page 235) for a true Italian-American feast.

Set the oven to broil.

Trim the bottom of the broccoli rabe stems if discolored and discard any yellowish leaves. Cut each stalk crosswise into three pieces (a stem, the middle, and the florets).

In a large pot, melt the butter over medium heat. Add the garlic, pepper flakes, salt, and black pepper. Increase the heat to medium-high and cook, stirring often, until the garlic is lightly toasted and the butter is foamy, 2 to 3 minutes. Add the broccoli rabe and stir well to combine, then stir in the lemon juice. Cook over medium-high heat, stirring often, until the rabe releases most of its liquid and it evaporates, 10 to 12 minutes.

Add the flour and stir well. Continue to cook over medium heat for about 2 minutes, stirring often. Stir in the milk and cook, stirring often, until the milk thickens, another 3 minutes. Add the sugar, provolone, and mozzarella and mix well to combine.

Pour the rabe mixture into a small broilerproof baking dish (such as a 12-inch oval gratin or 9-inch square). Broil until the top is browned and bubbling, 4 to 5 minutes. Remove from the oven and top with crispy shallots, if desired.

Serve immediately, straight from the cooking vessel. Leftovers keep, tightly covered in the refrigerator, for up to 3 days.

1 pound broccoli rabe

¾ cup (1½ sticks) unsalted butter, cubed

12 garlic cloves, finely chopped

½ teaspoon crushed red pepper flakes

4 teaspoons kosher salt

1 teaspoon freshly ground black pepper

¼ cup fresh lemon juice (about 1 large lemon)

2 tablespoons all-purpose or Wondra flour (see page 18)

1 cup whole milk

2 teaspoons sugar

½ cup coarsely grated sharp provolone cheese (grated on the large holes of a box grater)

½ cup shredded whole-milk mozzarella cheese

¼ cup Crispy Shallots (optional; page 305)

Roasted Potatoes Oreganata

SERVES 4 TO 6

Carb lovers, rejoice: This is a recipe for roasted potatoes with bread crumbs. It's not actually as heavy as it sounds, and there's a lot of textural contrast to keep things interesting. The potatoes are thinly sliced and roasted until soft, then tossed with a tangy bread crumb mixture and broiled crisp. The result is a sort of deconstructed gratin with all kinds of soft, crumbly, and crispy bits to enjoy. Pair these potatoes with seafood or veal for a balanced meal.

Preheat the oven to 425°F.

In a large bowl, combine the potatoes, 2 teaspoons of the salt, the pepper, olive oil, garlic, lemon zest, lemon juice, and anchovy. Mix well to ensure the potatoes are evenly coated. Arrange the potatoes in a single layer on a sheet pan (use two pans if necessary) and roast until they can be easily pierced with the tip of a paring knife, about 15 minutes.

Meanwhile, in a small bowl, combine the bread crumbs, ½ cup of the parmesan, the paprika, onion powder, dried oregano, and remaining 1 teaspoon of salt. Mix well and set aside.

Remove the potatoes from the oven and carefully transfer to a large bowl. Add the bread crumb mixture and toss to evenly coat the potatoes.

Turn the broiler on. Arrange the potatoes back on the sheet pan(s) and broil until browned and crispy, 2 to 3 minutes, watching closely as broilers vary in power.

Remove from the oven, top with the remaining 1 tablespoon parmesan, and serve immediately. Leftover potatoes keep, tightly covered in the refrigerator, for up to 3 days. Reheat in a toaster oven or low oven until crispy.

1½ pounds Yukon Gold potatoes (about 4 medium potatoes), sliced ¼ inch thick on a mandoline

3 teaspoons kosher salt

½ teaspoon freshly ground black pepper

½ cup extra-virgin olive oil

6 garlic cloves, grated on a Microplane

Grated zest of 2 lemons

3 tablespoons fresh lemon juice

1 anchovy fillet, finely chopped

½ cup Italian seasoned bread crumbs, store-bought or homemade (page 298)

½ cup plus 1 tablespoon finely grated Parmigiano-Reggiano cheese

2 teaspoons sweet paprika (preferably Hungarian)

2 teaspoons granulated onion powder

1 tablespoon dried oregano (ideally home-dried, page 301)

Angie's dad and his family on a trip to Italy

Mushrooms in Gorgonzola Cream Sauce

SERVES 4 TO 6

Between us, we refer to this dish as "mushroom noodles," but we realize that that name doesn't do justice to how unique and delicious they are. It's worth seeking out king trumpet mushrooms here, as they really do imitate the look and texture of pasta; they stay in firm tendrils the whole time. But plain old button mushrooms are fine to use, too, though they won't have quite the same visual impact. For best results, pair this rich, hearty side with steak or red meat on a chilly winter night.

———

Trim off the fibrous base of the king trumpet mushrooms (about ½ inch from the bottom of the mushroom). Slice the mushrooms in half down the middle with a knife, then carefully slice the mushroom halves lengthwise on a mandoline set at ⅛ inch thick to create long "noodles." It's okay if some of the "noodles" are shorter or break apart; use all of the mushroom. If using button mushrooms, clean them gently with a paper towel to remove any dirt. Cut large mushrooms into quarters and small ones in halves. Set aside.

In a food processor, combine the robiolina, Gorgonzola, and cream and process until smooth, about 1 minute.

In a large pot, heat the olive oil and butter over medium-high heat until the butter is melted. Add the mushrooms and stir with a silicone spatula, allowing them to gently brown on all sides, 3 to 4 minutes. Add the salt and pepper and stir to combine. Stir in the garlic and reduce the heat to medium, stirring occasionally, until the garlic is cooked through and the mushrooms release all liquid, 3 to 5 minutes.

Add the robiolina/Gorgonzola/cream mixture and mix vigorously to coat the mushrooms and create a creamy sauce. Stir in the lemon juice. Remove from the heat. Transfer the mushrooms to a serving bowl and garnish with chives.

Serve immediately. Leftovers keep, tightly covered in the refrigerator, for up to 2 days.

2 pounds large king trumpet or button mushrooms

5 ounces (about ¾ cup) robiolina (see page 19) or whipped cream cheese

3 ounces (about ⅓ cup) Gorgonzola cheese

½ cup heavy cream

¼ cup extra-virgin olive oil

3 tablespoons unsalted butter

1 tablespoon kosher salt

¾ teaspoon freshly ground black pepper

2 tablespoons finely chopped garlic (4 to 5 cloves)

1 tablespoon fresh lemon juice

2 tablespoons chopped chives, for garnish

Eggplant Agrodolce with Spiced Pignoli Brittle

SERVES 4 TO 6

Every time we visit Milan, we have a long-standing tradition of eating our last meal in the city's Chinatown, experiencing Chinese cuisine by way of local Italian ingredients. Our go-to trattoria, Hua Cheng, serves a sweet-and-sour eggplant dish that vaguely reminds us of caponata, a Sicilian eggplant specialty marked by its sweetened vinegar sauce. This is our riff on that dish, pulling in the flavors of some oft-seen caponata additions, such as pine nuts and mint.

We like to use Japanese eggplants here, which are firmer and meatier than their Italian counterparts. They do a much better job of maintaining their texture during broiling, which can reduce big eggplants to mush. The spiced pignoli brittle adds a welcome crunch, though if you don't have time to make the brittle, you can use toasted pine nuts for a similar effect.

1 pound Japanese eggplants (about 2 medium)

½ cup plus 1 tablespoon extra-virgin olive oil

1½ teaspoons plus ½ teaspoon kosher salt

2 garlic cloves, grated on a Microplane

Pinch of crushed red pepper flakes

3 tablespoons red wine vinegar

2 tablespoons fresh lemon juice

2 tablespoons sugar

2 tablespoons honey

Grated zest of 1 lemon

8 large mint leaves, roughly chopped

½ cup Spiced Pignoli Brittle (page 31), crumbled, or toasted pine nuts

---

Preheat the oven to broil.

Remove and discard the stems from the eggplants and cut them lengthwise into quarters, then crosswise into 2-inch lengths. On a baking sheet, toss the eggplant with ½ cup of the olive oil and 1½ teaspoons of the salt. Arrange in a single layer on the baking sheet, cut-sides up. Broil until the eggplant's edges are browned and the flesh is softened, 6 to 8 minutes.

While the eggplant is roasting, in a medium sauté pan, combine the remaining 1 tablespoon olive oil, ½ teaspoon salt, the garlic, and pepper flakes and cook over medium-high heat until the garlic is softened and aromatic, about 2 minutes. Add the vinegar, lemon juice, sugar, and honey and bring to a simmer.

Cook the sauce, stirring often, until it reaches a glaze consistency (its bubbles will get large as it reduces, and the mixture should coat the back of a spoon), about 2 minutes. Remove from the heat and stir in the lemon zest. Don't taste the sauce immediately, as hot sugar can burn your tongue.

Remove the eggplant from the broiler and use tongs to arrange them on a serving platter. Carefully drizzle the eggplants with the vinegar mixture. Top with fresh mint and spiced pignoli brittle and serve immediately.

This dish is best made and eaten day-of.

Saltimbocca-Style Fennel with Prosciutto & Fontina

SERVES 4 TO 6

Fennel doesn't always get the love it deserves, and there are a lot of raw preparations out there. But when roasted, this humble vegetable takes on a warm, mellow flavor, and we wanted to up the ante by layering it with cheese and prosciutto, as you would with saltimbocca.

Saltimbocca means to "jump or leap into the mouth." It's an Italian preparation commonly using veal or other thinly pounded meat cutlets; we've never seen it applied to a vegetable before. This is a cleaned-up version that feels a little fresher than usual, perfect for serving alongside a lighter protein like grilled chicken or fish. Feel free to omit the prosciutto for a vegetarian version, and swap the herbs (basil is also nice) and cheese (a melty provolone or Gruyère works, too).

¾ cup plus 3 teaspoons kosher salt

2 large or 4 small fennel bulbs, stalks and fronds discarded

4 large eggs

½ cup plus ¼ cup finely grated Parmigiano-Reggiano cheese

½ teaspoon freshly ground black pepper

1 cup Italian seasoned bread crumbs, store-bought or homemade (page 298)

1 tablespoon potato starch

⅓ cup all-purpose flour

6 to 8 thin slices Fontina cheese (about 3 ounces)

12 to 16 sage leaves

2 ounces thinly sliced prosciutto

⅔ cup extra-virgin olive oil

1 lemon, cut into wedges

In a large pot, bring 6 quarts water and ¾ cup of the salt to a rolling boil over high heat. Drop the fennel into the pot and reduce the heat to maintain a simmer. Cook until the fennel is translucent and soft, 5 to 7 minutes. Using tongs, remove the fennel from the pot and set aside to cool.

Meanwhile, preheat the oven to 350°F. Line a sheet pan with parchment paper.

Set up a breading station in three bowls: In one bowl, whisk together the eggs, ¼ cup of the parmesan, 1 teaspoon of the salt, and the black pepper. In a second bowl, mix the bread crumbs, potato starch, and remaining ½ cup parmesan. Place the flour in a third bowl. Set up the bowls in a row in this order: flour, egg, bread crumbs.

Place the cooked fennel on a cutting board, root-side down. Hold the fennel firmly with one hand while carefully slicing it into ¼-inch planks with the other, using a serrated knife and a gentle sawing motion to slice from top to root. Repeat for all the fennel. You should end up with 12 to 16 planks total.

On a clean surface, arrange half of the fennel in a single row, without overlapping. Place one small slice of the Fontina on each of the fennel slices and top each with 2 sage leaves. Divide the sliced prosciutto among the fennel planks, gently folding and placing on top of the sage, ensuring that the prosciutto does not hang over the sides. Match each fennel plank with a similarly sized plank of the remaining fennel to make a sort of sandwich. You should have 6 to 8 stuffed fennel.

Working with one at a time, bread the stuffed fennel, carefully but firmly holding each stuffed fennel like you would a sandwich. Dip it first in the flour on both sides, gently shaking off the excess. Then dip it in the egg, allowing the excess to drip off. Finally, press it gently into the bread crumbs on both sides.

In a large sauté pan, heat the olive oil over medium-high heat. Working in batches to avoid overcrowding, add the stuffed fennel and fry until golden, flipping once, 1 to 2 minutes per side. Transfer the fried fennel to the lined baking sheet.

When all of the fennel has been fried, sprinkle with the remaining 2 teaspoons salt. Transfer to the oven and bake for 12 to 14 minutes, or until the cheese is bubbling and starting to melt out of the sides.

Arrange the fennel on a platter and serve hot, with lemon wedges. Leftover fennel keeps, tightly covered in the refrigerator, for up to 3 days.

No Italian-American feast is complete without dessert, and this book wouldn't be, either, especially given our family history with baked goods.

The Rito family is descended from a long line of bakers: Angie's great-great-great-grandfather owned a bread shop in Catania, Sicily, and passed down his trade through the generations, eventually to her grandfather, who left Italy to start a new life in the US. Angie's family has run a bakery and deli, Rito's, in Cleveland since 1965, specializing in Sicilian pastries (think cannoli, cookies, cassata, and more).

Angie grew up in the bakery, quite literally: At thirteen she'd pile in with cousins and siblings to assemble cookie platters for the busy holiday season; at fifteen, she was working the storefront, bundling up tiramisù for customers; at seventeen, she was closing the shop and counting the money each night. A crew of burly men handled most of the heavy baking in the wee hours, but Angie delighted in decorating the cakes and cookies in the morning, and always wanted to see how they were made. It would be another few years before she started working in professional kitchens and began to work with fussy pastries and delicate doughs in earnest.

Today, we revel in developing desserts for the restaurant, but also in baking more at home, often using recipes that have been in the family for generations. The recipes here are a reflection of both, with some of our own tweaks: the cannoli shell recipe is the same one perfected by Angie's grandpa, with a whipped robiolina-based filling preferred by us; our tiramisù takes a staple of the genre on a trip to Vietnam with sweetened condensed milk. And we have an abundance of cookies, perfect for the holidays, because it's more fun to have a variety of little treats (remember how much we love antipasto at the start of the meal?).

While some of the recipes in this chapter are nostalgic, none of them are dated, and we've ensured that nothing here is a sugar bomb. We go for balance when it comes to the flavors in our sweets, so you can ideally eat more without feeling heavy. This chapter invites celebration; we hope to inspire you to bake with abandon.

Angie's grandpa & uncle baking at Rito's Bakery in the '70s

Angie's Aunt Maria packs up cakes with other ladies at the bakery

Rosemary & Lemon Pignoli Cookies

MAKES 10 TO 12 COOKIES

Angie's grandfather is very proud of his selection of Italian cookies, and justly so. He makes a mean pignoli, which is traditionally an almond paste cookie with pine nuts on top. But our version doubles down on pine nut flavor, with pine nuts ground into the actual dough, and on top. We also add a bit of rosemary and lemon for a twist. If desired, dust these with a bit of powdered sugar before serving, for an extra-decorative touch. *See photo on page 269.*

NOTE: Almond paste is made from equal parts ground almonds and sugar, with a bit of egg, syrup, or oil as a binder, and is usually sold in 7- or 8-ounce tubes or blocks in the baking aisle.

Preheat the oven to 350°F. Line a baking sheet with parchment paper and spray with nonstick cooking spray.

Grind the dried rosemary in a spice grinder or with a mortar and pestle into a coarse powder. In a food processor, blend ½ cup of the pine nuts until they form a paste, about 1 minute. Add the almond paste and process until well combined. Add the sugar and pulse to combine. Add the egg whites, lemon zest, salt, and rosemary and process to form a smooth dough. (At this point, the dough can be stored in an airtight container in the refrigerator for up to 3 days, or frozen for up to 2 weeks. Thaw completely before rolling.)

Place the remaining ¾ cup of pine nuts in a small bowl. Roll the dough into 1½-inch balls (about 2 tablespoons) and press the top of the ball into the whole pine nuts.

Arrange the cookies, pine nut–side up, on the lined baking sheet spacing them about 2 inches apart. Gently flatten the balls into discs about ¾ inch thick with the tips of your fingers. Bake until golden brown, rotating the pan from front to back halfway through, 15 to 17 minutes.

Let cool and serve. Leftovers keep, in an airtight container at room temperature, for up to 4 days.

1 teaspoon dried rosemary (ideally home-dried, page 301; if using store-bought use 1½ teaspoons for more flavor)

½ cup plus ¾ cup pine nuts

14 ounces almond paste (see Note), cut into 1-inch chunks (about 2 cups)

1 cup sugar

2 large egg whites

1½ tablespoons packed grated lemon zest (about 2 lemons)

1 teaspoon kosher salt

Angie's great-grandfather prepares bread in a bakery

Ginger & Lemon Ricotta Cookies

MAKES 30 COOKIES

One of the Rito Bakery's best-loved cookies is a decadent lemon number made with whipped cream and honey. Ours puts a gentle twist on the classic with the addition of ricotta and fresh ginger, which goes well with lemon and honey. The result is a moist, cakey cookie with a thin layer of zippy frosting. If you're so inclined, do as Scott's grandmother did with her version of these during the holidays, and sprinkle them with rainbow-colored nonpareils for a festive touch.

Make the cookies: In a medium bowl, whisk together the flour, baking powder, and salt. Set aside.

In a stand mixer with the paddle, cream the butter and granulated sugar on medium speed until pale and fluffy, about 2 minutes. Add the honey, ginger, and lemon zest and stir together for a few seconds to combine. Reduce the speed to low and add the ricotta and vanilla bean paste. Add the egg and mix until combined, about 1 minute. Scrape the sides as needed.

Slowly add the flour mixture with the machine running, mixing until fully combined, about 2 minutes. The dough should be thick, light, and fluffy. Cover the bowl with plastic wrap and refrigerate for at least 2 hours or up to 24 hours to chill.

Preheat the oven to 350°F. Line two baking sheets with parchment paper or silicone baking mats and spray with nonstick cooking spray.

Scoop 1-inch balls of dough (about 1 tablespoon), smoothing them gently with your hands (spray your hands with nonstick cooking spray to avoid sticking), and place on the baking sheets about 2 inches apart.

Bake until lightly golden around the edges, rotating the pans from front to back halfway through, 12 to 14 minutes.

Meanwhile, make the icing: In a small bowl, combine the milk, powdered sugar, lemon zest, lemon juice, ginger, salt, and vanilla bean paste and whisk thoroughly until smooth.

Cookies

1¾ cups all-purpose flour

1 teaspoon baking powder

2½ teaspoons kosher salt

½ cup (1 stick) unsalted butter, at room temperature

½ cup plus 2 tablespoons granulated sugar

¼ cup honey

1 teaspoon grated fresh ginger

Grated zest of 1 lemon (reserve the lemon to juice for the icing)

¾ cup whole-milk ricotta cheese

½ teaspoon vanilla bean paste

1 large egg

Icing

¼ cup whole milk

2 cups powdered sugar

Grated zest of 1 lemon

2 tablespoons fresh lemon juice

½ teaspoon grated fresh ginger (from a 1-inch piece of ginger)

½ teaspoon kosher salt

¼ teaspoon vanilla bean paste

Let the cookies cool completely on the baking sheets before icing. Transfer the cookies to a wire rack set over a baking sheet. Carefully pour the icing onto each cookie to coat, covering them completely. Allow the icing to set for about 15 minutes before serving.

Cookies keep, in an airtight container at room temperature, for up to 4 days.

Cocoa & Coffee Almond Cookies

MAKES 10 TO 12 COOKIES

Angie loves the way these Sicilian cookies look when they're finished—you coat the dough in powdered sugar before baking, so as it cooks, it expands and cracks, making a pretty design on the surface. Our version is a little more complex than the traditional cocoa-and-almond version, with coffee adding a savory note that complements the chocolate and nut flavors well. Instant coffee can be a little clumpy, so we like to hydrate it with egg whites before using.

———

In a small bowl, beat the egg whites and instant coffee together. Set aside and allow the coffee to dissolve.

In a food processor, mix the almond paste on high until it's broken into smaller pieces, about 30 seconds. Add the granulated sugar, salt, and cocoa powder and process to mix well. Add the egg white and coffee mixture and process again until smooth. Add the flour and mix well to combine. If necessary, stir in any streaks of flour with a rubber spatula.

Refrigerate the mixture for 30 minutes to chill. (At this point, dough can be stored in an airtight container in the refrigerator for up to 3 days, or frozen for up to 2 weeks. Thaw completely before scooping.)

Preheat the oven to 350°F. Line two baking sheets with parchment paper or silicone baking mats and spray with nonstick cooking spray.

Place the powdered sugar in a medium bowl. Once chilled, scoop the dough into 1½-inch balls (about 2 tablespoons) and transfer to the bowl of powdered sugar. Gently roll the cookies around to coat evenly on all sides, then place them on the baking sheets, about 6 cookies per sheet, with lots of space between them.

Bake until the cookies rise and feel slightly firm to the touch, rotating the pan from front to back halfway through, 14 to 16 minutes. The powdered sugar on the top will expand, creating a crackled pattern.

Let cool and serve. Leftovers keep, tightly covered at room temperature, for up to 4 days.

2 large egg whites

2 teaspoons instant coffee or espresso powder

¾ cup (6½ ounces) almond paste

1 cup granulated sugar

2 teaspoons kosher salt

⅓ cup unsweetened Dutch process cocoa powder

⅔ cup all-purpose flour

¾ cup powdered sugar

Pecorino & Pecan Shortbread Cookies

MAKES 20 TO 24 COOKIES

Angie's family makes these snowballs, or Italian wedding cookies, using walnuts, but instead we incorporated pecans for a sweeter flavor that reminds us of pecan pie, and added a savory element with pecorino cheese. Pecorino Romano is too sharp, salty, and lean to work for this recipe; it's worth seeking out Pecorino Toscano here, which has a softer, creamier texture and tangier flavor—all of which translates to compulsively snackable cookies.

In a stand mixer with the paddle, cream the butter, vanilla paste, and 1 cup of the powdered sugar on medium speed until light and fluffy, about 2 minutes. Add the pecorino and pecans and mix well to combine. Add the milk and salt. Mix to combine. Add the flour and mix well until fully incorporated. Refrigerate the dough for 1 to 2 hours to chill. (At this point, dough can be stored in an airtight container in the refrigerator for up to 3 days, or frozen for up to 2 weeks. Thaw completely before scooping.)

Preheat the oven to 350°F. Line two baking sheets with parchment paper or silicone baking mats.

Scoop cookies into 1-inch balls (about 1 tablespoon) and gently roll the cookie dough in your hands into smooth, even spheres. Arrange them 2 inches apart on the baking sheets.

Bake until the cookies are light golden brown on the bottom, rotating the pans from front to back halfway through, 14 to 16 minutes.

Meanwhile, place the remaining ⅔ cup powdered sugar in a medium bowl.

Remove the cookies from the oven and let rest until cool enough to handle but still warm, 3 to 4 minutes. Working in batches by hand, carefully toss the warm cookies in the bowl of powdered sugar, shaking off the excess. Return to the baking sheets to cool completely, another 10 to 15 minutes, then toss again in the remaining sugar.

Serve immediately. Leftover cookies keep, in an airtight container at room temperature, for up to 4 days.

½ cup (1 stick) unsalted butter, at room temperature

1 teaspoon vanilla bean paste

1⅔ cups powdered sugar

½ cup grated Pecorino Toscano cheese (2 ounces)

1 cup very finely chopped pecans

2 tablespoons plus 1 teaspoon whole milk

1 teaspoon kosher salt

1 cup all-purpose flour

the Rito family celebrates a birthday in the '60s

Polenta Snickerdoodles

MAKES ABOUT 20 COOKIES

Here's a play on a classic snickerdoodle—chewy, sweet, and rich, with an intense corny flavor. The polenta itself adds a nice textural element, amping up the chewiness and sandy texture, but it's worth seeking out freeze-dried corn, too, which enhances the sweetness and drives home the flavor of the polenta. (You can omit it and replace with the same amount of polenta, if you wish.) This isn't a family recipe—it's something we came up with as a new way to mash up American recipes with Italian ingredients, and the end result is a little sweet, a little savory, and exponentially craveable.

──────

NOTE: Freeze-dried corn is available at Whole Foods and many natural food stores or online; it can be ground in a spice grinder. You can also make your own with a food dehydrator. Ground freeze-dried corn can be used to enhance the corny flavor of recipes such as corn bread, corn muffins, corn cookies, and more. If you cannot find freeze-dried corn, use 5 tablespoons of instant polenta instead.

1 cup (2 sticks) unsalted butter, at room temperature

2 cups sugar

2 large eggs

2 teaspoons vanilla bean paste

2 teaspoons kosher salt

1½ cups all-purpose flour

1 cup instant polenta

5 tablespoons finely ground freeze-dried corn (see Note) or instant polenta

1½ teaspoons cream of tartar

½ teaspoon baking soda

3 tablespoons ground cinnamon

¼ teaspoon cayenne pepper

In a stand mixer with the paddle, combine the butter and 1½ cups of the sugar. Mix on medium-high speed until light and fluffy, about 3 minutes. Scrape down the bowl, add the eggs and vanilla paste, and mix on medium-high for 2 more minutes. Add the salt, flour, polenta, ground dried corn (or additional polenta), cream of tartar, and baking soda and mix briefly to combine. Cover the bowl with plastic wrap and refrigerate for 30 minutes to chill.

Preheat the oven to 350°F. Line two baking sheets with parchment paper or silicone baking mats and spray with nonstick cooking spray.

In a small bowl, stir together the remaining ½ cup sugar, the cinnamon, and cayenne. Remove the cookie dough from the refrigerator and, using your hands, roll it into 1½-inch balls (about 2 tablespoons). One by one, roll each ball in the sugar/cinnamon/cayenne mixture. Place the cookies on the baking sheets 2 to 3 inches apart. Gently press down on each cookie with the palm of your hand to slightly flatten them to ½ to ¾ inch thick.

Bake until just golden brown around the edges, rotating the pans from front to back halfway through, 10 to 12 minutes.

Let cool before serving. Cookies keep, in an airtight container at room temperature, for up to 3 days.

Clockwise from left:

Grandpa Rito's Cannoli 271
Rosemary & Lemon Pignoli Cookies 261
Tre Latte Olive Oil Cake 287

Grandpa Rito's Cannoli

MAKES 20 TO 25 CANNOLI

Making your own cannoli is a project, but it's worth it, because fresh ones are a world apart from the stale, chalky versions you find languishing in the pastry case. Angie's grandfather claims cannoli shells were the first thing he learned to make as a kid working in a bakery in Sicily. There, he mixed the dough on a big slab of marble, because the key to this dough is keeping it cold. The coldness of the dough contributes to the bubbles that form when you fry it, making for a light, crispy shell that's so delicate it almost melts in your mouth.

The shells are the trickiest part of this process; fortunately, they can be made in advance and held at room temperature for up to a week before filling. And if any of the shells come out funky or break in the process, keep them on the side and save for dipping in the filling—remember, this is supposed to be fun. (You can also make the dough and hold it in the refrigerator for up to 4 days, or freeze it for up to 1 month.)

Cannoli filling is often too sweet and heavy, but this one has whipped robiolina or cream cheese, which adds savoriness and lightens it up. There are plenty of flavor variations out there, but Angie's grandpa uses cinnamon, chocolate chips, and powdered sugar, so we do, too. Feel free to get creative with other mix-ins and decorations like toasted coconut, candied fruits, and/or nuts, and decorate the shells with chocolate, if you're so inclined. *See photo on pages 268–69.*

NOTE: You'll need a set of 5½-inch-long metal cannoli tubes (available on Amazon) to fry the shells; these help cook the dough on all sides and keep the temperature even throughout. The more tubes you can work with at a time, the faster the process will be, so consider investing in up to 10 tubes to move things along more quickly.

Make the shells: In a small bowl, mix together the sugar, honey, vinegar, lemon juice, and ice water. Stir until the sugar and honey dissolve. Set aside.

In a medium bowl, sift together the bread flour, cornstarch, allspice, and salt. Set the bowl over another bowl full of ice. Add the shortening to the flour mixture. With a plastic dough scraper or rubber

Special equipment

Pasta maker

5½ × ¾-inch metal cannoli tube forms

Shells

1 tablespoon plus 1 teaspoon granulated sugar

1 tablespoon honey

3 tablespoons white wine vinegar

1½ teaspoons fresh lemon juice

75 ml (5 tablespoons plus 2 teaspoons) ice water

2 cups bread flour, plus more for rolling out the dough

1 tablespoon plus 1 teaspoon cornstarch

Pinch of ground allspice

½ teaspoon kosher salt

2 tablespoons vegetable shortening or lard

2 large eggs

Neutral oil, such as vegetable, for deep-frying (about 8 cups)

Filling

2 cups whole-milk ricotta cheese, packed and drained overnight (see page 19)

⅔ cup plus 2 tablespoons robiolina (see page 19) or whipped cream cheese

1 cup powdered sugar

1 teaspoon kosher salt

¼ teaspoon ground cinnamon

⅔ cup mini semisweet chocolate chips

To assemble

¾ cup mini semisweet chocolate chips

½ cup powdered sugar

1 teaspoon ground cinnamon

Angie's grandfather Santo as a young boy in Sicily

spatula, cut the shortening into the flour mixture until the shortening breaks into tiny pieces no larger than a pea. In a small bowl, beat one of the eggs. Create a well in the middle of the flour mixture and add the beaten egg to the well. With a fork, stir to gradually incorporate the egg into the flour mixture, until combined. Gradually add the sugar-honey liquid mixture to the flour, mixing well with a fork, until you form a smooth but firm dough. Remove

RECIPE CONTINUES

the dough and wrap with plastic wrap. Refrigerate overnight or for up to 4 days.

Set a pasta maker to the thickest setting. Cut the dough (which should be moist and sticky) into quarters and work with one piece at a time, keeping the other pieces wrapped in plastic and set aside in the refrigerator.

Generously flour a clean surface with bread flour. With the palm of your hand, press the dough evenly on all sides into an oval shape, coating it liberally in flour.

Feed the dough through the pasta maker, rolling it smoothly with the crank. Fold the rolled dough in half crosswise, matching end to end, and gently press both sides together with your hands to seal it. Lightly flour the dough again.

Leave the pasta maker on the thickest setting and reinsert the dough, folded end first, rolling it through again smoothly with the crank. The dough should be about 10 inches long, as wide as your maker (probably 5 to 6 inches), and about as thick as two quarters. Dust again with the flour.

Repeat the folding, pressing, and rolling process two more times on the same setting, until the dough is a neat rectangular shape. Flour liberally as you feed the dough through each time. It should feel smooth and supple, and not sticky.

Adjust the setting on the pasta maker to one level thinner, then smoothly roll the dough through again.

Continue adjusting the setting on the pasta maker to one level thinner and passing the dough through each setting once, dusting with flour each time to avoid sticking, until the maker is on its thinnest setting. Cut the sheet in half if necessary for easier handling. Stop when the dough is the thickness of a dime. Set the sheet aside and cover with plastic wrap while you repeat the process with the remaining pieces of dough.

Using a pastry ring or wineglass, cut each sheet into 3½- to 4-inch rounds. You should get 20 to 25 rounds total. Dust the rounds lightly with flour and shingle them in layers on a baking sheet or large plate, then set them aside in the refrigerator, covered with plastic wrap.

In a small bowl, beat the remaining 1 egg to use as an egg wash. Wrap the dough rounds loosely around the metal cannoli tubes (see Note), sealing them shut with the egg wash. It's important to wrap loosely, so that the hot oil can get in between the tube and the dough, to help fry it on all sides.

Pour 3 to 4 inches oil into a large heavy-bottomed pot and heat until it reaches 340°F.

Working in batches, fry the cannoli shells on the tubes, stirring occasionally, until deep golden brown and little bubbles appear on the surface, about 1 minute. Using tongs, remove the shells from the frying oil and place on a plate lined with paper towels. Let cool completely on the tube before carefully removing from the tubes with your hands. To remove, hold the cannoli shell with one hand and gently twist and pull the tube with your other hand. Set aside on a clean plate. Repeat with the remaining dough until all of the shells are fried. Cannoli shells will keep, at room temperature, for 1 week.

Make the filling: In a stand mixer with the whisk, whip the ricotta on medium-high speed until smooth, about 30 seconds. Add the robiolina and whip again to combine. Add the powdered sugar, salt, and cinnamon and whip on high speed until combined, about 30 seconds. Remove the bowl from the mixer and fold in the chocolate chips. You should have about 3 cups of filling. The filling will keep, tightly covered in the refrigerator, for up to 4 days; do not add the chocolate chips to the filling until just before assembling, so they retain their texture.

To assemble: Do not fill the shells until just before serving. Transfer the filling to a piping bag fitted with a star tip, or a zip-top plastic bag with a ½-inch hole cut off one corner. Hold a cannoli shell gently in one hand and pipe the filling into one end. Turn the shell around and pipe it into the opposite end, until you feel the cream meet in the center. Gently place on a plate and sprinkle chocolate chips over the exposed filling on the ends.

In a small bowl, mix the powdered sugar and cinnamon together until incorporated. Place the mixture in a fine-mesh sieve and dust the cannoli. Serve immediately.

Ricotta Pie with Coconut & Lime

SERVES 8 TO 10

There's a ricotta and grain pie popular in Naples called *pastiera*, which is traditionally eaten around Easter. Every family has its own version, and it seems that many Italian Americans have adapted this recipe and dropped the grains from the pie entirely, resulting in a ricotta pie that's rich and creamy. Ours is adapted from Angie's great-grandmother Gemma's recipe, though we added the tropical flavors of coconut, rum, and lime to brighten up the overall flavor profile and give it an almost summery vibe. When mixed together, the flavors mellow into a comforting dessert that comes off as much lighter than you would expect from a cheese-based pie. This cake can be eaten once cooled to room temperature, though it's best after chilling overnight in the refrigerator.

Make the crust: In a food processor, process the coconut until finely chopped, about 1 minute. Add the sugar, flour, cinnamon, salt, and baking powder and pulse until combined. Add the cold butter and pulse 4 to 6 times, until the butter is the size of peas. Add the rum and vanilla paste and pulse 3 to 5 times to incorporate. Pour the egg yolks into the spout of the lid one by one, pulsing each time to incorporate. Pulse until the dough comes together in a ball. (If the dough is slightly crumbly, form together into a ball with your hands.)

Scrape the dough out onto a clean floured surface, roll into a ball, and flatten into a disc. Wrap with plastic wrap and refrigerate for at least 1 hour or up to 24 hours, until completely chilled.

Preheat the oven to 350°F.

Place a piece of clean parchment paper on a clean work surface and dust it with flour. Place the dough on the parchment, dust it with flour, and cover with a second piece of parchment. Using a rolling pin, roll the dough out between the two pieces of parchment paper into a large round, about 16 inches in diameter and ⅛ inch thick.

RECIPE CONTINUES

Crust

1 cup tightly packed sweetened shredded coconut

¼ cup sugar

1½ cups all-purpose flour, plus more for the work surface

1 teaspoon ground cinnamon

1½ teaspoons kosher salt

2 teaspoons baking powder

½ cup (1 stick) cold unsalted butter, cut into small cubes

1 tablespoon dark rum

1 teaspoon vanilla bean paste

4 large egg yolks (reserve whites for the filling)

Filling

4 large egg whites

2½ cups whole-milk ricotta cheese packed and drained overnight (see page 19)

Grated zest of 2 limes

2½ teaspoons kosher salt

1 teaspoon vanilla bean paste

1½ teaspoons ground cinnamon

1 (15-ounce) can sweetened cream of coconut (ideally Coco Lopez)

Gemma & Joseph Bruno on their wedding day

Spray an 8 or 9-inch pie dish with nonstick cooking spray. Remove the top layer of parchment from the dough and flip the dough into the dish, gently pressing the dough down so that it lines the bottom and sides of the dish. Trim the dough to within ½ an inch of the edge of the pie dish. (Reserve the trimmed dough scraps to create decorations on the top of the pie, if desired.) Flute the edge by pinching the dough between your thumb and forefinger or press around it with a fork. Prick the bottom of the crust all over with a fork.

Set aside in the refrigerator while you make the filling.

Make the filling: In a stand mixer with the whisk, whip the egg whites to stiff peaks on medium-high speed, about 5 minutes. Transfer to a small bowl and set aside. Do not rinse the bowl of the mixer.

To the mixer bowl, add the ricotta, lime zest, salt, vanilla paste, ½ teaspoon of the cinnamon, and the cream of coconut and whip on medium-high until very well combined and smooth, about 1 minute. Fold the whipped egg whites into the ricotta mixture with a rubber spatula, incorporating fully.

Scoop the mixture into the chilled prepared crust and spread into an even layer with the spatula. Sprinkle the remaining 1 teaspoon cinnamon over the top. If using leftover dough scraps to decorate the top of the pie, apply them now—a lattice pattern looks particularly nice.

Bake until the pie is set and slightly wobbly in the middle, 50 to 60 minutes. Cool completely on a cooling rack (the filling may deflate slightly, and will continue to set as it cools).

Cut into wedges and serve at room temperature, or chill overnight before slicing. Leftover pie will keep, tightly covered in the refrigerator, for up to 3 days.

Vietnamese Coffee Tiramisù

SERVES 6 TO 8

Tiramisù is a classic Italian-American dessert, but we wanted, perhaps unsurprisingly, to do something a little different. Angie loves Vietnamese iced coffee, made with a dark French roast coffee that's often enhanced with chicory, such as Café Du Monde, and thickened with sweetened condensed milk, so we found a way to incorporate those flavors into tiramisù. The sweetened condensed milk goes into two texturally distinct creams: a dense zabaglione-like custard, and an airy whipped mascarpone cream; while the chicory coffee is used for soaking the cookies. (Feel free to use store-bought ladyfingers here, though we are providing instructions for making your own should you so choose.)

Tiramisù is often slopped out of one big pan, but we wanted to show off all of the beautiful layers of this dessert in a trifle bowl instead.

———

Make the condensed milk custard: In a medium bowl, whisk the egg yolks and cornstarch together until well combined and pale in color, about 1 minute.

In a medium saucepot, whisk the whole milk and condensed milk together until very well combined. Set over medium heat and whisk continually until the mixture comes to a simmer, about 5 minutes. Remove from the heat. Very slowly, whisking the whole time, use a ladle to add the milk mixture little by little to the egg yolks, to temper the eggs. Once all of the milk mixture has been added, add the salt and vanilla paste and mix to combine. Pour the egg-milk mixture back into the saucepot and cook over medium heat, whisking continually, until thick and smooth, 4 to 5 minutes. Transfer the custard to a stand mixer with the whisk and whip on high speed until completely cooled, 4 to 5 minutes. Add the mascarpone and crème fraîche and whisk on medium speed until combined. Refrigerate for 1 hour or up to overnight to chill.

Condensed milk custard

3 large egg yolks

1 tablespoon plus 1 teaspoon cornstarch

1 cup whole milk

1 (14-ounce) can sweetened condensed milk

1½ teaspoons kosher salt

½ teaspoon vanilla bean paste

⅔ cup mascarpone cheese

⅓ cup crème fraîche

Mascarpone cream

1 cup heavy cream

1 cup mascarpone cheese

½ teaspoon kosher salt

¼ cup sweetened condensed milk

½ teaspoon vanilla bean paste

To assemble

18 (3½ × 1-inch) ladyfingers, store-bought or homemade (recipe follows)

2 cups brewed dark French roast coffee (preferably Cafe Du Monde), chilled

2 teaspoons ground cinnamon

RECIPE CONTINUES

Make the mascarpone cream: In a stand mixer with the whisk, whip the heavy cream on medium-high until stiff peaks form, 4 to 5 minutes. Fold in the mascarpone, salt, condensed milk, and vanilla paste until well combined. Refrigerate for 1 hour or up to overnight to chill.

To assemble: Place 1½ cups of the condensed milk custard in a 7-inch glass trifle or decorative glass bowl, spreading to cover the bottom in an even layer.

Break 8 to 10 ladyfingers into 1-inch pieces into a medium bowl. Slowly add 1 cup of the coffee, gently folding the ladyfingers while adding the liquid until the cookies are evenly coated in the coffee. Layer the soaked cookies over the condensed milk custard. Set the medium bowl aside. Top the cookies with 2 cups of the mascarpone cream, carefully spreading the cream in an even layer to coat the cookies. Break the remaining ladyfingers into the same soaking bowl, add the remaining 1 cup coffee, and fold to combine. Layer the soaked cookies on top of the mascarpone cream mixture, spreading them evenly across the surface of the cream. Add the remaining custard mixture on top of the layer of cookies. Sprinkle the cinnamon over the top.

Serve immediately. Leftovers keep, tightly covered in the refrigerator, for up to 2 days.

Ladyfingers

MAKES 20 LADYFINGERS

3 large eggs, separated

½ teaspoon vanilla bean paste

½ cup granulated sugar

¼ teaspoon cream of tartar

½ cup all-purpose flour

½ teaspoon kosher salt

2 tablespoons potato starch

¼ cup powdered sugar

Preheat the oven to 350°F. Line two baking sheets with parchment paper and spray with nonstick cooking spray.

In a stand mixer with the whisk, beat the egg yolks, vanilla paste, and ¼ cup of the granulated sugar on medium-high speed until pale in color and fluffy in texture, about 2 minutes. Set aside in a separate medium bowl. Wash the mixing bowl and whisk and dry well.

Return the whisk attachment to the stand mixer and whip the egg whites and cream of tartar on medium-high speed until fluffy, about 3 minutes. Add the remaining ¼ cup sugar in a steady stream, while still whipping, until shiny, stiff peaks form, about 1 minute. Gently fold the whipped whites into the whipped yolks with a spoon. Sift the flour, salt, and potato starch over the batter and gently fold to incorporate until homogeneous.

Fill a piping bag with the batter and cut ½ inch off the tip (or fit with ½-inch plain tip). Pipe cookies about 3½ inches wide and 1 inch long, spaced 1 inch apart, on the prepared baking sheets. (You should get about 20 ladyfingers.) Sift the powdered sugar across the tops of the cookies, going over the cookies multiple times to use all of the sugar.

Bake until light golden brown, rotating the pans from front to back halfway through, 12 to 14 minutes. Remove from the oven and set aside to cool. They should be crisp-edged but slightly soft in the center. Ladyfingers keep, stored at room temperature and tightly covered, for up to 3 days.

No-Bake Spumoni Cheesecake with Cherries, Pistachio & White Chocolate

MAKES ONE 10-INCH CAKE (SERVES 10 TO 12)

You may be familiar with spumoni, that delightfully retro molded gelato creation, usually consisting of chocolate, pistachio, and vanilla with cherry flavor. We aren't going to give you a recipe for spumoni, but we will give you a recipe for a spumoni-inspired no-bake cheesecake, swapping out regular chocolate for white, which adds a delicate sweetness to the whole endeavor.

The cheesecake is made with a rich, pistachio-laden crust, and layered with a homemade cherry filling, though you could substitute 2 cups of canned cherries, if so desired, or even skip the fruit altogether. Whipping the white chocolate into the cream cheese filling helps the cake set up and retain its structure as it cools, thanks to its high fat content, while sour cream helps balance the chocolate's sweetness, making for a gently sweet, slightly tangy, and altogether very delicious dessert. It must be made in advance and given time to chill, leaving you plenty of time to focus on the rest of dinner.

NOTE: If you cannot find sour cherries, sweet cherries may be used, but add 1 teaspoon of lemon juice to the cherry mixture.

Prepare the cherries: In a medium saucepan, heat the cherries, cornstarch, salt, lemon juice, vanilla paste, sugar, and 3 tablespoons water over medium heat, stirring well to combine. Bring to a simmer, stir, then reduce the heat to low. Simmer for 5 minutes, until the mixture thickens. Transfer the mixture to a medium bowl and refrigerate for at least 1 hour to cool completely.

Make the crust: In a food processor, process the graham crackers until finely ground. Add the pistachios and process until the nuts are finely ground and the mixture turns green, about 2 minutes. Add the granulated sugar and salt. While the processor is running, drizzle in the melted butter until all of it is incorporated, about 30 seconds. Press the crust into the bottom of a 10-inch springform pan.

Cherries

2 cups pitted fresh or thawed frozen sour cherries (about 12 ounces or 40 cherries)

1 tablespoon cornstarch

½ teaspoon kosher salt

2 teaspoons fresh lemon juice

¼ teaspoon vanilla bean paste

¼ cup sugar

Crust

12 whole graham cracker sheets (or 1½ cups ground graham cracker crumbs)

1½ cups pistachios

¼ cup granulated sugar

1 teaspoon kosher salt

½ cup (1 stick) unsalted butter, melted

Cheesecake

1 cup white chocolate baking chips (6 ounces)

½ cup heavy cream

3 (8-ounce) packages cold full-fat cream cheese

1 teaspoon vanilla bean paste

1 teaspoon kosher salt

½ cup sour cream

1½ cups powdered sugar

RECIPE CONTINUES

Make the cheesecake: In a microwave-safe container, combine the white chocolate chips and heavy cream and microwave for 45 seconds to 1 minute, until the chips have melted, stirring well to ensure everything is incorporated. (If you don't have a microwave, heat the cream in a small pot on the stovetop, let it sit for about a minute, and stir it into the chocolate chips until melted.) Refrigerate for at least 1 hour to cool completely.

In a stand mixer with the paddle, beat the cream cheese on medium speed until soft, about 1 minute. Add the vanilla paste, salt, and sour cream. Mix on medium speed until combined, scraping the sides intermittently, about 30 seconds. Add the powdered sugar and mix on medium speed until combined, about 30 seconds. Add the cooled white chocolate mixture and mix to combine, scraping the sides intermittently, until all the ingredients are smooth and combined, 30 to 45 seconds.

To assemble, spread the cherries evenly across the top of the prepared crust. Scoop all of the cheesecake mixture into a large dollop in the center of the pan, then carefully spread it outward in a circular motion to fill the entire pan to the edges, using a large offset spatula (or a rubber spatula). Smooth the cheesecake mixture as evenly as possible, while trying not to disturb the cherry mixture underneath. Cover tightly with plastic wrap and refrigerate overnight to set before serving.

To serve, run a knife around the edge of the cheesecake to loosen it from the springform ring. Remove the ring and slice the cake into wedges. Leftover cheesecake keeps, tightly covered in the refrigerator, for up to 4 days.

the Rito family enjoys dessert after a big meal

Honey Zeppole

SERVES 4 TO 6

While honey-soaked zeppole are a Rito family tradition around the holidays, using fried bread dough from the family bakery, the Tacinelli family makes honey *struffoli*, which are tiny little balls of fried dough served with honey and sprinkles. This is a marriage of the two, using robiolina or cream cheese, which adds moisture to the dough without weighing it down, and a welcome touch of savoriness to balance the honey. The pistachios are a nod to Italy's Greek neighbors, whose influences are seen in Sicilian cuisine.

The syrup and batter can be made in advance, though these zeppole, like most doughnuts, are at their best when fried to order.

Batter

16 ounces robiolina cheese (see page 19) or whipped cream cheese

1½ teaspoons vanilla bean paste

½ teaspoon kosher salt

½ cup sugar

4 large eggs

2 cups all-purpose flour

2 teaspoons baking powder

Honey syrup

1 cup honey

2 cinnamon sticks or ¼ teaspoon ground cinnamon

½ teaspoon kosher salt

To finish

Neutral oil, such as vegetable, for deep-frying (about 5 cups)

½ cup chopped pistachios (optional)

Make the batter: In a stand mixer with the paddle, mix the robiolina, vanilla paste, salt, sugar, and eggs on medium-high speed until homogeneous, 2 to 3 minutes. Add the flour and baking powder. Mix thoroughly to ensure that all ingredients are evenly incorporated.

Make the honey syrup: In a small pot, bring the honey, cinnamon, and salt to a boil over medium-high heat. Remove from the heat and stir in 2 tablespoons water. Set aside to cool slightly. Remove the cinnamon sticks before using.

To finish: Pour 3 to 4 inches oil into a large heavy-bottomed pot and heat to 340°F.

With a small spring-release ice cream scoop, carefully scoop zeppole batter into the hot oil. If you don't have an ice cream scoop, use two large spoons, and gently roll the batter between them to form a ball before dropping them into the oil. Fry only as many zeppole as will float freely in the oil at a time, flipping to ensure they cook evenly, until golden brown, 4 to 5 minutes (you will likely cook 4 to 5 batches, depending on the size of your pot).

Remove the zeppole from the oil with a slotted spoon to a large bowl. Toss the zeppole with about one-quarter of the honey syrup and set aside on a serving platter. Repeat the frying and tossing with a proportionate amount of honey syrup until all the batter and honey syrup are used. If desired, sprinkle with pistachios.

Serve immediately. Zeppole are best fried and eaten day-of. Uncooked batter keeps, covered in the refrigerator, for up to 4 days.

Hazelnut Torta Caprese with Sweetened Crème Fraîche

SERVES 8 TO 10

We felt it was important to offer at least one dessert for the chocoholics, and this is it: rich, dense, and almost fudge-like in texture, with a Nutella-esque flavor profile, but all grown up. It's based on a classic coastal Italian dessert called *torta caprese*, which is usually made with almonds, though we switched things up to incorporate hazelnuts and toasted brown butter instead. This cake is best served cold, in petite wedges, with a dollop of whipped crème fraîche to offset its luxuriant richness.

NOTE: Try to find chocolate with as close to 70% cacao content as possible (it will be labeled on the package), ideally in disc (aka feve) form, though chips or chunks will work.

Cake

¾ cup (1½ sticks) plus 1 tablespoon unsalted butter

1½ cups (10 ounces) dark chocolate discs (see Note)

2½ cups blanched roasted unsalted hazelnuts (12 ounces)

5 large eggs

1 teaspoon vanilla bean paste

1 cup granulated sugar

1 tablespoon kosher salt

1 tablespoon cornstarch

1 tablespoon plus 2 teaspoons buttermilk

Flaky sea salt, such as Maldon, for finishing (optional)

Topping

½ cup heavy cream

¾ cup crème fraîche

¼ teaspoon vanilla bean paste

¼ cup powdered sugar

¼ teaspoon kosher salt

Preheat the oven to 350°F. Lightly grease a 10-inch wide, 2-inch deep cake pan with nonstick cooking spray.

Make the cake: In a large sauté pan, heat the butter over medium-high heat until melted and large, foamy bubbles start to appear, 2 to 3 minutes. Swirl the pan to ensure even cooking. The butter will make loud sputtering noises, then the bubbles will dissipate and the noise will subside—this is when you should notice the white milk solids in the butter turning deep golden brown in color.

Remove from the heat, add the chocolate, and stir well until melted. Set aside to cool.

In a food processor, pulse the hazelnuts until they're ground as finely as possible, with the texture of wet sand, stopping to scrape down the sides of the bowl as needed. Set aside.

In a large bowl, whisk the eggs, vanilla paste, granulated sugar, kosher salt, cornstarch, and buttermilk until well combined.

When the chocolate mixture has cooled to room temperature, add the ground hazelnuts and stir well to combine. Pour the chocolate-hazelnut mix into the bowl with the egg mixture and stir well to combine

and create a smooth batter. Pour the batter into the cake pan.

Bake until set in the middle and a cake tester comes out clean, 25 to 30 minutes. Remove the cake from the oven and let it cool in the pan. It may deflate slightly as it cools.

Once cool, carefully remove the cake from the pan by placing an inverted plate on top and flipping it over. Place your desired serving plate on top of the now-upside-down cake and flip it once more, so that it's facing right-side up.

Make the topping: In a stand mixer with the whisk, whip the heavy cream on medium-high speed until stiff peaks form, 4 to 5 minutes. In a medium bowl, mix the crème fraîche, vanilla paste, powdered sugar, and salt with a rubber spatula until combined. Fold the whipped cream into the crème fraîche mixture with the spatula.

To serve, slice the cake into wedges and top with flaky sea salt, if using, and a dollop of whipped crème fraîche. For a more delicate texture, serve at room temperature. For a more dense, fudgy texture, serve chilled. Leftover cake keeps, tightly covered in the refrigerator, for up to 4 days.

Tre Latte Olive Oil Cake

MAKES ONE 9 × 13-INCH CAKE (SERVES 10 TO 12)

This is a tres leches-meets-olive oil cake, lightened up with a chiffon base to help soak in all of the milk. In Latin America, tres leches cakes are soaked in a mixture of evaporated milk, condensed milk, and heavy cream; we love their rich-yet-airy texture and wanted to combine that idea with the flavors of an olive oil cake, adding lemon for a bit of brightness. The finished result is in no way traditional, which is how we like things around here.

———

Preheat the oven to 325°F.

Make the cake: In a large bowl, whisk together the egg yolks, ¾ cup cold water, olive oil, vanilla paste, and ¾ cup of the sugar until well combined. In a separate bowl, sift together the flour, baking powder, and salt. Mix the flour mixture into the egg yolk mixture, carefully folding with a spatula until well incorporated.

In a stand mixer with the whisk, whip the egg whites, cream of tartar, and lemon zest on medium-high until very frothy and thickened, 2 to 3 minutes. Gradually add the remaining ¾ cup sugar, little by little, to incorporate it into the egg whites. Keep whipping the eggs until they're slightly shiny, have some volume, and just barely hold their shape (soft peaks), about 2 minutes.

Remove the bowl from the mixer and add the egg yolk/flour mixture little by little, folding with a rubber spatula, until very well combined.

Pour the batter into an ungreased 9 × 13-inch baking pan. Bake until a knife inserted into the center comes out clean, 35 to 45 minutes. Cool upside down, in the pan, on a wire rack. (This will help the cake retain its height.)

Meanwhile, make the soaking liquid: In a large bowl, stir together whole milk, condensed milk, evaporated milk, olive oil, vanilla paste, salt, and lemon zest. Set aside.

Once the cake is cool, carefully run an offset spatula or butter knife around the sides of the pan to release the cake from the sides, but leave the cake in the pan.

Cake

7 large eggs, separated

½ cup extra-virgin olive oil

2 teaspoons vanilla bean paste

1½ cups sugar

2 cups all-purpose flour

1 tablespoon baking powder

1½ teaspoons kosher salt

½ teaspoon cream of tartar

Grated zest of 1 lemon

Soaking liquid

1½ cups whole milk

1 (14-ounce) can condensed milk

1 (12-ounce) can evaporated milk

½ cup extra-virgin olive oil

½ teaspoon vanilla bean paste

½ teaspoon kosher salt

Grated zest of 1 lemon

Mascarpone topping

1 cup heavy cream

1 cup mascarpone cheese

½ teaspoon vanilla bean paste

2 tablespoons sugar

½ teaspoon kosher salt

For serving

½ cup extra-virgin olive oil

Grated zest of one lemon

Poke holes all across the surface of the cake with a cake tester or toothpick and pour the milk mixture slowly and evenly over the top (it may take a few minutes for the mixture to soak all the way in). Cover the cake and refrigerate overnight.

Just before serving, make the mascarpone topping: In a stand mixer with the whisk, whip the heavy cream on medium-high speed until thickened and it just barely holds its shape, about 2 minutes. Add the mascarpone, vanilla paste, sugar, and salt and whip briefly to combine.

Spread all of the topping across the top of the cake with an offset spatula or the back of a large spoon.

To serve, slice the cake into roughly 3-inch squares. Drizzle with the olive oil and top with lemon zest. Leftovers keep, tightly sealed in the refrigerator, for up to 3 days.

After-Dinner Drinks

We love to end a meal with

an after-dinner drink, and fortunately, this is an area in which Italy excels, with a wide range of post-meal drinks both bitter and sweet. *Digestivi*, the category of after-dinner drink involving herbs and spices that allegedly help settle the stomach, are often referred to as *amaro* (Italian for "bitter"). In Italy, many regions, and sometimes even individual towns, have their own special *amaro* recipe, making use of local ingredients, and we love to try new ones whenever we visit. Italians and Italian Americans are also known for an array of sweet fruit or nut-enhanced liqueurs intended for after-dinner consumption, another category we're quite fond of for a special treat after a big meal.

A few years ago, we started playing around with making our own *digestivi* and liqueurs, using just a basic 190-proof grain alcohol or neutral spirit, such as Everclear, as the base. We've incorporated nuts, fruits, herbs, spices, and even unexpected ingredients like artichokes, coffee, and peppercorns in our creations. All of them are very easy to make; the most challenging part is waiting for at least a month before cracking into them. And guests are blown away when we bust out a homemade bottle, not knowing how easy the process really is.

Use the brief collection of recipes here as a starting point for your own experiments—after you get the hang of these, branch out to incorporate other fruits or herbs. Like spicy? Add some chiles. Love citrus? Try one with yuzu. With after-dinner drinks, the bottle is your oyster. *Salute.*

Nocino with Espresso Beans & Lemon

MAKES ABOUT 7½ CUPS (25 TO 30 SERVINGS)

Nocino is an aromatic, bittersweet liqueur made from green (unripe) walnuts steeped for months in a strong alcohol base and sweetened with simple syrup. In Emilia-Romagna, where this *digestivo* is from, it's a straightforward walnut affair, but we add lemon peel, coffee beans, and cinnamon to ours for more flavor. The finished result is a unique drink with a complex caramelly, slightly astringent flavor.

———

NOTES: Green walnuts are available only for a brief window of about 2 weeks, usually in the third week of June, and this *digestivo* takes 4 to 6 months to steep. That's why nocino is usually consumed around Christmas, when it's finally ready. We order our green walnuts from Haag Farm in California, which ships nationally. You'll want to wear gloves when you cut them, as they secrete a clear gel that can stain your hands black if you're not careful.

We call for using an entire 750-milliliter bottle of alcohol here, figuring that since the green walnuts are available only for such a short period, you might as well make a big batch, though you could halve this recipe if you'd prefer.

1 (750 ml) bottle 190-proof grain alcohol or neutral spirit, such as Everclear

20 green walnuts (see Note), cut into quarters

6 to 8 strips of lemon zest (from 1 lemon)

¼ cup medium or dark roast coffee beans

2 cinnamon sticks

2 cups sugar

⅛ teaspoon kosher salt

Clean and dry a glass jar large enough to accommodate all the ingredients without being filled to the brim—there should be about 2 inches of space for air. A gallon jar usually does the trick. Add the alcohol, walnuts, lemon zest, coffee beans, and cinnamon sticks to the jar, seal tightly, and let steep at room temperature in a cool, dry place for at least 4 months and up to 1 year. The liquid will turn very dark brown in color.

When the nocino has steeped sufficiently, in a small saucepan, combine the sugar, salt, and 2 cups water and bring to a boil over medium-high heat. Remove from the heat and stir well, ensuring all the sugar is melted. Transfer to a heatproof bowl and place in the refrigerator to cool.

Strain the alcohol infusion through a fine-mesh sieve into a clean, dry bowl. Add the chilled sugar syrup and whisk well to combine. Using a funnel, transfer to a decorative bottle. Store in the freezer.

Serve nocino chilled in cordial glasses. Nocino keeps indefinitely in the freezer.

Homemade Sambuca

MAKES ABOUT 3¼ CUPS (12 TO 14 SERVINGS)

You may be familiar with sambuca, a clear, anise-flavored liqueur commonly served alongside an espresso, a popular combination among Italian men of a certain age (like Angie's grandfather). It's sometimes garnished with an espresso bean, a style referred to as *con la mosca*—with the fly.

—————

NOTE: The word *sambuca* comes from the Latin word for elderberry, which is the traditional flavoring agent here, but if you can't find it, feel free to increase the star anise to ¾ cup instead. Dried elderberries are available online at sources like Amazon or Kalustyan's.

1½ cups 190-proof grain alcohol or neutral spirit, such as Everclear

½ cup whole star anise

2 tablespoons dried elderberries (optional; see Note)

2 cups sugar

⅛ teaspoon kosher salt

Espresso beans (optional), for serving

In a clean, dry 32-ounce glass jar, combine the alcohol, star anise, and elderberries (if using). Seal tightly and let steep at room temperature in a cool, dry place for at least 1 month and up to 1 year.

When the liquid is ready, in a small saucepan, combine the sugar, salt, and 2¼ cups water and bring to a boil over medium-high heat. Remove from the heat and stir well, ensuring all the sugar is melted. Transfer to a heatproof bowl and place in the refrigerator to cool.

Strain the alcohol infusion through a fine-mesh sieve into a clean, dry bowl. Add the chilled sugar syrup and whisk well to combine. Using a funnel, transfer to a decorative bottle. Store in the freezer.

Serve sambuca chilled in cordial glasses, with 2 espresso beans per glass, if desired. Sambuca keeps indefinitely in the freezer.

Scott's mom and her brother on her First Communion Day

Toasted Hazelnut & Orange Liqueur

MAKES ABOUT 2⅓ CUPS (ABOUT 10 SERVINGS)

Frangelico—that classic hazelnut liqueur in the funny monk-shaped bottle—was the inspiration for this drink, which uses the technique of fat-washing (a method of infusing alcohol with fatty flavors by soaking them together, then straining the fat out); in this case, using the natural fat from nuts. We toast the hazelnuts first to heighten their aroma and release some of their oils, then blitz them up with the alcohol before freezing the mixture. Once frozen, the fat-infused alcohol separates from the solids and is easy to drain off. Paired with fresh orange, it's a more sophisticated take on the classic, with a sweet-but-balanced nutty flavor.

Preheat the oven to 400°F. Line a sheet pan with parchment paper or a silicone baking mat.

Spread the hazelnuts in a single layer on the lined pan. Place in the oven and toast until dark golden brown and the oil is released, about 12 minutes.

Carefully transfer the hazelnuts to a food processor and add the alcohol. Process for 20 to 30 seconds to form a puree.

Transfer to a clean, dry 64-ounce glass jar and let cool to room temperature. Seal tightly and let steep at room temperature in a cool, dry place for at least 1 month and up to 1 year. When ready, transfer to the freezer overnight.

When the liquid has frozen overnight, in a small saucepan, combine the sugar, salt, vanilla paste, orange zest, orange juice, and 2 cups water and bring to a boil over medium-high heat. Remove from the heat and stir well, ensuring all the sugar is melted. Strain the liquid through a fine-mesh sieve and refrigerate until cooled.

Remove the hazelnut-infused alcohol from the freezer. The nut mixture should have separated from the alcohol, sinking to the bottom and revealing the clarified alcohol on the top. Strain the alcohol infusion through a fine-mesh sieve into a clean, dry bowl.

3 cups blanched roasted unsalted hazelnuts

1 (750 ml) bottle 190-proof grain alcohol or neutral spirit, such as Everclear

2 cups sugar

¼ teaspoon kosher salt

½ teaspoon vanilla bean paste

Strips of zest of 1 large orange, plus more for garnish, if desired

½ cup freshly squeezed orange juice, strained (from 1 large orange)

Add the chilled vanilla-orange syrup and stir well to combine. Using a funnel, transfer to a decorative bottle. Store in the freezer.

Serve the liqueur chilled in cordial glasses. Garnish each glass with a twist of orange peel, if desired. Liqueur keeps indefinitely in the freezer.

Citrus 'Cello

MAKES ABOUT 4½ CUPS (16 TO 20 SERVINGS)

You typically see *limoncello* on the Amalfi coast, which is famous for its citrus—lemons, of course, but there are other *"cellos"* there made with everything from oranges (*arancello*) to grapefruits (*pompelmocello*) and other citrus varieties. It's usually made with just the zest of the fruit, which is steeped in alcohol until its flavor is extracted, then strained and mixed with simple syrup. The result is often quite sweet, so in our version, we like to include the juice of the fruit in the syrup, too, which adds acid and flavor, creating a more balanced drink. We love to make big batches of different creative *"cellos,"* and put them in small, decorative bottles to give away as gifts during the holidays.

———

NOTES: Since the syrup will keep in the refrigerator for the month it takes the alcohol to steep, if you'd like, you can prepare the syrup at the same time as the alcohol infusion, using the same fruit for both.

You can also add an additional layer of flavor to the base recipe with the inclusion of 1 to 2 tablespoons of aromatics such as pink peppercorn or chamomile, or a few sprigs of fresh herbs such as basil or thyme. This is a fun project to get creative with, so feel free to experiment.

1½ cups 190-proof grain alcohol or neutral spirit, such as Everclear

½ cup grated zest from the desired citrus (about 15 small citrus, such as lemons or tangerines, or 10 large citrus such as blood orange)

⅔ cup juice from the same citrus

2 cups sugar

¼ teaspoon kosher salt

½ teaspoon vanilla bean paste

In a clean, dry 32-ounce glass jar, combine the alcohol and citrus zest. Seal tightly and let steep at room temperature in a cool, dry place for at least 1 month.

In a small saucepan, combine the citrus juice, 2 cups water, the sugar, salt, and vanilla paste and bring to a boil over medium-high heat. Remove from the heat and stir well, ensuring all of the sugar is melted. Strain the liquid through a fine-mesh sieve into a heatproof bowl to remove any pulp and place in the refrigerator to cool.

Strain the alcohol infusion through a fine-mesh sieve into a clean, dry bowl. Add the chilled sugar syrup and stir well to combine. Using a funnel, transfer to a decorative bottle. Store in the freezer.

Serve 'cello chilled in cordial glasses. Homemade 'cello keeps indefinitely in the freezer.

VARIATION: Crema di 'Cello

This modified *crema* version includes heavy cream, which takes the edge off the alcohol flavor and makes a creamy, rich drink. The citrus 'cello is cleaner and crisper, while the *crema di 'cello* is more like a dessert in a glass. When combining the strained infusion and the chilled sugar syrup, simply add ¾ cup heavy cream and stir well to combine. *Crema* di 'cello also keeps indefinitely in the freezer.

Basics

These are the foundational

recipes for essential building blocks, like stock, bread crumbs, dressings and more, that we turn to time and time again. The recipes in this chapter are all called for in several places throughout the rest of the book, so use this as your reference. Most of these recipes are simple and straightforward, and some are for ingredients you could buy in the store, but it's worth it from a flavor perspective to take the time to make your own.

Homemade Bread Crumbs

MAKES 2 CUPS FINE CRUMBS AND
3 CUPS COARSE CRUMBS

We make two kinds of bread crumbs—coarse and fine—which are used as the base for our Italian Seasoned Bread Crumbs (fine), and our Crispy Garlic Bread Crumbs (coarse).

———————

2 (13-ounce) baguettes (21 inches long)

Preheat the oven to 250°F.

Halve the bread horizontally. Using your hands, scoop out the soft inner part of the baguettes. (The soft bread from inside the baguettes can be used for meatballs. Seal it in a zip-top bag and store in the freezer until ready to use in a meatball recipe.)

Place the baguette crusts on a sheet pan. Bake until the bread is totally crispy, with no soft spots, 20 to 25 minutes. Remove from the oven and let sit until cool enough to handle.

Break the dried bread into small pieces with your hands. Working in batches, pulse the dried bread in the food processor until broken into even smaller pieces, no larger than a nickel. Pour the processed crumbs into a sieve set over a bowl. Repeat the process until all the bread is ground.

Sift the crumbs to separate the coarse crumbs from the fine ones and reserve both separately, using the fine crumbs for Italian Seasoned Bread Crumbs (recipe follows) and the coarse crumbs for Crispy Garlic Bread Crumbs (opposite).

Italian Seasoned Bread Crumbs

MAKES ABOUT 2½ CUPS

Seasoned fine bread crumbs are a staple in many Italian-American stuffing and breading recipes. You can of course use the store-bought kind, but these are worth going the extra mile for, especially if you dry your own herbs. Use these to bread chicken or veal cutlets, in meatballs, or anywhere fine seasoned bread crumbs are called for.

———————

NOTE: We add tomato powder (dehydrated tomatoes ground into a powder) to our crumbs for added depth of flavor and a hint of tanginess; it's optional, but available for purchase on Amazon or at Kalustyan's.

2 cups finely ground bread crumbs (from Homemade Bread Crumbs, at left)

1 tablespoon granulated onion

1 tablespoon granulated garlic

3 tablespoons dried oregano (ideally home-dried, page 301)

2 teaspoons dried thyme (ideally home-dried, page 301)

2 teaspoons freshly ground black pepper

2 teaspoons tomato powder (optional)

In a small bowl, whisk together the bread crumbs, onion, garlic, oregano, thyme, pepper, and tomato powder (if using) until combined. Store in a sealed container in a cool, dry place for up to 4 weeks.

Crispy Garlic Bread Crumbs

MAKES ABOUT 3 CUPS

This variation makes use of coarse bread crumbs, pan-frying them in olive oil and butter with garlic and thyme to crisp them up while infusing them with additional flavor. We sprinkle them atop pastas like the Sorpresine with Mussels, Guajillo, Cilantro & Lime (page 153) and Amatriciana with Braised Pork Shoulder (page 107), and on our Chrysanthemum Caesar (page 75) for added texture and flavor.

---

1 large head garlic	1 teaspoon freshly ground black pepper
½ cup extra-virgin olive oil	3 sprigs thyme
½ cup (1 stick) unsalted butter	3 cups coarse bread crumbs (from Homemade Bread Crumbs, opposite)
2 teaspoons kosher salt	

Cut the garlic just above its base to detach individual cloves, and reserve the cut part. Smash each clove with the side of a wide knife but leave the peels on.

In a large pot or large sauté pan, combine the reserved garlic base and unpeeled smashed cloves, the olive oil, butter, salt, pepper, and thyme and heat over medium-high heat, moving often. Cook until the butter is melted and starts to form large bubbles, about 2 minutes.

Add the bread crumbs and stir immediately to combine. Continue stirring and cooking over medium-high heat until the bread crumbs have turned light golden brown in color, 3 to 4 minutes. Remove from the pan and place on a plate lined with paper towels to cool.

Once cool, discard the garlic pieces. The crumbs can be used immediately, or stored in an airtight container at room temperature for up to 5 days.

Chicken Stock

MAKES ABOUT 8 CUPS

Our chicken stock is fairly straightforward, with the addition of a bit of garlic, because we're Italian and can't help ourselves. And we like to leave the clear onion skin on (not the papery outer shell, but the interior layer just beneath that), because it adds a nice golden color.

If you can find chicken backs and necks, grab them, as they have more gelatin and make for a richer stock. You can intermittently skim the fat off the top while the stock simmers if you're so inclined, but don't worry about it too much, because when the liquid cools, the fat will solidify and be easy to separate.

We don't season our stock at all, so you can season the recipes calling for it accordingly; if you're going to use a store-bought substitute, we recommend seeking out an unsalted version.

---

2 pounds raw chicken bones (preferably backs and necks, but wings can be substituted)	4 celery ribs, cut into 2-inch pieces
1 medium onion, outer layer peeled, quartered	2 heads garlic, halved horizontally
1 large carrot, peeled and cut into 2-inch pieces	1 tablespoon black peppercorns
	5 sprigs thyme
	2 bay leaves

Thoroughly rinse the chicken bones in cold water until the water runs clear.

In a large stockpot, combine the chicken bones and 12 quarts water and bring to a boil over high heat. Reduce the heat to medium-low to maintain a simmer and add the onion, carrot, celery, garlic, peppercorns, thyme, and bay leaves. Simmer for 2 to 2½ hours, skimming any white foam that rises to the surface occasionally, until the stock is a dark amber color and the liquid has reduced by about one-third. Strain through a fine-mesh sieve.

Cool immediately in the refrigerator for 2 to 3 hours, until the fat is solidified on the top. The fat can be scraped off and discarded at this point. The stock will keep, tightly covered in the refrigerator, for up to 5 days, and can be frozen for up to 3 months.

Roasted Garlic Puree

MAKES ABOUT 2 CUPS

This is one of our favorite ways to process garlic to give it a mellow, deep, caramelized flavor, as opposed to the sharp, strong taste of raw garlic. We sometimes use it alongside raw garlic for multiple layers of garlic flavor, as called for in the dressing for Chrysanthemum Caesar (page 75); or use the puree as is in many of our meatball recipes. Do keep the garlic-infused oil that's left over after roasting the heads, as it's ideal for vinaigrettes or dipping bread into.

————

12 heads garlic, tops trimmed off to expose the cloves

2½ cups neutral oil, such as vegetable

Preheat the oven to 275°F.

Place the garlic heads cut-side down in a 9 × 13-inch baking dish. Pour the oil into the pan. The garlic should be covered about halfway up with oil. Cook until the garlic has turned golden brown in color, 1½ to 2 hours. Remove from the oven and let cool.

When cool enough to handle, pour the oil off into a sealed container and set aside in the refrigerator for up to 1 week for future use.

Gently squeeze each garlic head until the roasted cloves come out of the papery skins. Transfer to a blender and puree until smooth.

Refrigerate until ready to use. Garlic puree keeps, refrigerated, for up to 1 week, or in the freezer for up to 3 months.

Garlic & Chile Soffritto

MAKES ABOUT ½ CUP

In Italian-American cooking, we use garlic as the base of so many things, and this *soffritto* gives a warmer, softer flavor than using raw cloves. The garlic flavor seeps into the oil while it's cooking, and the chiles add a hit of heat, allowing the infused fat to carry those flavors throughout whatever dish you add it to. We like to use it on the Charred Broccoli with Pecorino & Toasted Sesame (page 249) and in the Garlic Focaccia (page 29).

————

⅓ cup extra-virgin olive oil

⅓ cup finely chopped garlic (about 10 cloves)

½ teaspoon crushed Calabrian chiles in oil

½ teaspoon kosher salt

In a sauté pan, combine the oil, garlic, chiles, and salt and gently cook over low heat, stirring continually with a wooden spoon to avoid sticking. Cook until the garlic is lightly toasted, 8 to 10 minutes.

Set aside to cool before using. Soffritto keeps, in the refrigerator, for up to 4 days, and in the freezer for up to 3 months.

Home-Dried Herbs

MAKES 1 TO 2 OUNCES

We dry our own herbs so they're more potent and flavorful—some of the stuff sitting on shelves at the grocery store has been there for years, and they taste like nothing. Although it sounds like an oxymoron, freshly drying herbs concentrates and intensifies their flavor (plus, it's how Angie's grandma does it). We use dried herbs in marinades or cook them in oil at the start of a recipe, treating them more like spices, as opposed to fresh herbs, which we usually add at the end to finish a dish. If you have a dehydrator at home, feel free to use that, but the simplest method uses a low oven.

2 to 3 ounces oregano, mint, basil, or rosemary sprigs

Preheat the oven to 200°F. Line a baking sheet with parchment paper.

Wash and dry the herb completely. Pick the leaves and discard the stems. Place the leaves in a single layer on the lined baking sheet. Place in the oven until the herbs are completely dried and slightly crispy, and their color has darkened, about 1 hour. There should be no damp or soft parts when the herb is touched.

Remove from the oven and let cool. Store the dried herbs in an airtight container at room temperature. Dried herbs keep for up to 3 months.

Besciamella

MAKES ABOUT 2½ CUPS

Besciamella is just the Italian word for béchamel, though our version involves more savory aromatics than the classic. We use this to add stability and richness to the filling in our lasagnas (see pages 168–89), allowing us to add a lot of cheese without breaking the sauce into a greasy mess.

————

½ cup (1 stick) unsalted butter, cubed

1 head garlic, halved horizontally

⅓ cup thinly sliced shallots (about 1 medium shallot)

1 bay leaf

1 thyme sprig

¼ teaspoon black peppercorns

1 teaspoon kosher salt

½ cup all-purpose flour, "00" flour, or Wondra (see page 18)

2 cups cold whole milk

In a small heavy-bottomed pot, melt the butter over medium heat. Add the garlic, shallots, bay leaf, thyme, peppercorns, and salt. Cook over low heat until the shallots are translucent, about 2 minutes.

Add the flour and stir well. Increase the heat to medium and cook, stirring continually with a wooden spoon or silicone spatula, until the flour forms a smooth paste and turns lightly golden brown, about 5 minutes. Stir in the milk and cook for 5 minutes, stirring continually, until the besciamella is thick enough to coat the back of a spoon. Remove from the heat and strain through a fine-mesh sieve.

Place in the refrigerator to cool. Besciamella keeps, tightly covered in the refrigerator, for up to 3 days, or in the freezer for up to 3 months.

Oven-Dried Tomatoes

MAKES ABOUT 1 CUP

These sweet-tart little tomatoes are delicious on their own, as part of antipasto, on toast with fresh mozzarella, or anywhere that sun-dried tomatoes are called for. We always have some on hand for tossing into salads and onto sandwiches. Don't discard any leftover oil from the marinade—it takes on a lovely tomato-basil flavor and can be used in dressings or for dipping bread.

————

½ cup sugar

2 tablespoons kosher salt

2 teaspoons freshly ground black pepper

2 cups cherry tomatoes, halved

1¼ cups extra-virgin olive oil

2 sprigs basil

Preheat the oven to 250°F. Line a sheet pan with parchment paper.

In a small bowl, mix together the sugar, salt, and pepper. In a large bowl, drizzle the cherry tomatoes with ¼ cup of the olive oil, tossing to coat evenly. Add the sugar/salt/pepper mixture to the tomatoes little by little, alternating between tossing and adding more until the tomatoes are coated with all of the mixture. Work quickly so the sugar mixture does not dissolve.

Arrange the tomatoes on the lined sheet pan, cut-side up. Top the tomatoes with any remaining salt/sugar/pepper/oil mixture. Transfer to the oven and roast until the tomatoes are partially dried and deep red in color, 1½ hours for small tomatoes, 2 hours for larger tomatoes. Let cool.

When the tomatoes are cool, store in a sealed container and cover with the remaining 1 cup olive oil (a pint-sized plastic or glass container is ideal, so that the olive oil can cover the tomatoes). Slightly bruise the basil with the back of a knife to release its flavor and add to the container. The tomatoes will last in the refrigerator for up to 2 weeks, submerged in the olive oil.

Crispy Shallots

MAKES ABOUT 1½ CUPS

A great crispy topper to have on hand, crispy shallots can be used on everything from salads (like the garlicky Broccoli Salad with Oregano Vinaigrette, Olives & Crispy Shallots on page 73) to baked casseroles (like the Broccoli Rabe & Provolone Gratin on page 250). As an added bonus, the oil you fry the shallots in can be reserved for future use in vinaigrettes or for sautéing vegetables.

---

4 medium shallots, sliced into rings about ⅛ inch thick (preferably on a mandoline)

2 cups neutral oil, such as vegetable

Pinch of kosher salt

Place the shallots in a 2-quart saucepan. Add enough oil to come up 3 to 4 inches. Set the pot over a very low flame and cook, stirring frequently, until the shallots are an even dark golden brown, 20 to 25 minutes.

Drain the shallots (reserve the oil for other uses). Spread the shallots on a plate lined with a paper towel to cool. Season with the salt.

The shallots will crisp up as they cool. Shallots keep, stored in an airtight container at room temperature, for up to 1 week. Store the oil in a separate sealed container in the refrigerator for up to 1 week.

Creamy Italian Dressing

MAKES ABOUT 2 CUPS

This is our take on store-bought creamy Italian dressing, a low-brow favorite that we loved at salad bars growing up. Our version today has Japanese Kewpie mayo, a slightly sweeter and thicker style of mayonnaise, which lends a smooth texture and rich flavor to the mix. In addition to the Sardine Polpette (page 207) and Japanese Sweet Potatoes with Creamy Italian Dressing (page 245), use it as a dip for vegetables, pour it on a salad, or really swap it out anywhere you'd put the bottled stuff to use.

⅓ cup crème fraîche

¾ cup Kewpie mayonnaise

¼ cup white wine vinegar

⅓ cup finely grated Parmigiano-Reggiano cheese, plus more for serving

1 tablespoon garlic powder

1 tablespoon onion powder

1½ teaspoons dried oregano (ideally home-dried, page 301)

½ teaspoon freshly ground black pepper

1 teaspoon kosher salt

2 teaspoons sugar

½ cup neutral oil, such as vegetable

⅓ cup extra-virgin olive oil

In a blender, combine the crème fraîche, mayo, vinegar, ¼ cup water, the parmesan, garlic powder, onion powder, oregano, pepper, salt, and sugar and mix on high until well combined, about 30 seconds. If any ingredients stick to the sides, scrape down with a rubber spatula and blend again.

With the blender running on low, slowly drizzle in the neutral and olive oils and blend until well incorporated, about 20 seconds. The dressing keeps, tightly covered in the refrigerator, for up to 1 week.

Cured Lemons

MAKES 1 CUP

This simple recipe yields a very versatile product that can quickly add a citrusy pop to salads or grilled meats, or can be eaten straight from the jar. Once cured, the lemons will keep for several weeks in the refrigerator; just be sure they remain submerged in their own liquid.

———

2 lemons

2 teaspoons kosher salt

¼ cup sugar

Wash the lemons, then trim ½ inch off the tops to make them easier to slide across the mandoline. Hold each lemon cut-side down on a mandoline and carefully slice on the thinnest setting. Remove all the seeds.

In a small bowl, mix the lemons well with the salt and sugar. Let sit for at least 15 minutes before eating. Cured lemons keep, tightly covered in the refrigerator, for up to 4 weeks.

Lemon Aioli

MAKES ABOUT 2 CUPS

We choose not to make aioli the "classic" French way because we find that it doesn't keep well and takes on off-flavors after a day or two. We first began playing around with premade mayo—ideally Japanese Kewpie, which is sweeter and thicker than most—and flavoring that instead. The result is more shelf stable and, in our opinion, ultimately tastes better. Use this lemon-enhanced version anywhere you'd use regular mayo for an extra dash of rich, citrusy flavor.

———

1½ cups Kewpie mayonnaise

4 garlic cloves, grated on a Microplane

Grated zest of 4 lemons

⅓ cup fresh lemon juice

2 tablespoons extra-virgin olive oil

2 tablespoons sugar

1 tablespoon kosher salt

Freshly cracked black pepper

In a small bowl, combine the mayo, garlic, lemon zest, lemon juice, olive oil, sugar, salt, and pepper to taste and whisk well. Store in the refrigerator until ready to use. Aioli keeps, in the refrigerator, for up to 4 days.

Ricotta Infornata

MAKES ABOUT 2½ CUPS COARSELY GRATED

Ricotta infornata, or oven-baked ricotta, is a specialty of Catania, Sicily, where it's so ubiquitous it's even sold at the airport. It's traditionally made with local, salted and dried sheep's milk ricotta left to brown slowly in an oven overnight, so it dries out and hardens up, and is then used to grate over the classic Pasta alla Norma. We make ours with ricotta salata—which is typically made with sheep's milk, and is already salted and dry in texture—and toast it in the oven; it's called for in the Eggplant Sugo alla Norma (page 97) and the Eggplant Polpette (page 198).

NOTE: This recipe calls for a pound of cheese, though you can make a smaller quantity if you'd like.

1 pound ricotta salata

Preheat the oven to 450°F. Line a baking sheet with parchment paper or a silicone baking mat.

Cut the ricotta into wedges about 1½ inches thick. Arrange on the lined baking sheet, leaving 1 to 2 inches of space between the wedges. Roast until the cheese starts to brown, about 10 minutes. Flip the cheese over and roast until evenly browned, an additional 5 to 10 minutes.

Remove from the oven and let cool before using. Ricotta infornata keeps, covered in the refrigerator, for up to 1 week.

further reading

We're constantly learning as we continue to redefine and refine what Italian-American cooking means to us. As we explore both our own and the cuisines of other cultures, we often turn to expert sources for knowledge and inspiration about history, ingredients, and techniques. Here's a brief overview of some of the texts we've found useful in expanding our minds and our recipes.

Books

Communion: A Culinary Journey Through Vietnam, by Kim Fay

Cooking South of the Clouds: Recipes and Stories from China's Yunnan Province, by Georgia Freedman

Creole Italian: Sicilian Immigrants and the Shaping of New Orleans Food Culture, by Justin A. Nystrom

Cucina Paradiso: The Heavenly Food of Sicily, by Clifford A. Wright

The Elements of Taste, by Gray Kunz

Encyclopedia of Pasta, by Oretta Zanini de Vita

The Flavor Bible: The Essential Guide to Culinary Creativity, Based on the Wisdom of America's Most Imaginative Chefs, by Andrew Dornenburg and Karen A. Page

Japan: The Cookbook, by Nancy Singleton Hachisu

La Cucina: The Regional Cooking of Italy, by The Italian Academy of Cuisine

On Food and Cooking: The Science and Lore of the Kitchen, by Harold McGee

Peppers of the Americas: The Remarkable Capsicums That Forever Changed Flavor, by Maricel E. Presilla

Sicily: Food & Cookery, by Pamela Sheldon Johns

Websites/Blogs

African Renewal. "Black-Eyed Peas: A Taste of Africa in the Americas," by Franck Kuwonu (un.org/africarenewal/magazine/december-2019-march-2020/black-eyed-peas-taste-africa-americas)

Arab America. "Arab Contributions to Sicilian Cuisine," by Habeeb Salloum (arabamerica.com/sicilys-unique-contribution-italys-cuisine)

Best of Sicily Magazine. "Sicilian Chickpeas," by Roberta Gangi (bestofsicily.com/mag/art433.htm)

The Culture Trip. "A Brief History of Som Tum, Thailand's Popular Green Papaya Salad," by Kelly Iverson (theculturetrip.com/asia/thailand/articles/a-brief-history-of-som-tum-thailands-popular-green-papaya-salad)

Hickswrites: A Journal of Epicurean Adventures in New Orleans. "New Orleans Dining: Pascal's Manale," by Steven Wells Hicks (hickswrites.blogspot.com/2010/08/new-orleans-dining-pascals-manale.html)

Hungry Huy. "How to Make Pour Over Coffee," by Bryan Huy Vu (hungryhuy.com/pour-over-coffee)

Just One Cookbook. "Tsukune," by Namiko Hirasawa Chen (justonecookbook.com/tsukune)

Momentum Travel Blog. "The Secret History of Thai Food," by Rebecca Seal (momentum.travel/food-drink/secret-history-thai-food/#)

NPR's The Salt. "Hacking Iconic New Orleans Barbecue Shrimp Far From The Gulf," by John Burnett (npr.org/sections/thesalt/2015/07/19/423605844/hacking-iconic-new-orleans-barbecue-shrimp-far-from-the-gulf)

Pocket Worthy. "Eating the Arab Roots of Sicilian Cuisine," by Adam Leith Gollner (getpocket.com/explore/item/eating-the-arab-roots-of-sicilian-cuisine)

"Reinventing Habsburg Cuisine in Twenty-First Century Trieste," by Daša Ličen (folklore.ee/folklore/vol71/licen.pdf)

Serious Eats. "Seriously Asian: Chrysanthemum Greens," by Chichi Wang (seriouseats.com/2011/05/seriously-asian-chrysanthemum-greens.html)

Viet World Kitchen. "Vietnamese Iced Coffee Tips," by Andrea Nguyen (vietworldkitchen.com/blog/2012/05/vietnamese-iced-coffee-tips-ca-phe-sua-da.html)

What's Cooking America. "Collard Greens History and Recipe," by James T. Cotton Noe (whatscookingamerica.net/Vegetables/CollardGreens.htm#)

acknowledgments

From Angie

Thank you to my entire family, whose unremitting love and support have made me the person I am today. Endless thanks to my amazing parents, Dawn and Jim, who have always nurtured my creativity, believed in me, and put the needs of me and my siblings above everything else. Thank you to my little sisters and big brother, and to my many aunts, uncles, and cousins for surrounding me with so much love throughout my entire life—I'm so lucky to have all of you. Very special thanks to "G & G" Romaine who have taught me the meaning of true hospitality and taking care of others from a young age, just by being the incredibly loving and generous people they are; and to Grandma and Grandpa Rito for inspiring me for my whole life with their delicious food and passion for making and sharing it.

From Scott

Thank you to my mother, father, and brother for believing in me and supporting me when I decided to give up my career, change my life, and follow my heart. I'm also very thankful for having the best grandparents a kid could ask for. Grandma Tacinelli was the ultimate dinner party host—serving everyone else first and never sitting down to enjoy the fruits of her labor—and I will never forget Grandpa Tacinelli's post-dinner card games and stories about growing up in New York City. Thank you to Grandma and Grandpa Addario for giving me my initial taste of how special family heritage recipes could be, for passing on the torch of our Easter pie tradition, and for all the memories (including those very special sardine sandwiches). I miss you all very much every day; I hope I am doing our family recipes justice.

From Both of Us

Huge thanks to Jamie Feldmar, who has always kept us on track as she guided us through the writing process. Thanks for putting up with the two of us, especially when we talked over each other at the same time, and for always brightening our day with a constant flow of vintage El Camino photos from the streets of LA. We look forward to our glorious reunion at Sunny's in Red Hook one of these days.

Thank you to our stellar team at Clarkson Potter, especially Jenn Sit, who believed in our vision and helped us tell our story in the best way possible, and to Marysarah Quinn, whose talent for design brought it to life in a more beautiful way than we could have ever imagined.

Thank you to Michael Stillman, who has been the best partner we could ask for, and has allowed us to make all of our dreams become reality at Don Angie. Without you, none of this would be possible. Thanks to Sloane, Evie, and Alli Stillman for taste-testing our frittata in its early stages!

Thank you to Caroline Lange, whose precision and attention to detail helped us hone our recipes for ultimate accuracy. A special thanks to Annette Tacinelli and Andrea Feldmar, who pulled through with extra recipe testing when we needed it. Thanks to all of the friends and neighbors out there who sampled the products and gave their feedback to our testers!

To Allison Good—Thank you for always lending a helping hand throughout this entire process, from conception and pitching, to writing and designing, to sorting out logistics and communication. Thank you to Sara Mavec and her keen eye for all of the assistance with visual inspiration, and to Bianca Kenworthy, who got the ball rolling on the PR front.

We are forever grateful to Christopher Testani for his unparalleled talent in photography and willingness to work with us on this project. We were lucky enough to also work with his lovely wife Carla Gonzalez-Hart, who set the stage for these gorgeous photos with her incredible prop styling. A major shout-out to Barrett Washburne, food stylist extraordinaire, who made everything look extra beautiful and taught us so many new tips and tricks. We will always think of you when it comes to fancy citrus zesting and whipped cream styling!

David Black—We are eternally grateful for your hard work on this project to help make it a reality, and for your guidance to us newbies in navigating the publishing process. We look forward to our next red-sauce feast and fine Sicilian wine together. Thank you also to Dorothy Kalins, who was instrumental in the early conception of this project and helped us tell our story to publishers.

Thank you to Adam Richardson and Jose Medina, our right-hand guys, who held down the fort at Don Angie, and who assisted us throughout the process of writing this book, from shuttling us ingredients during quarantine to prepping for the photo shoots. We're incredibly lucky to work with you both. A special thank-you to Adam for his additional assistance in developing the Savory Pizzelle Crackers with Black Pepper, Fennel & Parmesan and Honey Zeppole recipes.

Thank you to the entire Don Angie team, whose continual hard work has made the restaurant what it is today. Thank you to our resident pasta maker Carmen Guaman, whose beautiful pasta appears in some of these photos, and to Damien Good, who has embodied the warm hospitality and spirit of generosity that connect us with our guests on a daily basis.

A big thank-you to Nick Gaube, Rodrigo Rodriguez, and the team at Quality Italian, who lent us their kitchen and space to shoot these beautiful photos. Thank you to Evan Young, who was a tremendous help to us in the kitchen throughout the photoshoot process.

Thank you to Roman Grandinetti and his mother Regina, who were kind enough to let us hang out and shoot some photos at their shop, Regina's Grocery.

Thank you to our close friends P.J. Damiano and Erin "Palisino," who are basically family, for their continual love and support, and for being great companions on the many food adventures that have inspired the recipes in this book. Special thanks to Julie Rose Loketi, who took the fabulous Polaroid shot of Don Angie during our opening, and to Ashley Sears, whose awesome photo of us in the Don Angie kitchen also appears in this book.

Thank you to the chefs who have taught and inspired us throughout the years, especially Craig Koketsu, Kevin Lasko, Rich Torrisi, Mario Carbone, and Eli Kulp—your guidance and mentorship has made us into the cooks that we are today. Thank you to our purveyors who supply the restaurant on a regular basis with high-quality ingredients and who provided their superior products for the photos in this book: Strassburger Meats, Greenpoint Fish and Lobster, Prime Food Distributor, and Natoora. Thank you to Mutti for all of the beautiful tomatoes. It's easy to make good food when you are working with great products!

Last, a big thank-you to the folks who have gifted and lent beautiful plates, casseroles, and other serviceware that helps make our food look so good: the Dansk company, our friend Nate Mell at Felt + Fat, and our friend and casserole guru, Caroline Hatchett.

INDEX

Copyright © 2021 by Angie Rito and Scott Tacinelli
Photographs copyright © 2021 by Christopher
Testani

Published in the United States by Clarkson Potter/
Publishers, an imprint of Random House, a
division of Penguin Random House LLC, New York.
clarksonpotter.com

CLARKSON POTTER is a trademark and POTTER
with colophon is a registered trademark of
Penguin Random House LLC.

Library of Congress Cataloging-in-Publication Data

Names: Rito, Angie, author. | Tacinelli, Scott,
author. | Feldmar, Jamie,
   author. | Testani, Christopher, photographer.
Title: Italian American : red sauce classics and new
essentials / Angie
   Rito & Scott Tacinelli with Jamie Feldmar ;
[photographs by Christopher
   Testani].
Description: First edition. | New York, NY :
Clarkson Potter/Publishers,
   [2021] | Includes index.

Identifiers: LCCN 2021015189 | ISBN
9780593138007 (hardcover) | ISBN
   9780593138014 (ebook)
Subjects: LCSH: Cooking, Italian. | Cooking,
American. | LCGFT: Cookbooks.
Classification: LCC TX723 .R528 2021 | DDC
641.5945--dc23
LC record available at https://lccn.loc.
gov/2021015189

ISBN 978-0-593-13800-7
Ebook ISBN 978-0-593-13801-4

Printed in China

Photographs: Christopher Testani
Digital Tech: Christine Shevlin
Food Stylist: Barrett Washburne
Prop Stylist: Carla Gonzalez-Hart
Prop Assistant: Todd Henry

Editor: Jennifer Sit
Designer: Marysarah Quinn
Production Editor: Abby Oladipo
Production Manager: Heather Williamson
Composition: Merri Ann Morrell and Nick Patton
Copyeditor: Kate Slate
Indexer: Elizabeth Parson

10 9 8 7 6 5 4 3 2 1

First Edition